Containing States of Mind

Wilfred Bion's insights into the analytic process have had a profound
influence on how psychoanalysts and psychotherapists understand emotional change and pathological mental states. One of his most influential
ideas concerns the notion that we need the minds of others to develop our
own emotional and cognitive capacities.

In *Containing States of Mind*, Duncan Cartwright explores and develops
some of the implications that Bion's container model has for clinical
practice. He argues that the analyst or therapist best fulfils a containing
function by negotiating irreconcilable internal tensions between his role as
'dream object' and 'proper object'. The container model is also used to
illustrate different 'modes of interaction' in the analytic field, the nature of
particular pathological states and some of the key dilemmas faced in
attempting to make unbearable mental states more bearable.

As well as addressing key theoretical problems, *Containing States of Mind* is
a clinical text that renders complex ideas accessible and useful for psychotherapeutic and analytic practice and as such will be essential reading for all
those involved in the fields of psychoanalysis and psychotherapy.

Duncan Cartwright is head of the Centre for Applied Psychology, University of Kwa-Zulu Natal, South Africa. He is in part-time private practice
and is the author of *Psychoanalysis, Violence and Rage-Type Murder:
Murdering Minds*, Routledge, 2002.

Containing States of Mind

Exploring Bion's 'Container Model' in
Psychoanalytic Psychotherapy

Duncan Cartwright

Routledge
Taylor & Francis Group

LONDON AND NEW YORK

First published 2010 by Routledge
27 Church Road, Hove, East Sussex BN3 2FA

Simultaneously published in the USA and Canada
by Routledge
270 Madison Avenue, New York, NY 10016

Routledge is an imprint of the Taylor & Francis Group, an Informa business

Typeset in Times by Garfield Morgan, Swansea, West Glamorgan
Printed and bound in Great Britain by TJ International Ltd, Padstow,
Cornwall
Paperback cover design by Lisa Dynan

This publication has been produced with paper manufactured to strict
environmental standards and with pulp derived from sustainable forests.

British Library Cataloguing in Publication Data
A catalogue record for this book is available from the British Library

Library of Congress Cataloging-in-Publication Data
Cartwright, Duncan, 1968–
    Containing states of mind : exploring Bion's container model in
psychoanalytic psychotherapy / Duncan Cartwright.
        p. cm.
    Includes bibliographical references.
    ISBN 978-1-58391-878-4 (hardback) – ISBN 978-1-58391-879-1 (pbk.)
    1. Psychoanalysis. 2. Psychodynamic psychotherapy. 3. Bion, Wilfred R.
(Wilfred Ruprecht), 1897–1979. I. Title.
    RC480.5.C365 2009
    616.89'17–dc22

                                                            2009006828

ISBN: 978-1-58391-878-4 (hbk)
ISBN: 978-1-58391-879-1 (pbk)

For Gabriel and Jamie

Contents

Preface

I consider Bion's theory of the container as an invaluable starting point to understanding how change occurs both in the 'nearness' of the clinical hour and in more abstract formulations about psychic transformation. Ideas expressed in this book represent many years of engaging with Bion's work in clinical practice. I remember, as a trainee, puzzling over how 'containing' might be translated into technique. The answers did not come easily and my thinking started with how Bion's concept appeared to be used in clinical settings in a somewhat idealized way. This appeared to have particular implications for technique. To this end, the first paper I wrote on the subject was a version of 'idealizing the container' (Chapter 8 in this book).

Clearly, Bion's contribution to psychoanalysis is much broader than his ideas about the container and the contained. In this book, however, I make them central to the analytic process and see his ideas as outlining a 'container model' that represents an ongoing clinical reality, an ongoing process in the analytic relationship, and a particular way of working with patients. I have tried to make my ideas available for clinical application both in terms of psychotherapeutic process and understanding some aspects of pathological thinking. My hope is that they express some useful clinical 'truths' that resonate with trainees, analysts and psychotherapists. In this sense, the book is about 'clinical thinking' as opposed to just an attempt at theoretical elaboration. As there is a clinical focus to most of the book, some theoretical arguments and literature reviews have been deliberately limited.

It is often said that Bion's work underwent different periods of development. In many ways his 'container model' can be located in his earlier work. In my thinking on the topic, I pay little attention to the historical development of his ideas. In fact, on reflection, it appears I read him 'backwards' and tend to bring some of his later ideas (e.g., 'becoming', 'O', the ephemeral nature of experience, and his thoughts on clinical practice) to bear on his earlier notions of the container.

Like most psychoanalytic theory, many of the concepts Bion developed were derived from experiences in traditional psychoanalytic settings (the use of the couch, frequency of sessions, etc.). Clearly this has an influence on how psychoanalytic concepts are understood and applied in other modes of psychoanalytic treatment. In this regard, one may question the usefulness of Bion's containing model in chair-to-chair psychoanalytic psychotherapy. For instance, following Bion, the analyst's reverie is seen as an important means of engaging the containing function. In traditional analytic practice the analyst is permitted more privacy and space to contemplate states of reverie, thoughts at the periphery of awareness. In a chair-to-chair setting can the therapist make use of his reverie in similar ways? I never address this directly in this book. In my experience, many of Bion's ideas are applicable to psychoanalytic psychotherapy but greater demands are made on the therapist to actively engage with the patient while still considering his own fleeting internal thoughts and responses. The ongoing challenge in psychoanalytic psychotherapy is finding ways of applying such concepts in a useful way. In this sense, implicit in many of the ideas presented in this book are considerations about using 'containment' in psychoanalytic psychotherapy.

Acknowledgements

I am grateful to John Steiner and Antonino Ferro for their helpful comments regarding queries about some of their work. I thank Sia Antonakas and Jeff Ward for their assistance in reviewing various sections of the manuscript. Heartfelt gratitude to Ros Kernoff, dear friend and colleague, for her support and commentary on final versions of the book. Finally, I express deep appreciation to Fiona Grayer, family and friends, who have been so patient, understanding and supportive throughout the writing process.

Permissions

The author and publisher are grateful to the following for their permission to reproduce passages from copyright material as follows:

'Autistic defenses in agoraphobic syndrome: "flat" objects and the retardation of projective identification', *Journal of the American Psychoanalytic Association*, *54*, 109–135. Copyright © SAGE Publications, 2006. 'Beta-mentality in the Matrix Trilogy', *International Journal of Psychoanalysis*, *86*, 179–190. Copyright © Institute of Psychoanalysis, 2005. 'Love Me!' by Stevie Smith, from *Collected Poems of Stevie Smith*, copyright © 1942 by Stevie Smith, reprinted by permission of New Directions Publishing Corporation, New York; Estate of James MacGibbon, London, for World rights excluding USA and Canada. Extracts from 'Burnt Norton' and 'The Hollow Men' are reprinted by permission of Faber and Faber Ltd, London, for World rights excluding the USA; Houghton Mifflin Harcourt Publishing Company for rights in the United States, its territories, and the Philippine Republic. The poem 'Dead Alive' is reproduced by kind permission of its author.

Chapter 1

Encountering unbearable states of mind

Wilfred Bion's ideas about psychoanalysis and psychotherapy continue to enrich our thinking about how we should approach analytic encounters. In this book I explore and develop his model of the container and related ideas. Bion's ideas about the container stand out as a major contribution to understanding the invariants of analytic experience and the transformatory conditions for generating psychic meaning and change. Grotstein (1979) goes so far as to say that the container–contained configuration uncovers 'a new natural law' (p.110), a new way of organizing material that exposes new ways of seeing the order of things. However, despite the usefulness and popularity of the idea of 'containing' in various forms of psychoanalytic practice, understanding and application of 'the container model' varies greatly and still remains relatively under-theorized. The focus of this volume is twofold: first, I explore various theoretical aspects of the container model putting forward ideas about how I apply it in the therapeutic setting; second, I explore and develop some implications that the model has for understanding the development of pathological states or ways of thinking.

Developing Melanie Klein's (1946) ideas about projective identification, Bion thought that projective identifications, split-off parts of the self that are located in other objects, required containment in another mind if they were to be modified in some way. His thinking introduces a particular dynamic that he based on the prototype of a sexual union denoted by ♀♂ (container–contained).

Bion's container model can be applied in various ways at different levels of abstraction. In the clinical setting it translates into a model whereby the analytic pair (predominantly the analyst) attempt to make unbearable mental states more bearable, in turn, enriching the scope of the experiential field. Because unbearable mental states remain separated, split off, from the patient's core self, the therapist's containing function relies on attending to thoughts and feelings at the periphery of his awareness. For this reason the therapist's reverie, his dream thoughts, become a gateway to accessing unprocessed experience that requires further psychic work. In this way the therapist's container function becomes part of broader psychic processing system, picking up on and attending to parts of the patient's internal world that for various reasons cannot be tolerated or given meaning. There are many questions here:

- How does one apply Bion's container–contained configuration to the clinical setting?
- What is the difference between the 'container' function and the container–contained configuration?
- How does the analyst make use of his reverie in this process?
- What implications does the container have for understanding pathological processes?

It could be said that Freud chartered a metapsychology that had as its driving force the energetics of the unconscious pitted against reality. Klein, on the other hand, sought to understand the concrete nature of internal objects, phantasy, and their management through projective and introjective processes. Bion's point of entry is quite different. It lies at the interface between objects and thinking, between individuals' minds, in search of transformative links that make change possible. In this way, Bion brought to psychoanalysis a unique perspective on what might be called the *psychoanalysis of encounter*. Although his work underwent a number of transformations it is the encounter between minds, and how this generates change, that remains a constant fascination to Bion. He emphasizes, particularly in his later work, the idea that the mind is always in transit and is constantly in a state of 'becoming' something else. External reality is not thought of as being a stable, consistent, objective entity, suitable for Cartesian apprehension. Rather, it is always mediated through the mind of an other. From this perspective we are left with a difficult set of parameters to work with: a mind is dependent on another mind for meaning but this necessarily remains ineffable, opaque, and always in flux.

Perhaps along with Winnicott, Bion was a true innovator of the *in between*. Rather than getting mired in theoretical dilemmas about the role of affect, sexuality, the drives and so forth, much of his thinking focused on understanding how the encounter between subjectivities is able to transform psychic occurrences (bearing influences from internal and external experience) into meaningful experience, in turn, leading to growth of the personality. In many ways Bion's thinking can be seen to pre-empt some of the current debates on intersubjectivity[1] in psychoanalysis (e.g. Beebe *et al.*, 2005; Benjamin, 1990; 1998; Gentile, 2007; Mitchell, 2000; Stolorow *et al.*, 2002).

---

1 Intersubjectivity has been used in such different ways that it is perhaps best to refer to 'forms of intersubjectivity' as Beebe *et al.* (2005) suggest. I follow them in using the term in its broadest sense to connote all that occurs *between* minds.

Unlike much of the thinking about intersubjectivity, however, which tends to emphasize a 'harmonious mutuality' between patient and client, Bion's ideas attempt to articulate the struggle we are engaged in when we are truly engaged with an other. For Bion, a real human mental connection is like an emotional storm caused by the coming together of minds that crave and resist each other. Although we are equipped with some kind of primary awareness of sensory objects and emotions, the ability to think and generate meaning demands that the encounter be subjected to a series of transformations that Bion made central to his work. The task becomes finding ways of tolerating this emotional storm for long enough so that it can be thought about and given particular personal meaning. As put by Bion, it involves working out how 'to make the best of a bad job' (1987, p.247). It is here that he locates the model of the container.

Despite Bion's often abstruse use of abstract terms and complex theoretical notions, it seems to me that the essence of his contribution lies in his struggle to articulate the transformatory qualities of *lived experience* always unfolding at the cusp of our awareness. He is interested in the minutiae of experience, how we come to know our experience and learn from it, use it, and be transformed by it. I read him as constantly puzzling over dilemmas about how to engage or encounter the 'nearness' of analytical experience. In his words:

> I am not very interested in the theories of psychoanalysis or psychiatry or any other theories; the important point is what I call 'the real thing', the practice of analysis, the practice of treatment, the practice of communication.
>
> (Bion, 2005b, p.16)

Unfortunately, this 'radical experiential view' (Godbout, 2004, p.1125) is often obscured by Bion's marshalling of 'empty' nomenclature in an attempt to avoid the 'penumbra of associations' linked to the concepts he is discussing.[2] Despite this, however, a number of his theoretical contributions have markedly changed the way one might think about psychoanalytic experience, bringing the 'nearness' of the clinical encounter into full focus. To this end he replaces 'invisible' instincts with the emotional links between objects (Loving, Hating and Knowing), the formation of thoughts cannot be considered apart from affective experience and its inherent link to 'other

---

2 *Transformations* stands out as his most audacious attempt at understanding the analytic encounter through the use of near-mathematical formulae but, in doing so, it fails as an attempt to remain close to analytic experience 'usable' to the practising analytic therapist (Meltzer, 1975b). Further, as Matte-Blanco (1988) has pointed out, the fact that they are 'empty' concepts does not make their 'emptiness' or the signs that Bion employs devoid of meaning.

minds', the analyst's 'free floating attention' is given 'subjective depth' in his use of the term reverie. Further, Bion's focus on dream-work-alpha and the 'waking-dream' draws the analyst's attention to the real-time processing of analytic experience and the creative aspects involved in transforming raw experience into mentation. Similarly, in the heat of the analytic encounter, the concept of the container becomes a means of tolerating and transforming unassimilated experience through building meaningful commentaries about the self in interaction, the self in the encounter. Put simply, the container makes unbearable mental states more tolerable through making them meaningful as they emerge.

The container function

In order to locate the container function I start with a very brief sketch of mental functioning as conceptualized by Bion. He used the terms 'dream-work-α' (Bion, 1992)[3] and later 'alpha-function' (Bion, 1962b) to isolate a function in the psyche that transforms sense impressions into elemental psychic impressions (alpha-elements) or proto-thoughts and proto-emotion. Alpha-function is responsible for animating the psyche, imbuing it with a sense of subjectivity (Symington and Symington, 1986). To use an example, let us say I observe a couple kiss. It impacts my senses, creating sensory impressions on the mind (beta-elements). To this I have an unconscious response which involves transforming the experience into pictograms (Rocha Barros, 2000) using alpha-function. This, in turn, leads to the emergence of images and psychic impressions, largely unconscious or preconscious. For example, we may imagine that this experience simultaneously elicits arousing physical sensations and 'pleasant undefined feelings', undefined 'bad' feelings associated with the image of an evil figure, images of a child alone, a vague sense of feeling alone, images of babies, images of my mother, a sense of deadness or hate, and so forth. These alpha-elements are best thought of as being the 'components of thought' (Ferro, 2005a, p.1) that can then be stored in memory and used to create dream-thoughts and later, reflective conscious thought. These components of thought may appear in consciousness in the form of momentary 'flash' images (similar to those experienced by trauma victims) but lack any particular narrative or developed meaning.

With the capacity to create basic proto-thoughts or pictograms set in motion, further psychic operations are required to develop these pictograms into dream-thoughts which eventually form coherent narratives. For this Bion deduced Ps$\leftrightarrow$D[4] and the container function as the mechanisms that

---

3 Term first used in notes made in 1959 and published in *Cognitions* (Bion, 1992).
4 Bion (1963) derives Ps$\leftrightarrow$D from Klein's paranoid-schizoid and depressive positions. However, the double-headed arrow is used to depict a more fluid, dynamic process where psychic elements constantly move between moments of disintegration and integration.

make psychic change possible, processes used to work on the relationships between psychic objects in order to generate psychic growth. 'Ps' represents a process of fragmentation or disintegration that allows psychic elements to be reintegrated (D) in different ways, creating a changed relationship between disparate elements. Through the process of disintegration (Ps) and integration (D), psychic impressions or pictograms integrate and recombine into constellations that await meaning. In terms of the above example, this might include: 'I love my father and my mother is evil and I feel left out' or, 'I feel evil witnessing such intimacy,' or, 'I feel hate towards my parents but I also feel pleasant loving feelings', and so forth.

The containing function, on the other hand, works to hold these thoughts in mind so that they can be 'detoxified' and permitted to gather new meaning. Ps↔D and the container essentially work in a dialectical way. In Bion's words: 'On the Ps↔D operation depends the delineation of the whole object: on the successful operation of ♀♂ depends the meaning of the whole object' (1963, p.90).

In sum, the container comprises a mental function that allows such thoughts to be held in mind long enough so that these dream-thoughts, in the processes of integration and disintegration, can be thought about. To continue with the example, perhaps with the aid of my therapist's 'containing' capacities I begin to think about the idea that I have feelings of hate towards my mother and I feel rejected by how my father seems to prefer her. From this, a meaningful narrative begins to form that can then be recycled through the same process in search of other 'selected facts' (Bion, 1962b) or sources of meaning that allow these narratives to reconfigure. Put simply, the containing function represents an area of mind or a mental connection that attempts to find ways of tolerating undeveloped psychic content and emotions so they can be held in mind and understood. But how is this to be applied to the therapeutic situation? What does the analyst actually do when he says he is using his containing function in working with the patient?

Bott Spillius (1988) argues that the container model along with Bion's alpha-function is the most widely accepted and best understood idea in Bion's work. In my experience it certainly seems to be tacitly accepted by most (across a number psychoanalytic orientations), but I would not concur that it is well understood. Although the idea of the therapist's 'container function' has taken hold as a key psychoanalytic concept, it has undergone relatively little development in theory and practice. Caper (1999) has similar concerns about the theory of 'the container':

> Considering the impact that this theory has had on psychoanalytic thinking, it is surprisingly sketchy, and it is remarkable how little it tells us about how containment is actually supposed to work.
>
> (p.141)

Caper (1999) wonders if this was deliberate on Bion's part; another of his concepts that require the analyst to fill in the details using his or her own experience. As mentioned earlier, Bion deliberately uses the signs ♀♂ for container–contained in an attempt to prevent the meaning of the concept being saturated by fixed ideas that prevent ongoing thought. In my view, however, there seem to be other important factors at play here that relate to its intuitive appeal.

Bion's 'containing analyst' often seems to be used as a saturated term where assumptions about it as a theoretical and technical idea are simply assumed. In my experience, it is often said that 'we need to contain emotions and thoughts' or 'contain the patient' and there are many nods of acknowledgment but little unpacking of what this might actually mean. There may be a number of reasons for this. First, Bion's often schematic descriptions of the containing process have an almost seductive ring to them where objects can be transformed through allowing the mother to metabolize them. To quote Bion:

> The infant projects a part of its psyche, namely its bad feelings, into a good breast. Thence in due course they are removed and re-introjected. During their sojourn in the good breast they are felt to have been modified in such a way that the object that is re-introjected has become tolerable to the infant psyche.
>
> (Bion, 1962b, p.90)

How this actually occurs is often not apparent in Bion's writings. It appears that this sometimes leads to the idea that containment, along with projective identification, is quite a magical and mysterious process. How projections are 'detoxified' is simply taken for granted. One possible reason for the tacit acceptance of the analyst's container function might be that it parallels deep unconscious phantasies, inherent preconceptions, about the maternal object and about the need to be 'contained'. In Chapter 8, I explore how such phantasies contribute to countertransference states that I call 'idealizing the container', a psychic state often employed defensively to avoid thinking about intolerable affects. The second reason why the container appears to be taken for granted is related to the idea it represents a three-dimensional object, a near-physical repository. This conception has technical implications for the therapist. For instance, from this point of view, 'containing' is often viewed as being synonymous with the therapist being 'silently and passively receptive' to the patient's emotions and projections. Alternatively 'containing' often takes on a 'protective function' or a sense of empathizing and needing to 'be there' for the patient. All these are associated with the idea that the container is a near-physical, 'concrete' object with an interpersonal emphasis. The above may be important therapeutic factors in some cases, but Bion had in mind a much more active, transformative psychical process. To this end he makes clear that 'containing' demands much more than the dutiful presence of the therapist or mother (Bion, 1959). Here Bion is developing the idea that the containing function represents a mental connection that goes beyond reified or interpersonal conceptions of the container. From this perspective it is the mother's ability to retain 'a balanced outlook' (1959, p.313) that seems to be important. But what might a 'balanced outlook' mean? In this book I make this idea central to informing what might be considered to be 'containing' aspects of the analyst's mind when applied to the clinical setting.

Following Bion, there appears to be broad agreement that the process of containing involves an interchange between patient and analyst whereby the analyst, receptive to the patient's projections, introjects them, somehow 'detoxifying' them making them available to the patient via interpretation so they can be taken back in a more manageable form. This model, as it stands, seems to make intuitive sense, especially when it is seen as analogous to the process that occurs between mother and infant. But what does this actually all mean? What do I mean when I say I needed to contain my patient's hate? How is it possible that projections are 'exchanged', modified, and 'given back'? How does all this differ from Winnicott's much used concept of 'holding'? How should we understand the role of interpretation in the containing process? What are the precursors to the containing function? One of the main problems here is making clear the distinction between psychic reality and external reality in therapeutic interaction. Although we may conceive of projections as 'flying across the room' and being contained by the therapist in terms of phantasy (psychical reality), the reality of how this impacts on technique and therapeutic interaction is a different story.

In Chapter 2, I consider the relationship between projective identification and the container, as well as the role of countertransference, as a starting point to exploring what might constitute 'containing' in the analytic relationship. In essence Bion could be understood as introducing two related ideas that bring the idea of 'containment' to life. First, he introduces the idea that some phantasies of projective identification encompass a wish not only to split-off parts of the self, but also a wish for containment. Second, Bion introduces the notion that the container has a 'transformational' function. These ideas first emerge in 'Attacks on Linking': Bion is making the point that the infant *seeks* 'to investigate his own feelings in a personality powerful enough to contain them' (Bion, 1959, p.314). Statements like this appear to mark the start of one of Bion's most profound contributions: the idea that knowing (K) the other (and by implication, self), and being known by them, constitutes an emotional link intimately connected to the growth of the personality. Here the role of 'truth' and curiosity become a crucial means of reframing emotions, desires, and thought in the service of the reality principle (Grotstein, 2004).

One of the central ideas I consider further in Chapters 3 and 4 is the idea that the containing function is best understood as a fragile mental connection, a process through which the analyst attempts to negotiate irreconcilable tensions within himself. I conceptualize these tensions to be principally between the analyst's role as 'proper object' and 'dream object'. Within this the analyst strives to maintain his position as a 'real contemplative object' in an effort to make unbearable mental states more bearable. My intention here is to free the containing function from being conceptualized in three-dimensional terms, emphasizing it as an ongoing mental connection that is characterized by a state of 'becoming'.

The container–contained configuration

Bion uses the container and contained at different levels of abstraction. At a more local level he uses the model to refer to a mental function involved in making psychic states more bearable and thinkable, as discussed above. But it is also a model that can be applied to any relationship between objects. For my purposes I will use the terms 'container function' and 'container–container configuration' to represent these different levels of abstraction respectively. Although both concepts are related, there are important differences that require clarification. Differences between the concepts can be stated as follows:

1   The container–contained configuration refers to an abstraction that can be applied to all asymmetrical relationships between objects. The container function, on the other hand, refers to part of a set of mental apparatus that enables the creation of thoughts so as to give rise to new meaning.[5]
2   The container function is intimately related to the concept of projective identification where the container refers to the receptive mind of the recipient. The container–contained configuration, on the other hand, does not necessarily involve projective identification.
3   The container–contained is an abstraction to be applied after sessions and should not intrude on the therapeutic interaction. The container function forms part of the 'meaning-making' process that operates unconsciously and preconsciously in the 'here-and-now' of the therapeutic process.

---

5 For those familiar with Bion's (1962b) *Grid*, the container–contained configuration is probably best classified as a concept (Row F), whereas the container function is best understood as being a mental function that facilitates movement down the rows in the grid from inchoate components of thought (alpha-elements) and beta-elements to more abstract conceptualizations (Row A-H).

4   The container–contained configuration is an abstraction that generates spatial imagery, delineations of 'inside' and 'outside' the area of enquiry (e.g. the analyst contains the patient's anger, the maternal object contains his love). The container function, on the other hand, represents an unknowable entity that does not lend itself to representation in three-dimensional space.

5   While the container–contained configuration can be used as an abstract representation of the dynamic relationships between the container function and its contents, or between analyst and patients (e.g. the patient projects into the analyst), the reverse cannot be applied.

I consider these to be important differences. Conflating the use of the container function and the container–contained configuration leads to a number of misunderstandings. Notably, if the container function is conceptualized as a three-dimensional object (similar to the configuration) it easily fosters misguided clinical thinking where the therapist's containing mind is seen as being synonymous with qualities of robustness, passivity, protectiveness, or with fantasies that the mind can literally contain parts of the patient. This kind of reasoning has a seductive ring to it that we will discuss further in later chapters. In my understanding, it runs contrary to more accurate views of the container function as representing a fairly precarious relational link or mental attitude that attempts to hold in mind unbearable psychic states so they gather meaning and understanding.[6]

The basic premise behind the container–contained configuration is deceptively simple: one object (container) external to another (the contained) influences the contained in some way, whilst the contained, in turn, alters the qualities of the container. Here interaction between the two gives rise to various possibilities: the container may compress the contained, the contained may overwhelm the container, the contained may resist containment, and so forth. Bion meant container–contained configurations to be 'abstract representations of psychoanalytic realizations' (Bion, 1962b, p.90) that serve to illuminate particular relationships between objects. The relationship between language and emotion, for instance, has different outcomes depending on if language 'contains' emotion or vice versa. If the patient's speech can contain emotions, language used will convey emotions meaningfully. If on the other hand emotions overwhelm the patient's speech, language is not able to contain emotions meaningfully and might be expressed as stuttering or incoherent speech. To use another example, the 'containing' establishment or group may restrict the growth of an individual's ideas or

6 This problem led Meltzer (1986) to propose that the 'container' concept be reserved for abstract conceptualization and separated from clinical work and its links to projective identification. I have chosen to retain the use of the 'container' concept but emphasize the distinction between 'the configuration' and 'the container function'.

beliefs (contained) and prevent further development unless the container expands or a new container is sought. Alternatively, the individual may be so destructive or influential that his or her action destroys the existing establishment or group (container). In a similar way, Bion uses the configuration to illuminate group dynamics, the relationship between the mystic and the establishment, between the individual and culture, preconception and realization, society and the individual and so forth.

The idea of a containing object is of course not something unique to Bion or psychoanalysis and often emerges in everyday usage: 'I feel like I'm going to explode','I need to hold these feeling inside me', or 'I wish you would contain yourself'. All these make use of the containing image as a three-dimensional form representing our minds or bodies. But implicit in the container–contained configuration are a number of factors. First, the configuration suggests that inherent in each mental object is the capacity to contain and be contained. For example, the image of my father may contain anger (contained), or he could be contained by my image of an angry family. Here the image of my father has the capacity to be container or contained depending on the point of view.

Second, the configuration generates a way of understanding emerging boundaries that give rise to conceptions of what is inside or outside, background or foreground. Where the figurative boundaries lie would depend on how objects separate and interact to generate dynamic qualities. Third, as a model of change, the container–contained configuration implies the acceptance of what could be called a *necessary or 'forced' asymmetry* between objects for change (destructive or growth promoting) to occur: one object has to assume the containing or background position in order for the other to be 'contained'. This appears to represent a distinguishing feature of Bion's model of change contributing particular qualities to the dialectical relationship between container and contained. Above all Bion's emphasis is on *the relationship* between container and contained as core to understanding all analytic objects of study:

> The breast [container] and the mouth [contained] are only important in so far as they serve to define the bridge between the two. When the 'anchors' usurp the importance which belongs to the qualities which they should be imparting to the bridge growth is impaired.
>
> (Bion, 1989, p.26)

Bion is making the point that the container and the contained signify the qualities of a particular kind of relationship, a basic relational unit. This is disrupted or breaks down when the container and contained act as separate objects or when individual qualities of an object are privileged over their relationship to other objects.

Container–contained configurations can be applied to relationships between objects as part of a systemic model representing different levels of abstraction. For instance, thoughts may contain emotions, some thoughts may contain other thoughts, internal objects are contained or contain others, each having influence on the other. The result is an infinite number of configurations of the container–contained that, in turn, have relationships with each other so that a dynamic nesting process emerges (Billow, 2003), an image of expanding concentric circles of different qualities that set up complex systems within and between minds. It therefore seems possible to begin to think about *containment systems* here. To use an example, a patient's understanding of marriage may be contained by his cultural identity. This may, in turn, be contained by differing dominant societal values. We could imagine that this might impact his need to contain or be contained by his wife's ideas about marriage. Further, if the patient's beliefs about marriage contain his wife's understanding in such a way that they cannot be expressed, this may influence other object relationships such as his relationship with his son and so forth.

In this volume I restrict myself to exploring the clinical implications of the container–contained configuration. To this end, in Chapter 7 I return to the idea of 'forced asymmetry' and how this plays itself out in 'modes of relating' between container–contained that can be applied to understanding core organizing phantasies between therapist and patient.

Key features of the container model

Some introduction is required to the way I conceptualize the container model throughout the book and some of the key dilemmas and issues this presents. I consider the container to be part of an analytic field where it finds representation at different levels of psychic experience. In exploring what constitutes 'containing' in the analytic relationship I also want to make some introductory comments about the relationship between the container and psychic space, the emotions, internalization and pathology.

The bi-directional field and containment systems

I conceptualize the container function, the therapist's containing mind, as being embedded in a field of complex interpersonal and intrapsychic relationships. The idea of the therapist and patient being part of a bi-directional field has been emphasized by Baranger *et al.* (1983). In Madeleine Baranger's view analysis is conducted

> within an intersubjective relationship in which each participant is defined by the other. In speaking of the analysis, we are referring to the formation of a structure which is a product of the two participants in the relationship but which in turn involves them in a dynamic and possibly creative process.

> (Baranger, 1993, p.16)

The idea that interaction takes place in a bi-directional field means that the analyst and patient both contribute to a field of meaning that is bigger than the sum of its parts. The meeting of two minds generates new meaning that can be understood by trying to understand how both therapist and patient are drawn into the field and the transference–countertransference response. From the field theory perspective transference and countertransference have their source in underlying organizing phantasies co-created as a product of the field in which patient and analyst personify different positions or roles. Through tolerating and thinking about his position of being embedded in the field, the analyst attempts to broaden the analytic field using his containing function.

Part of the analytic field comprises cycles of introjective and projective communications (Hamilton, 1990; Klein, 1957; Money-Kyrle, 1956; Schafer, 2000) between therapist and patient that exist at different levels of intensity. The analyst's containing mind functions to make bearable emotions and thoughts that are communicated via projective identification because they cannot yet be thought or rendered meaningful. Although the analyst's role is to make thinkable the unthinkable, the containing function exists in a field of intrapsychic and interpersonal relations and, as Bion suggested, is recip- rocal and recursive in nature. In moment-to-moment interaction the patient also attempts to hold in mind unbearable states of mind and calls on his or her containing function to assimilate the analyst's interpretations. What is hoped for, prompted mostly by the therapist, is an expansion to the analytic couple's containing capacity. Therefore, from a field theory perspective, the containing function depends on two or more minds and cannot be located solely in the mind of the analyst.

Field theory also permits a dynamic systems view of the encounter between minds. The analyst and patient meet each other at conscious and unconscious levels of experience, creating multiple tracks that organize inchoate sensory experience, the components of thought (alpha-elements), verbal communications and consequent interpersonal processes. It is also possible to think about how different tracks of experience might influence each other, in turn, generating emergent new experience. Here, non- conscious interpersonal processes, psychic functions and processes, internal objects, form a complex influencing system. From this perspective the ability to hold unbearable psychic states in mind so that they become thinkable and meaningful is dependent on complex psychical and inter- personal processes that occur at different levels, each level having non- linear influences on the other.

This can be further conceptualized by making use of the principle of *self- similarity* from non-linear systems theory (Gleick, 1987; Marks-Tarlow, 1999; Schroeder, 1991). Simply put, I use self-similarity to refer to the way different elements of the system, in part, take on the form of each other leading to the emergence of patterns, fractals, that repeat themselves at various levels of psychic organization. In other words it provides a way of thinking about how different levels of psychic experience, psychic functions, processes in the bi-directional field, have a referential influence on each element of the psychic system. In this way we can start to think about the fractal effects of container–contained configurations, containment systems, that can be applied to internal or external relationships.

Fractals can be readily observed in clinical material. A controlling patient, for instance, may relate to his words, emotional well-being, thoughts, money, his dreams, others, the session, in invariant controlling ways. The repetition of control occurs like a fractal in the person's experience. In thinking about the experiential field, I am making the assumption that a similar process can be applied to psychic functions and structures. The assumption here is that each psychic process or relationship reverberates through multiple dimensions, creating fractals that mimic some of the features of other systems of generating experience. Furthermore, assuming the principle of self-similarity allows for some understanding of how aspects of the psyche acquire some stability through 'mimicking' the form and function of other psychic elements (Quinodoz, 1997).

Considering the fractal or emergent effects of psychic processes is implicit in many psychoanalytic ideas. To mentions a few, Freud's (1900) 'return of the repressed' can be understood as a way of examining fractal effects of repressed ideas as they manifest at different levels of the psyche or in different symptoms. Ogden's (1992) and Grotstein's (2000) ideas about how multiple tracks or levels of generating psychic experience work in a synchronous fashion offer views of psychic development that cannot be understood in a linear fashion. Further, Matte-Blanco's (1988) courageous attempts at exploring the psyche using mathematical principles draws on ideas that the symmetrical and asymmetrical modes gives rise to emergent properties in the psyche.

The principle of self-similarity is also evident in Bion's (1963) theory, particularly when he considers how the psychic process of disintegration–integration (Ps↔D) often mimics the container–contained where disparate thoughts (disintegration) take on the form of the container and vice versa. Bion also suggests that sense impressions (beta-elements) may have the capacity to become 'abortive prototypes' of the container function proper. In locating the containing function in a field of experience we can start to consider what non-linear effects the containing function may have on other psychic processes.

Based on the above assumptions my understanding is that components of the containing function occur in the analytic field at different levels of psychic complexity. Invariant at all levels, and following Bion, is the drive to 'know' or apprehend the object. Below I outline three different levels of psychic experience to help locate representations or fractal elements of the container. Although inseparable and always having reciprocal influences on each other, for the sake of exploration I divide these levels into non-symbolic, preverbal and symbolic.

My understanding of non-symbolic processes is influenced by Bucci's multiple (1997a, 1997b) code theory. Bucci makes use of cognitive and developmental research to account for various psychoanalytic processes and concepts. Non-symbolic activity involves the processing of sensory patterns, continuous gradients of experience (through perceptual, affective and motoric channels). At this level there are no specified categories of experience. This would include the analyst's abilities to make fine non-conscious distinctions on sensory and bodily levels without being able to express this in any clear way. Sub-symbolic processes often cannot be directly experienced and yield a sense of being 'outside the self' (1997b, p.159). They are 'non-conscious' in the sense that they remain largely out of awareness as opposed to being unconscious due to intrapsychic forces (the dynamic unconscious). This level of experience includes procedural mental activity regarding behaviour and emotion (Clyman, 1991; Emde, 1993), interpersonal learning based on action schemas that grant us implicit ways of being with an other. Important for my purpose is the assumption that there exists a form of primary intersubjectivity derived from sensorimotor attunement, a non-symbolic attentiveness to the actions and movements of the other. This occurs in the immediacy of interaction forming a sense of 'self-resonating-with the other' (Bråten, 2003; Stern, 2000). Clearly, there is a great deal of debate in psychoanalysis regarding non-conscious activity and findings from cognitive science, developmental psychology and neuro-science. I will not debate these issues in this book. I do, however, take the position that these findings have important implications for psychoanalysis. In terms of the container model, I am interested in speculating about the emergent psychic effects these implicit interpersonal processes have on the mind. To this end I link the non-symbolic level of generating experience to what I call proto-containing experiences (see Chapter 6). Here action-movement systems, ways-of-being-with-the-other, give rise to emergent experiences based on the patterning of 'sameness' and 'difference' in the analytic field. I argue that because this level of mind has no concept of negation such experiences generate a sense of 'flow' or 'moving along' in interaction. Further, I put forward the idea that such experiences generate preconceptions of the containing function proper.

The second level of psychic organization might be called the preverbal level. Here psychic impressions based on sensory information assume a different level of organization. Inchoate images, feelings, sounds, begin to form psychic representations that refer to particular internal objects. Using Bion's model, this is an area of mind where sensory impressions pass through alpha-function transforming them into inchoate psychic objects (alpha-elements). The organization of such experiences depends primarily on splitting and cycles of projective and introjective identification between internal objects, processes that are broadly part of the dynamic unconscious and preconscious experience. This level of mind depends on the containing function to give meaning to, and make more bearable, unformulated experience.

Finally, the third level of psychic organization, the symbolic level, allows for the full use of symbolic meaning through language. Here, following Bucci, symbols 'have properties of reference and generativity; they refer to or represent other entities, and they can be combined to generate infinite varieties of composite images and meanings' (Bucci, 1997a, p.159). At this level of mind, once unformulated experience has been rendered bearable and 'thinkable', symbols themselves become the containers of meaning, allowing the verbal communication of shared meaning systems.

In this book I focus mainly on the first two levels in the analytic field: the emergence of proto-containing experience and the containing function proper. Consistent with a dynamic systems perspective it appears that all three levels interact in complex ways. For instance, it appears that characteristics of proto-containing experiences can be appropriated at more mature levels of mind to shut down representational experience and projective processes (see Chapters 10 and 11) or can be used to mimic the containing function (Chapter 9). Alternatively the psychic 'movements' of projection and introjection might be understood to rupture or disrupt proto-containing experiences. Further, symbolic objects may be seen to lose their meaning if removed from their experiential proto-containing context or if their meaning is not continually revised or reconfigured by the containing function. We shall return to some of these possibilities in other sections.

Psychic space

What is the relationship between psychic space and the container model? The container–contained configuration easily lends itself to being conceptualized in spatial terms. When applied to the clinical setting the mechanism of projective identification easily assumes a crude form of three-dimensionality and the phantasy is coupled with the idea of projection into a receptacle. Implicit in this is the idea that the container has an 'inside' and 'outside'. It emerges as a three-dimensional image similar to that of a real physical vessel. This in itself is not unusual in the sense that most of our thinking takes place in three-dimensional psychic space: 'in my family', 'in my mind', 'getting these thoughts out of my head'; all suggest a distinction between inside and outside and a sense of space that is three-dimensional (with the addition of time). In psychoanalysis we often use terms like internal and external, introjection and projection. These terms portray the three-dimensional perspective within which most thinking takes place. The restrictiveness of three-dimensional space impressed Matte-Blanco (1988) and led him to explore the theoretical and clinical implications of this. He used principles of basic mathematical logic to show how psychic space exists in multiple, if not infinite, dimensions. Matte-Blanco argues it is virtually impossible to discuss our thoughts without referring to metaphor or pictorial representations. However, it does not necessarily follow that internal space should be based on conceptions of three-dimensional space just because it is a somewhat inevitable consequence of the limitations of our capacity to think. There are shortcomings to limiting the container–contained model to three-dimensional space.

Bion was aware of these limitations. In a footnote in *Learning From Experience* he explains that he is using the container–contained configuration with reluctance because it is more 'appropriate to immature than mature scientific thinking' (1962b, p.102). He is referring here to the limitations of using three-dimensional models or metaphors to explain complex multidimensional mental processes.

It appears that due to the pictorial qualities that the container–contained readily elicits – contained being inside a container – Bion was also concerned that it conveyed a 'static condition' that did not convey its essential dynamical qualities:

> Considering now whether it is necessary to abstract the idea of container and contained as an element of psycho-analysis I am met with doubt. Container and contained implies a static condition and this implication is one that must be foreign to our elements; . . . I shall therefore close the discussion by assuming there is a central abstraction unknown because unknowable yet revealed in an impure form in statements such as 'container or contained' and that it is to the central abstraction alone that the term 'psycho-analytic element' can be properly applied.
>
> (1963, p.7)

Although Bion demonstrated the dynamic qualities of the container–contained and understood it to exist as a reciprocal relationship, often the container does appear to take on static three-dimensional qualities, the very problems he sought to avoid by conceptualizing it as an 'unknowable' abstraction.

It appears more accurate to view psychic space and the container model as multidimensional in nature: our thoughts can be in many places at the same time (through projection), we can experience many different thoughts about the same object at the same moment, ideas and thoughts disappear and re-emerge and so forth. Bion (2005b) appears to be referring to such complexities in describing how the analyst does not approach his task by simply listening or interacting with one (physical, three-dimensional) person. Rather, 'it is like having the whole of one person at all ages and at all times spread out in one room at one time' (Bion, 2005b, p.32).

Matte-Blanco (1988) argues that multidimensionality occurs because unconscious reasoning is governed mainly by principles of symmetrical logic where symmetrical qualities of the object cause concepts of space, time, boundaries and difference to disappear. More conscious levels of experience, on the other hand, operate in accordance with asymmetrical principles where differences between objects define processes of reasoning and deductive logic. We will return to Matte-Blanco's theory in attempting to understand the 'containing connection' between therapist and patient. Using his model I explore how the psychoanalytic object exists in a system of complex dimensionalities that can be applied to the container model.

In sum, while applying the container–contained in three-dimensional terms may illuminate various relationships between objects, this idea is limited when it comes to thinking about psychic space and the analyst's containing function. This idea runs throughout this book where I consider how rigid adherence (implicit or explicit) to the container's existence in three-dimensional space generates various forms of pathology and limits the nature of the psychoanalytic process.

Emotions and the container

What role do emotions play in the containing function? In essence, the fabric of the container model, when applied to the analytic situation, is founded on emotional links. Bion thought that analytic goals should be orientated toward increasing the patient's capacity for suffering. Although at face value this may appear unduly pessimistic, his emphasis lies on the assumption that through 'suffering' emotions, sustaining mental contact with them, we are able to transform such states into meaningful experience. Further, 'suffering' acts like a signal or register, similar to pain in physical medicine, that orientates and illuminates areas of psychic experience that require attention. For Bion, encounters with another mind are inevitably painful in the sense that patient and analyst are always being asked to assimilate new experience and adjust their emotional preconceptions. It is also inevitably difficult because the patient has to constantly grapple with the opaque nature of the other's mind and the reality that he can never know it as a thing-in-itself. Whether the analytic couple are able to attend to this 'suffering' is another matter. The analyst and patient have a choice: face or avoid psychic pain, an inevitable consequence of facing reality. Although Bion relies heavily on Freud's (1911) 'two fundamental principles' (reality vs pleasure principle), his approach is quite different. For Bion, genuine reflective thought is not a means of postponing gratification thus avoiding unpleasure (through sublimation), it is a means of making unpleasure more tolerable. In addition, derivatives of primary process thinking, dream-thoughts and reverie, form part of the containing process and are not simply viewed as being a medium through which impulses or instincts can be discharged.

Bion (1962b) borrows Elliot Jaques' concept of the reticulum to depict the emotional nature of the containing function. It acts like a loosely knit net that allows for the entry of emotional variables that can be replaced forming a connective between minds and allowing for the container to reconfigure in different ways. Here, preconceptions and 'pre-emotions' constitute the analyst's receptive mind. Bion is clear, however, that emotions never exist in isolation and can only be conceived of in the relationship between two objects. He uses K (Knowing), H (Hating), L (Loving) links to isolate broad emotional mediums through which objects, analyst and patient, are linked. These links represent the 'musical key' in which two minds come together. We might say that analyst and patient 'fall into' particular emotional linkages that organize the way they relate, in turn, influencing all levels of psychic experience.

Emotional states of this nature are responsible for animating the containing function. They have an essential probing or searching function that implicitly 'nudges' or draws the therapist into personifying particular roles in the transference. Through 'containing' such occurrences the therapist initiates a process whereby he begins to think about (generate alpha-elements) emotions engendered in him. Regardless of whether the emotional link is H, L or K these links stimulate the containment system and the ability to think. On the other hand, the active stripping away of these respective emotions leaves the container inanimate. Bion (1962b) uses –K, –H and –L to represent such attacks on the containing function. Describing the implications of –K on the container, Bion writes about a sense of ' "without-ness". It is an interior without an exterior. It is an alimentary canal without a body' (p.97).

In considering the containing function, Bion privileges the K-link over other emotions. The drive towards knowing, curiosity, the ability to think amidst strong affect, is a central part of the containing process. This is in keeping with the idea that mental growth is dependent on confronting the 'truth' about our experience. Although the concept of 'truth' is awkward and loaded with philosophical baggage, Bion simply meant it to mean the nearest one can get to the reality of experience, what is *actually* being experienced in the here-and-now. In this sense Bion's subject is not driven principally by life and death instincts, the search for a good object or attachment needs, he is driven by curiosity, a need to 'know'.

Aside from these basic emotions working to link objects and make 'containing' a possibility, Bion also draws our attention to how difficult it is to tolerate mental contact with such links so that they can evolve and create the emotional context in which we can have meaningful thoughts. These difficulties are easily evoked when we consider the complexities of what it means to think in the presence of someone else. Bion emphasizes how much analyst and patient try to avoid inevitable difficulties in bearing such emotional turmoil. An important aspect of the containing function in this regard is the emergence of 'passion' (Bion, 1963) in the relationship. 'Passion' involves the ability to maintain a kind of mental contact that engages these emotional links (implicitly and explicitly) so that they are not split off from other mental processes. Passion, for Bion, is the ultimate sign that two minds are linked. Within the therapeutic context this has important associations with tolerating countertransference states and the therapist being able to embrace his own presence as an 'emotional agent' in the therapeutic relationship. In my view, 'passion' is an essential part of the containing function in that it allows the patient to engage with the analyst's subjectivity and his struggle to make the patient feel understood. In Chapter 5, I explore the importance of 'passion' and the subjectivity of the analyst's interpretive stance in making 'containing' interpretations.

It could be said that the apparent need to bear unpleasure, to think about it so as to afford psychological growth, is more easily avoided in our era of high technology. Cyberspace and high-tech gadgets seem to easily become repositories for split-off parts of the self. Such opportunities appear to make it easier to mimic and simulate experience rather than 'suffer it'. I explore some aspects of this cut-and-paste mentality in Chapter 9 where I consider a perverse form of 'pseudo-containing' as represented in the *Matrix* movies.

The internalization of the container function

It is often said, modelled on the infant–mother dynamic, that the therapist as container needs to be internalized by the patient. How might this occur? Bion thought that the containing function is derived from basic bodily processes such as feeding and breathing:

> φ^n represents a late stage in a series of stages that commences with a few relatively simple undifferentiated preconceptions probably related to feeding, breathing and excretion.
>
> (Bion, 1962b, p.93)

With these preconceptions already inherent in the infant, it is the presence of a caring and attentive caregiver that leads to the facilitation and growth of the container function. Through this process the infant is able to reinternalize psychic states that are made more manageable. Over time this not only leads to the internalization of a 'receptive containing object' but also leads to the internalization of the container function itself. Bion (1970) suggests in *Attention and Interpretation* that the internalized container function 'is not related to father or mother but can be related to fragments of both' (p.122). The implication here appears to be that it is more accurate to think of the internalization of a 'function' that transcends real and internalized objects and need not be specifically associated with the maternal object.

Based on the theory of projective identification, as mentioned earlier, it is often assumed that projections are detoxified and 'given back' to the infant so they can be reinternalized in a more manageable form. The processes involved here often remain unclear and it is worth considering why, from this perspective, the containing function should be 'internalized' if this function is already being performed by external objects. This is especially the case if projections are linked with unbearable psychic pain. Within the analytic process, the analyst needs to find a way of being receptive to the patient's projective identifications by subjecting them to thought and generating understanding and meaning. Once unbearable or unassimilated psychic states find a receptive object, the patient's anxiety begins to diminish. But at this stage, the patient is still dependent on an external containing object. Containing occurs in the presence of the analyst but cannot occur in his absence because it has yet to be internalized. The quandary here involves the difficulty of giving up a containing object (through internalizing its capacities) that brings about psychic relief. The answer appears to lie in the precarious nature of the analyst's containing function.

It appears to me that the inevitable fallibility of the analyst's 'containing' mind and the need to mourn the loss of an 'ideal' containing object are intimately linked to the withdrawal of projective identifications and the internalization of the containing function. I am influenced greatly by Steiner's (1993) observations regarding the importance of mourning in facilitating psychic growth and reintegration. Although creating in the patient a sense of feeling understood is an important part of containing, he argues that this is not enough and 'the patient continues to need the object to act as the container. . . . Projections are not truly withdrawn until a second stage is reached' (Steiner, 1993, p.60). According to Steiner, what is initially internalized is a narcissistic object relationship, an object containing parts of the self where no real separateness has been achieved. This accounts for why anxiety initially diminishes once the containing process is engaged. The second stage of 'containing' involves beginning to mourn the object, so separateness (and the 'taking back' of projections) can be achieved and a process of sorting out what belongs to the object and what belongs to the self can begin. Here, facing the *fear of loss* of the object and *experiencing the loss* of the object become very important parts of the analytic work if real integration in the depressive position is to be achieved. I extrapolate from this the need for the analyst's containing function to work with an ongoing tension, a dialectic, between succumbing to the patient's narcissistic object relations and maintaining a mind of his own. As will be discussed later, this is represented in the analyst's containing function in negotiating tensions between relating to himself or herself as 'proper object' and 'dream object'.

The idea that the containing object needs to be receptive to projections as well as facilitate mourning allows us to conceptualize the containing function as performing a bridging function between the paranoid-schizoid position and the depressive position. I understand the specifics of the mourning process to involve the patient mourning idealized phantasies of a containing object. It is the process of tolerating and working though the analyst's deficiencies, imperfections and fallibilities that usher in the internalization of a more realistic containing function.

Thinking, mentalization and the container function

Whereas Freud taught us to consider how repressed and unconscious we are of the true meaning of our behaviours, Bion wants us to consider how much of our lives we live without genuine thought, mindless. This is less about suffering amnesias due to repressed ideas and more about our difficulties in sustaining emotional connections with our objects so as to render them meaningful and part of lived experience. What interests Bion is the move from the capacity for primary awareness of an object (something we share with all animals) to the capacity to transform this into psychic experience.

Influenced by his work with psychotic patients with thought disorders, Bion (1962a, 1962b) began to question the idea that the ability to think was an inherently biological development. He makes two broad assumptions. First, he argues that thinking does not produce thoughts. Counterintuitively it is the other way round: thoughts emerge in the psyche through the processing of experience, and thinking emerges as a secondary means of managing thoughts. Second, he makes the assumption that thought is born out of relationships with other minds and is intricately linked with the processing of emotional experience.

In engaging the containing process, the analyst is particularly interested in what happens to his thinking when sitting with the patient: how are thoughts formed, what thoughts are generated, his ability to have his own thoughts. Importantly, Bion emphasized the idea that genuine thought emerged in the 'absence' of the object. We shall explore this further in Chapter 4. Important here is the idea that if 'absence' of the object is made bearable, it generates an awareness of psychic objects, a turning towards the internal world leading to a curiosity about thinking. The external object is replaced by searching thoughts that ultimately enrich the psyche and move psychic growth beyond fixed or saturated thoughts that are informed by what is already known (preconceptions).

In my understanding, there are a number of ways that the mother assists in dealing with frustration. The first emerges from the soothing rhythmic qualities born out of non-conscious aspects of interaction between mother and infant that impart a sense of 'moving along' (see Chapter 5). The second involves the caregiver's ability to regulate the infant's affect through accommodating to her immediate needs. In this way the caregiver shields the infant from too many intrusive environmental impingements. This process is what Winnicott (1965) called 'holding'.

Although both these processes work in different ways to regulate affect, they need to be differentiated from the containing function, the third way of managing frustration. The crucial difference here is that the container refers to a mind–mind connection with the infant. It is based on attuning to intrapsychic qualities, a curiosity about mental states, that regulates frustration. Put simply, affect is regulated through thinking about it. This separates the container function from interpersonal processes aimed at regulating affect or frustration. Following Bion, through this process the emergence of thought 'bridges the gulf of frustration between the moment when a want is felt and the moment when action appropriate to satisfying the want culminates in its satisfaction' (1962a).

With a focus on psychic experience, current thinking about 'mentalizing' has much in common with Bion's containing function. Mentalizing involves the capacity to intuit and track emotional and mental states in the self and others (Allen *et al.*, 2008; Bateman and Fonagy, 2004, 2006). The ability to mentalize remains largely unconscious or preconscious and involves attempts to perceive and interpret the intentional mental states that lie behind behaviour or conscious thought. Similar to the containing function, mentalizing is an imaginative activity that respects the opaque nature of minds. It necessarily involves imprecise attempts at making meaning that focuses on mental states rather than on the physical world directly. Our ability to mentalize allows us to have multiple perspectives on an object, an idea similar to Bion's use of the term 'correlation' to refer to the ability to hold in mind and contain multiple views on an object.

When our ability to focus on mental states as meaningful in themselves collapses, we move towards what Bateman and Fonagy (2004) call 'psychic equivalence' where internal and external experience, psychical and physical experience, are seen as the same. Once this occurs the ability to hold things in mind or 'contain' is lost and mental states verge towards being treated like physical objects. Indeed, the idea of containing itself is translated into physical terms when this occurs. 'I just need to hold things together' or 'I just keep things inside', are examples of how the container is represented as a near-physical entity as a means of regulating affect when mentalizing begins to collapse.

Container pathology

Ferro (2005a) develops Bion's theories of psychic functions and thinking into a model for understanding different types of psychopathology. In his view pathological states can take three forms. The first involves the impairment of alpha-function where sense impressions cannot be transformed into rudimentary psychic forms or pictograms. With this, the apparatus for thinking has little to transform or act on. The consequences are most evident in psychotic and autistic states where sense impressions take the place of thoughts and are either evacuated through projective processes or used as objects of encapsulation. Without an ability to produce rudimentary thoughts, distinctions between internal/external and conscious/ unconscious experience are seriously impaired.

The second category of pathological states emerges when the individual is able to produce pictograms or alpha-elements but lacks the capacity to think about them through using the container function and processes of integration and disintegration (Ps↔D). The third form of pathology is related to traumatic states which arise when alpha-function is overwhelmed by sense data which it cannot process.

In this book I use Ferro's model but focus particularly on the role of the container. In doing so I consider how modes of interaction between container–contained can be applied to the clinical situation representing internal psychic states that are enacted in the therapeutic relationship. Bion considers three different relationships between container–contained interaction: symbiotic, commensal and parasitic. To this I add autistic, and pseudo-containing strategies.

In later chapters I consider various manifestations of container pathology and their particular consequences. Prominent in my thoughts about container pathology is the location and use of the container as a near-physical object synonymous with autistic and 'self-containing' strategies. In terms of Bion's model, what seems to occur here is confusion between beta-elements and alpha-elements. My sense is that when alpha-function or the containing function are immobilized, somewhat more primitive organizations linked to beta-elements and non-symbolic proto-containing capacities take hold and are treated like psychic objects. This leads to particular pathological states where sensory objects mimic thoughts. I relate this to the existence of a 'mimetic function', a primitive counterpart to alpha-function, responsible for generating near-physical non-symbolic experiences in the psyche. I consider this to constitute the emergence of a pathological process when containment breaks down. Because thoughts are treated like objects and sensory objects are treated like thoughts, the containing function proper is replaced by near-physical or fabricated versions of the psychic container. In later chapters I use the term *beta-mentality* to refer to various manifestations of this pathological process.

Chapter 2

Projective identification, countertransference and the containing function

In this chapter I want explore what we mean when we say we are utilizing a containing function in analytic practice. Apart from being confused with Winnicott's concept of 'holding', the containing function is often taken to refer to the maintenance of a somewhat passive, empathic connection with the patient. One supervisee of mine once described containing as 'just sitting with the patient, absorbing things in a calm and quiet way'. In this way it is associated with attempts to gain access to the patient's mind by 'absorbing' or 'taking on' unassimilated, often volatile, emotional states. This easily leads to the idea that the therapist needs to offer himself or herself as a passive receptacle for the patient's projections. Even more, 'absorbing things in a calm and quiet way' seems to introduce subtle pressures for the analyst to maintain silences and a 'calmness' that can appear rather contrived and stilted. From this perspective the analyst's 'containing' stance is unwittingly close to outdated analogies that portray the analyst as a 'blank screen'.

At the other extreme, 'containing' is often used as shorthand for active interventions aimed at reassurance, conveying empathy, or simply attempting to calm the patient down. It is associated with active attempts to protect the patient. This occurs through excessive or gratuitous attempts at empathizing with the patient to attain a sense of 'being there' with the patient. This forms part of a countertransference state that I call 'idealizing the container' which I explore further in Chapter 8.

While all the above may at times have some place in the therapeutic process, these approaches need to be separated from Bion's use of the term. In my understanding, Bion has in mind a generative process that involves intuiting, engaging and naming unarticulated experience through complex interpersonal and intrapsychic exchanges. The complexity of the process, as I understand it, involves both the 'presence' and 'absence' of the analyst's mind in the analytic field, a tension between engaging with states of reverie and presenting oneself as a more 'present' object closer to the demands of external reality. Bion thought that the containing process demanded much more than the simple presence of the therapist and depended on a particular mental connection between minds (Bion, 1967). This brings us to question how we understand, theoretically and technically, the nature of this mental connection. In 'Attacks On Linking', Bion (1959) begins to describe the containing process as follows:

> My deduction was that in order to understand what the child wanted the mother should have treated the infant's cry as more than a demand for her presence. From the infant's point of view, she should have taken into her, and thus experienced, the fear that the child was dying. It was this fear that the child could not contain.
>
> (p.313)

Here Bion refers to the containing process as being related to the therapist's ability to 'take in' projective identifications and experience them in order to connect with the infant's inchoate experience. A sentence later he alludes to what this might mean for the containing mind of the mother or the therapist:

> An understanding mother is able to experience the feeling of dread that this baby was striving to deal with by projective identification, *and yet retain a balanced outlook* [my emphasis] . . . To some this reconstruction will appear to be unduly fanciful.
>
> (1959, p.313)

What might Bion mean here about retaining *a balanced outlook*? Bion is aware that the above statements may appear 'unduly fanciful' and how much his formulation moves away from a psychoanalysis that is focused on the analysis of memories and the past to one that focuses on *transforming experience* through the immediacy of encounters with another mind. Many questions could be raised about his formulation: how are projections actually 'taken in'? What actually happens? How are projections given back? What is transformed in this process and how? It seems as though much of the very schematic language used in analytic texts has led to a great deal of confusion regarding how these ideas are translated into technique. Bion's work is far from exempt of such confusions. Nevertheless, his ideas on the analyst's containing mind, as being closely linked to reverie and negative capability, suggest a state of mind that attempts to experience each session anew. It is a state of mind that attempts to apprehend experience that is felt at the edges of consciousness but cannot yet be understood, fully experienced, or held in mind. In this way Bion's view of analytical containment concerns a process of transformation whereby previously unbearable states of mind that prevent thinking and development are made more bearable and thinkable. As Bion put it, the containing process works on parts of the individual (or the analytic couple) that 'feel the pain but will not suffer it and so cannot be said to discover it' (1970, p.9). In considering various aspects of the 'containing function', in effect I want to consider further what Bion might have meant by the analyst's 'balanced outlook' in the containing process. I arrive at the idea that, both theoretically and clinically, the containing function is a bridging construct, a caesura that is best conveyed through attention to the analyst's and patient's inchoate experiential states or reveries. I develop this idea by viewing the containing function as a mental connection that is maintained through balancing tensions between the analyst's function as 'proper object' and 'dream object' (Chapter 3). First, I consider projective, identification, 'holding' and countertransference and their links to the containing function.

The container and projective identification

Although Bion developed the idea of 'the container' as a coherent psychoanalytic concept, ideas about the mind or body acting as a container for thoughts and feelings are implicit in many psychological writings. From a psychoanalytic perspective, Melanie Klein (1932) put forward the idea that infants possess an innate curiosity about the insides of their mothers' bodies. She believed that children based their early understanding of the world on primitive phantasies about their mothers' insides. In this sense, from the infant's perspective, the mother is conceived of as a container of concrete objects that are experienced in preverbal interactions with the mother. Developing this idea further, Klein (1946) assumed that the internal image of the mother or analyst can act as a receptacle for the child's mental contents or projections via the mechanism of projective identification. The idea that the phantasy of projective identification had particular interpersonal or external consequences (through cycles of projective and introjective identification) was developed further by a number of Kleinians, notably Heimann (1950), Money-Kyrle (1956, 1971), Rosenfeld (1952) and Jacques (1953). Central to their arguments was the idea that the analyst can make use of countertransference states to understand and interpret projective identifications so projected parts of the self can be reintrojected by the patient. Implicit here is the notion that the analyst becomes a container for the patient's projections. Writing during a similar period, Bion began to develop this idea further.

In 'Notes on the Theory of Schizophrenia' (Bion, 1954) and 'Differentiation of the Psychotic and Non-Psychotic Personalities' (Bion, 1957), Bion makes use of Klein's concept of projective identification to illustrate how parts of the self can, in phantasy, be projected into other parts of the personality or external objects. Here he alludes to the idea that external objects can become receptacles for fragments of experience or psychic functions. In his words: 'particles of the ego lead an independent and uncontrolled existence, either contained by or containing the external objects'

(Bion, 1957, p.268). This, as far as I am aware, is the first time we see Bion playing with ideas that seem to be forerunners to the full development of his idea of the container–contained configuration.

One of Bion's major contributions to theory and technique came in the wake of his extension of Klein's concept of projective identification where he makes the analyst's containing function an 'essential feature of Melanie Klein's conception of projective identification' (1962b, p.3).

Klein (1946) introduced the term projective identification in 'Notes on Schizoid Mechanisms'. She thought that schizoid mechanisms, combined with unconscious persecutory phantasies, caused the infant to split off and locate good or bad parts of the self in other internal objects, particularly the mother. Through this primitive defensive process the infant, in phantasy, rids herself of unwanted parts of the self and uses them to control, damage or take over other objects. Klein saw this as a template for aggressive object relations with the mother, particularly concerning the projection of unbearable bad aspects of the self in which 'she [the recipient of projective identification] is not felt to be a separate individual but is felt to be the bad self' (p.9).

Klein also recognized that this inevitably led to a depletion and frag-mentation of the self due to continually locating parts of the self in other objects. Later she advanced the idea that projective identification could be viewed as an essential means to managing excessive envy by destroying good or idealized parts of the object (Klein, 1957). In both of these con-tributions Klein alludes to projective identification as having multiple functions and aims.

Developing Klein's thinking, Bion (1959) put forward an important dis-tinction between normal and abnormal forms of projective identification which appeared to pave the way for thinking more broadly about the analyst's containing function. Klein's version of projective identification is similar to what Bion called pathological or abnormal projective identification where projections are motivated by phantasies of intrusion, omnipotence, destructiveness and control. In contrast, normal or realistic forms of projective identification involve the projection of intolerable or unassimilated states of mind that intend to communicate something to the object that can be held in mind and transformed by a receptive other. It could also be argued that implicit in Bion's idea here is an extended phantasy associated with normal forms of projective identification. It involves a sense of unconscious hope that unbearable mental states can be received and 'metabolized' by the receiver's mind before they are returned.

The link here between a 'containing object' and normal forms of projective identification has a number of implications for theory and technique. Most importantly it shifts Klein's version of projective identification from being essentially defensive and intrapsychic to one that better captures a devel-opmental process within an interpersonal context. From this perspective, projective identifications are received and transformed by the containing mother in a way that leads to psychic development. In Bion's (1962a) words:

> Normal development follows if the relationship between infant and breast permits the infant to project a feeling, say, that it is dying, into the mother and to reintroject it after its sojourn in the breast has made it tolerable to the infant psyche. If the projection is not accepted by the mother the infant feels that its feeling that it is dying is stripped of such meaning as it has. It therefore reintrojects, not a fear of dying made tolerable, but a nameless dread.
>
> (p.306)

The infant actively seeks communication with the object, enlisting the person in attempts to read, feel and transform affective states or psychic activity that feel incomprehensible and threatening. The mother's containing function involves being receptive to the infant's unassimilated affective states so as to make them more tolerable and thinkable. If the mother is not receptive to what the infant feels, more forceful aggressive means are used in an attempt to enlist the object. As opposed to pathological or abnormal projective identification, where aggression might be seen as inherent in the individual, aggression evident in normal forms of projective identification is more likely to have its origins in interpersonal or environmental influences (Bott Spillius, 1988). Of course, in reality such distinctions are usually a matter of degree, and it is often the case that projective identifications aimed primarily at communicating unassimilated experience can develop into pathological forms of projective identification should the receptivity of the object be unavailable. Either way, Bion's consideration of the importance of the mother's container function in normal development creates a crucial link between mother and infant.

But the influence of the analyst's or mother's containing mind goes further than simply processing and 'returning' unbearable mental states. It ultimately leads to the internalization of the containing function itself so as to become part of the patient's mental apparatus. In Bion's terms, the containing relationship is introjected 'as part of the apparatus of alpha-function' (1962b, p.91). It is not clear precisely how Bion conceptualized the relationship between alpha-function and the container. They appear to have different functions at times, but in some of his work he makes little distinction between the two. For my purposes, following Ferro (2002, 2005a), I see them as having different psychic functions. Whereas alpha-function transforms sensory impressions and affect states into primitive psychic forms (alpha-elements), the containing function gives meaning to such psychic elements as they begin to aggregate. With this in mind I would not see the container as introjected as a part of alpha-function, rather it is internalized as a separate function that supports alpha-function.

The process involved in communicating through projective identification is perhaps best understood as occurring in three different phases where projective identification is viewed as intrapsychic, but with interpersonal components. First, as just mentioned, projections occur in the mind of the projector. In other words, the individual projects into his or her internal image of the object. For example, the patient may project hate into a psychic representation of the therapist, turning the internal image into an aggressive and dangerous object. The effect this has on the other person, the therapist, as an external object, does not occur by virtue of an actual projection.

A second phase occurs at an interpersonal level whereby the manipulation of the internal image sets in train a process of interpersonal 'nudging' or influencing that impacts the relationship so as to realize aspects of the patient's intrapsychic phantasy (Ogden, 1986; Grotstein, 2005). To return to the example above, the patient may, for instance, engage in behaviours that subtly irritate the therapist, inducing him to act out in a way that can be perceived as 'hateful'. For example, the patient may be consistently late, avoid acknowledging the therapist's presence, or adopt mannerisms that 'get under the therapist's skin'. These are but a few instances of how the patient may translate and confirm his or her phantasies through 'interpersonal nudging'. Often much of this escapes our conscious awareness and we only become aware of this through exploring countertransference states. Here induction or transformation of the object occurs at a sensory motor level through gesturing, prompting, and the tone, prosody and rhythmic components of verbal interaction.

The third aspect of this process occurs when 'hard-wired' capacities for empathic attunement activate similar phantasies in the receiving object. Recently, Grotstein (2005) has put forward the concept projective *trans*-identification to help clarify the subtle non-conscious aspects of this process:

> In projective transidentification, the analyst, upon experiencing the evocative or provocative induction (sensory, ultra-sensory, or even extrasensory) stimulus from the analysand, summons within himself those corresponding symmetrical phantasies that match the analysand's experience. This is how the mother functions in maternal reverie when attending to her infant. Thus, when the analyst seems to act as a container for the analysand's reported experiences, I postulate that the analysand unconsciously projectively identifies his emotional state into the image of the analyst with the hope of ridding himself of pain and of inducing this state in the analyst by manipulating his image of the later.
> (p.1064)

Returning to the example, as a result of the interpersonal nudging that occurs, we might imagine that the projection of hate unconsciously activates corresponding object relationships in the analyst which involve the self in relation to internal bad hateful objects. As Grotstein puts it, this occurs when 'the projecting subject evokes something already extant and dormant within the external object whose latent capacity for empathic resonance with the subject's intrapsychic identification could be elicited' (p.1061). Important here is that although the patient, in phantasy, wants the therapist to contain his split-off feelings, the therapist can only connect with this through his own feelings; he can only feel his own feelings.

The above has important implications for our understanding of the analyst's function as a container. It attempts to set right slippages in understanding projective identification as implying that something 'real' is moved from patient to therapist. This, in turn, implies that the therapist functions to literally contain parts of the patient, an 'actual' container.

Much of the confusion here appears to be due to an overly schematic usage of the term 'projective identification' that loses sight of the fact that it is essentially an intrapsychic phantasy. Perhaps it goes without saying that we can only in phantasy split off aspects of our self and put them into other internal objects. Unfortunately, references to projective identification often unwittingly confuse issues here by referring to the process as if they were real physical happenings in time and space. It appears that at least part of this problem occurs due to extension of the term to include interpersonal components. These are clearly important but, in my view, need to be clearly separated from projective identification itself.

The idea of 'being projected into' also sets up the overly schematic idea that we need to 'hold on' to projections, keep them 'inside' us, and then give them back. Further, it seems that this view leads to conceptions of the therapist's container function as being a means of ameliorating turmoil or bringing about 'a sense of calm and security' in the patient by offering oneself as a protective receptacle for the patient's unbearable feelings. Although this may be important at times when the patient is distressed, this is not the essence or goal of the containing function. Such truncated perspectives on the container model, as I understand it, are far from the clinical reality of how the containing process actually occurs and tend to undervalue the complexity of the process that Bion attempts to focus on. Furthermore, the image of the container as a three-dimensional reified vessel better explains the way it is appropriated in pathological processes. It occurs in the therapeutic process when the therapist idealizes the idea of 'holding' the patient's feelings. It also arises in pathological states where thoughts and feelings are used to shore up the self, treating the self like an actual object. Alternatively, it occurs when objects are experienced as inflexible, impenetrable, leading to excessive use of projective identification and violent action.

There is one final important implication to using projective identification and the container in overly schematic ways. It leaves the impression of a rather linear 'containing' process whereby the therapist goes through a process of receptivity-metabolization-interpretation. In clinical reality, however, various versions of these 'containing activities' occur simultaneously and cannot be conceptualized as discrete tasks. This is partly why in later sections of the book I formulate the analyst's containing mind in dynamical, non-linear terms and see the role of interpretation as more iterative in nature (see Chapter 5).

In my brief exploration of the link between projective identification and the container I hope to have made it clear that Bion depicted the 'container' as essentially having a transformational function that aims to give meaning and thought to unbearable states of mind. It is important to bear in mind that although an interpersonal 'nudging' process accompanies the communication of projective identification between projector and recipient, the containing process itself refers to an intrapsychic function.

In addition to the overly schematic image of 'the container', the therapist's containing function is also often confused with Winnicott's concept of 'holding'. Before continuing to explore the main features of the containing process it is worthwhile setting out the difference between these two concepts.

'Holding' and the container function

Although often used interchangeably, 'containing' and 'holding' refer to very different clinical processes that exist at different levels of conceptualization. Symington and Symington (1986) make the following distinctions between the container and holding:

> The container is *internal*, whereas holding or the holding environment is external or in the transitional stage between internal and external; the container is non-sensuous but the holding environment is predominantly sensuous; the container together with the contained is active. This activity may be either integrating or destructive, whereas the holding environment is positive and growth promoting.
>
> (p.58)

By 'internal' I take the Symingtons to be referring to the containing process as a mental process whereby unnamable psychic states are given meaning and can begin to be thought about. Because Bion formulated the container as a psychical concept, it differs from the sensuous nature of holding that represents something interpersonal and actual. In fact Bion thought that sensual experience could be used defensively to ameliorate the intensity of the container–contained dynamic. In his words:

> The sense of touch is usually employed as an antidote to the confusion that can be incidental to the employment of ♀♂. [It is used] to establish

the reassurance obtained from feeling there is a barrier between two objects, a limiting boundary that is absent in the container–contained relationship.

(Bion, 1963, pp.95–96)

Bion goes on to argue that this 'produces the paradoxical effect that the topographically closer relationship implied by tactile contact is less intimate, i.e. less confused, than the more distant "container–contained relationship"' (p.95).[1] By implication, the container is not directly dependent on the physical proximity of the object. Put simply, holding someone or something in mind and allowing it to gather psychic meaning does not directly depend on interpersonal processes or the physical proximity of the object. Although, as discussed earlier, projective identification is dependent on an interpersonal 'nudging' process for transmitting feeling states, containing and transforming such projections does not depend on the physical presence of the object.

It seems to me that one of the implications of considering the container link as being an intrapsychic process still remains to be fully explored in analytic writings. It concerns the idea that a containing mind need not be conceptualized as being 'housed' in one person or individual, the mother, for instance. Because it is not dependent on the physical sensuous world it can be formulated as being part of 'many minds' in considering the individual's mental state. In other words, the container function may be carried out by mothers, fathers and others, and is not housed in a closed two-person system. Bion seems to be making reference to these qualities when he writes:

> There is a field of emotional force in which the individuals seem to lose their boundaries as individuals and become 'areas' around and through which emotions play at will. . . . That state of mind is easier to understand if it is regarded as the state of mind of a group rather than of an individual but transcending the boundaries we usually regard as proper to groups or individuals.
>
> (Bion, 1967, p.146)

This seems to link with Bion's thoughts about the analyst ignoring the psychology of the group at their peril (Bion, 1992). Further, if we conceptualize the therapeutic space as a bi-directional field, the containing function occurs in a field of experience generated by both participants and cannot be easily located in the therapist. From this perspective the intrapsychic nature of the container transcends physical boundaries.

---

1 By quoting Bion here, I am not suggesting that Winnicott's 'holding' is synonymous with physical touch. I understand Bion to be referring to all sensory experience.

A further related implication that separates the containing function from 'holding' pertains to the idea that 'containing' continues, as a process beyond the physical constraints of the session. Depending on a number of different factors (the analyst's psychological make-up, the degree to which projective identification is used with excessive force), the therapist continues to psychically digest unassimilated experiences engendered in him by his contact with the patient outside sessions. In some cases, as part of a pathological process, the patient succeeds in annexing parts of the therapist's mind for the purpose of denying reality. However, it is likely that this process continues with all patients but remains largely unconscious and unobtrusive.

To return to the distinction between the container and 'holding', whereas 'holding' is always growth promoting, the same cannot be said for the container. The container function attempts to make unformulated experience understandable. The outcome might give rise to positive or destructive effects. 'Holding', on the other hand, relies on the therapist's ability to accommodate to the patient's needs in order to foster safety and security in an interpersonal setting. In this way 'holding' is an attempt to meet the patient's regressive dependency needs and to protect them from impingements apparent in the environment. It is expressed in terms of the mother's 'primary maternal preoccupation' (Winnicott, 1965) where she ablates herself, her needs, so that they don't get in the way. As Ogden (2004b) puts it, 'the mother's early psychological and physical "holding" includes her insulating the infant in his state of going on being from the relentless, unalterable otherness of time' (p.1350). In this safe place everything is measured by the rhythms of the infant. Although 'holding' is always growth promoting, containing involves, to quote Ogden again, 'the full spectrum of ways of processing experience from the most destructive and deadening to the most creative and growth-promoting' (Ogden, 2004b, p.1349). For this to happen the mother needs a mind of her own in order to intuit and help the infant 'name' unarticulated experience, not the suspended or ablated self evident in 'holding'. This point best clarifies the differences between these two terms: the containing function is dependent on the mother's mind, her imaginative speculations, whereas 'holding' is dependent on accommodating to the needs of the infant or patient. Here, differences between minds are diminished as much as possible and the mother's mind is seen as a potential impingement.

Recognizing the differences between these two concepts, some analysts have particular ways in which they put them to clinical use. Grotstein (1991, 2000), for instance, sees 'holding' as more directly related to affect regulation, whereas container–contained interaction is seen as a dynamic 'meaning-making agent', ultimately giving us symbolic language to understand our lives. Although useful, this distinction appears somewhat limiting as it could be argued that 'meaning-making' and the ability to name unassimilated experience also impacts affect regulation. This is primarily the result of a mental connection, not an interpersonal one. In other words, mentalization, attending to mental states and understanding them, also impacts on affect regulation in the analytic field (Bateman and Fonagy, 2004; Fonagy, 2004). Caper (1999) introduces another way of using the concepts of 'holding' and 'containing' in clinical practice that does not necessarily contradict Grotstein's view. He suggests that we see the therapeutic process as moving from the accommodating 'holding' position, where the patient feels secure, to the containing relationship where a sense of 'insecurity', something different from the patient's perspective, is introduced via interpretation. Both these approaches uphold the distinctions between these two concepts as being clinically useful.

Countertransference

Freud (1910) understood countertransference to be the 'result of the patient's influence on his unconscious feelings' (p.144). In this, his initial engagement with the topic, he recognizes the influence of the patient on the analyst, elaborating his idea that this occurs mainly through an unconscious–unconscious linkup between both parties. Although he recognized these influences, Freud thought that the evoked responses on the part of the analyst largely emerged in the form of his own conflicts and thus should be expunged through personal analysis and self-analysis if the analyst is to have a 'clear view' of his patient. The historical development of countertransference is extensive and I do not intend reviewing it here. I am concerned with considering how countertransference intersects with the therapist's containing function.

During the late 1940s and 1950s the tide of how countertransference should be used in clinical practice began to change perhaps most significantly due to Winnicott's (1949) paper on 'Hate in the counter-transference' and Heimann's (1950) 'On counter-transference'. Both, in different ways, take up the idea that the countertransference is more than a problematic obstacle and can act as a rich source of information about the patient. In Heimann's words:

> My thesis is that the analyst's emotional response to his patient within the analytic situation represents one of the most important tools of his work. The analyst's countertransference is an instrument of research into the patient's unconscious.

(p.74)

Here begins the idea that the countertransference is 'the patient's *creation*, it is part of the patient's personality' (p.77). This position unfortunately led to a great deal of misunderstanding in the management of countertransference. It is often misinterpreted to mean that the analyst should make statements along the lines of 'You are making me feel . . .'. This, in effect, amounts to simply giving back what is being projected into the analyst but also 'blames' the patient for what can only be the analyst's feelings albeit evoked by the patient. Heimann (1956) never advocated such an approach. Although words like 'the patient's *creation*' easily lead to misinterpretation, Heimann was making the point that the analyst's feelings bear impressions of the patient's personality. Perhaps in response to this confusion, other Kleinian authors at the time, particularly Money-Kyrle (1956), went about emphasizing the complex tangle between the analyst's and the patient's feelings in the countertransference. It raises important questions regarding how the analyst engages with his countertransference as a source of 'evocative knowledge' (Young, 1994). In Bion's model, the mother or therapist acts as a container for these emergent forms of meaning. He put forward the idea that we are able to best access and understand such countertransference states through making use of analytic reverie. We return to this in the next section.

Broad acknowledgement of the usefulness of the countertransference response has been interpreted in many different ways across psychoanalytic schools, but there is some consensus that the analyst's engagement with his own emotional experience contributes to how he intervenes and what he chooses to express (consciously or unconsciously). Further there is also general agreement that for countertransference to evolve as a useful source of knowledge, the therapist has to guard against 'acting out' the countertransference. That being said, some, including myself, have also illustrated how deliberate or spontaneous countertransference disclosure may have therapeutic benefits in particular cases (e.g. Bollas, 1983; Cartwright, 1997; Coltart, 1992; Ehrenberg, 1995; Symington, 1983). It should be said, however, that such claims do not advocate disclosure on a continuous basis and warn against its abuse. What is meant by 'countertransference disclosure' also varies a great deal. It might involve directly enacting the countertransference, consciously revealing personal details about one's self, disclosing one's feeling about the patient, or simply making evident to the patient the way the analyst is thinking about a matter.

More recently there is growing awareness that a degree of countertransference disclosure or enactment is an inevitable part of the analytic process. If one accepts that countertransference is mostly unconscious and therefore remains somewhat undefined, unknowable, partial enactment is inevitable. The therapist begins with only a fleeting or blunt awareness of his own feelings and thoughts in terms of how they relate to a particular patient. In this way countertransference is usually experienced first as a source of 'pressure', vague affective states that cannot yet be thought about or understood. As a result the enactment of such 'pressures' is to some degree inevitable. There are two points here. Not only are partial enactments inevitable, but they also give rise to important information about unconscious processes that are only made conscious through enactment. Because such states are always evolving, the therapist, in my view, should not rely on a 'dictionary' of ready-made countertransference states as Baranger (1993) seems to suggest. Rather the countertransference should be approached as always idiosyncratic, textured with different meanings that match the uniqueness of each patient.

Partial enactments of the countertransference are increasingly being understood as also having important therapeutic value. I find Carpy's (1989) paper, 'Tolerating the Countertransference: A Mutative Process', to be an excellent exposition of this line of reasoning. In his understanding:

> The analyst's partial acting out allows the patient to see, consciously and unconsciously, that she is affecting the analyst and inducing strong feelings in him, and it allows her to observe him attempting to deal with these feelings.
>
> (p.292)

Carpy's argument about the mutative effects of countertransference enactment is based on the idea that the analyst grapples with tolerating his own feeling states so as to grant the patient a degree of evidence on two fronts. First, the patient is granted evidence that she is getting through to the analyst. Second, the partial enactment subtly confirms the patient's world view. For example, let us say the therapist grapples with feelings of irritation that cannot be fully understood. The therapist struggles with these feeling states, perhaps appearing slightly uncomfortable, signalling to the patient that she is affecting the therapist and getting through to him. In addition, this also activates, in subtle ways, her fear that others cannot bear her feelings and will reject her (her world view). In this way, the process is mutative because it sets in motion ongoing vicarious contact with split-off parts of the self, gradually permitting the patient to internalize them in a more tolerable way *through non-verbal interaction*. This differs from a model advocating the 'return' of split-off parts of the self through interpretation. We will return to this issue in discussing the role of interpretation in the containing process (Chapter 5). From this point of view, we might say that the patient begins to witness, mostly unconsciously, the therapist's struggle with difficult unknown experiences that mirror her own internal world. It is made more bearable through witnessing the therapist's implicit and inevitable communications that he remains engaged with this unarticulated aspect of himself. Brenman Pick (1995) indicates that the patient constantly monitors the therapist's movements in avoiding or engaging emotional turmoil and is very skilled in projecting into particular parts of the analyst that unconsciously elicit the desired feeling. The fact that there is always a part of the therapist that wishes to avoid psychic pain makes this necessarily a struggle that inevitably reveals itself in the therapist's demeanour, vocal tone, degree of eye contact, fumblings, choice of words and so forth.

How might the above be related to the containing function? As an intrapsychic concept, the containing function, in my opinion, predominantly refers to the therapist's internal processing of countertransference states. First, this involves the therapist's capacity to attend to countertransference states along with wilfully attempting to curtail destructive 'acting out'. Second, the therapist turns his attention to states of reverie, waking dream-thoughts that serve as a textured commentary on what countertransference states might mean thereby processing them.

As suggested by Carpy (1989), the internal process is continually being communicated at a non-verbal level through his tolerating the countertransference. As an interpersonal process, however, this does not form part of the containing function per se but a way of communicating the container function at work. In this way the 'fall-out' from tolerating the countertransference, always failing to some degree, gently begins to implicitly expose the patient to an imperfect but more bearable struggle. This is an image of a therapist who is able to think and connect while struggling with feelings that are vicariously linked to the patient's internal states. Returning to Carpy (1989), in terms of the mother–infant model, this concerns the mother being able to tolerate panic in order to feed the infant:

> If she is able to tolerate such a panic, she will feed the baby. In my opinion what is 'containing' about this is that the baby will have an experience of being fed by a mother in whom he can sense panic, but who is nevertheless able to give him milk. This is what makes the panic tolerable.
>
> (p.293)

There are two points I wish to add to the above. First, in my experience the analyst's subjectivity is an essential part of this process. As the patient or infant begins to sense the analyst's struggle and his attempts to speak from within himself, he begins to connect with the analyst's subjective experience, the analyst as subject. Implicit in Carpy's words, 'an experience of being fed by mother [object] in whom he can sense panic [subjective],' is a dual process. It concerns a play between mother as 'object', containing split-off parts of the self, and mother as 'subject' through whom he gains vicarious contact with the experience of these split-off states. Put simply, sensing the analyst's subjectivity is an important means through which the patient begins to think about and tolerate his own uncontained mental states.

Second, tolerating the countertransference reiterates the idea that the containing process is constantly being communicated via the struggle to put words to experience. It is dependent on a particular kind of mental connection that differs from the idea that the containing function is simply lodged in the mind of the therapist who separately 'metabolizes' it and gives it back to the patient once it is more manageable.

Opposing views on the containing function

So far we have explored how countertransference might be conceptualized as part of the containing process and established that the therapist's containing function aims to achieve a lot more than simply forming an empathic or ameliorating connection with the patient. Differences between 'holding' as Winnicott defined it and the containing function have also been set out. The containing function as Bion conceptualized it is much more about making the unbearable thinkable. Caper (1999) puts this well when he says: 'Analytic containment converts a state of mind that is unbearable . . . into a state of mind that is merely insecure' (p.155). This is in keeping with Bion's view that psychoanalysis should aim to expand the patient's capacity for suffering. But there is less clarity when it comes to how these ideas are applied to the analytic encounter in understanding how projections are 'detoxified' by the analyst's containing function and 'returned' to the patient in a more manageable form.

Analysts differ as to what aspects should be considered essential features of the containing function. It has been understood to include such qualities as:

- a capacity for active observation, clarification and emotional resonance (Charles, 2004; Sorensen, 1995)
- a sanctuary that imparts a sense of being 'inside' a good object (Britton, 1992a; Luzuriaga, 2000)
- a unique, private area of mind, sheltered from irrelevant stimuli that imparts a sense of comfort for the purpose of modulating psychic pain (Meltzer, 1986)
- a transformative meaning-giving function making use of the analyst's reverie (Ferro, 2002, 2005a, 2006; Grotstein, 2000; Ogden, 1997, 2004b)
- a process of 'taking the transference' that involves reverie, transformation and publication (Mitrani, 2001)
- a form of projective identification from analyst to patient (Hamilton, 1990).

Analysts also differ on how the concept translates into particular analytic techniques or the adoption of a particular analytic stance. I shall not review all contributions here. Rather, I intend to focus on two opposing views on the subject, Ogden's and Caper's, as they represent what I consider to be polar dimensions, 'points in the containing process'. Ogden, on the one hand, privileges the therapist's reverie as essential in the containment process, whereas Caper focuses on the role of the therapist as a real 'proper' object.

Caper (1999) is of the view that the therapist, while being receptive to projections, needs to maintain his separateness, resisting identification with such projections so as to be able to think about them. This, according to Caper, instils a healthy boundary between the patient and the analyst. Whilst being receptive to projections, the ability not to identify with the patient's phantasies shows the patient, through the process of analysis, that 'there is something in the analyst that he cannot penetrate with his projections' (p.114). This requires being 'role-unresponsive' to projections and, according to Caper, through his interpretative action, the analyst is best off treating these phantasies as 'objects of knowledge' (p.114). It entails the analyst maintaining a sense of 'integrity' or conviction in order to distance himself or emerge from the folie à deux brought about by projective identification. By doing so the analyst aims to introduce himself as a 'proper object' (p.117) in the sense that his comments are distinct, private and peculiar to himself. 'Containing', from Caper's perspective, comprises the ability to bring together two separate capacities: the ability to be receptive to projections and the analyst's ability to act and think separately and realistically in relation to them. In his words: 'The idea I propose is that the object contains or detoxifies what has been projected into it simply by being realistic about it' (p.141). Here the nature of what is projected is altered by helping the patient see that his phantasies are not real and are not immutable concrete objects. In this way the containment function is working to sort out confusions between external and internal reality. Caper is clear that this is an ongoing process with the analyst's interventions constantly chipping away at the unrealistic hold that phantasy has on external objects. Containing is about putting intractable narcissistic phantasies (extensions of the self) in their place so they can be located and understood as products of the patient's internal world.

Carl

It was clear very early in therapy that Carl perceived me as being a threatening figure. He would say very little about himself and deny any sense of fear or threat when I mentioned this to him, even though at times he was clearly very anxious when he sat with me. In one particular session I was very aware of the threat he felt and I tried to think about whether my attempts to make him feel a little more at ease were somehow confirming his projection. I came up with very little but realized that I was feeling helpless in trying to reach him. In time it seemed clearer that the very fact that I was making 'his threat' the centre of our work was unconsciously confirming his view of me as immensely threatening. This realization seemed to free me somewhat from trying to address his anxiety so directly.

Most of what Carl spoke about related to a sense of feeling disconnected from others and a feeling that others were largely disinterested in him and his work. Relationships with men always appeared somewhat strained and he often described a sense of having 'unfinished business' in these situations. This appeared related to how he always wanted to participate more in discussions with men but felt he could not. Finding it very difficult to engage with me, much of our discussions seemed to centre around thoughts about the 'exceptional bond' he had with his father. I was often aware of how he appeared to talk about this relationship in overstated and idealized ways. Although his idealized thinking appeared to create a barrier to me exploring this relationship further with him, his father appeared to be a particularly harsh disciplinarian and a very dominating figure. This led me to start thinking about what might lie behind his tenacious need to hold on to this particular view of his father. With this is mind I interpreted that I thought underlying the 'goodness' in his relationship with his father there appeared to be some 'unfinished business' that we appeared to be avoiding. I said that I sensed that this was a very real threat to him, so much so that he felt similarly threatened by me when I attempted to explore his anxiety. I then went on to ask him to consider what it was about our situation, about me, that made him feel so anxious. He began to consider some of my actions that made him feel that I was being hostile. Gradually he appeared to gain a sense that not all of my actions and thoughts had hostile intent and in some cases Carl began to see that they were attempts to help him.

After repeating various versions of this interpretation over the next three months, the sense of threat that dominated our sessions for a long period was clearly diminished. The shift in our relationship seemed to ignite a different kind of relational dynamic where he would describe a benevolent sense of 'feeling listened to like an uncle'.

In the above brief example, 'containing' aims towards respecting and demarcating the integrity of part of the therapist's mind as separate from projections. Initially I appeared to be drawn into playing the role of an extremely threatening object simply by making this the focus of our work together. However, in time, once he was able to sense the absence of real threat, Carl was better able to focus on the idea that his anxiety emanated from destructive phantasies related to his father (which made themselves present through projective identification). The shift that occurred as a result appeared to make me more available to him as a more real, caring 'uncle' object.

Caper (1999) emphasizes the idea that self-esteem is derived from relationships with love objects as separate objects, rather than through narcissistic intrusion or treating the object as an extension of the self. Here, the love and support of an external object does not itself account for healthy development. The infant has to overcome the intrusiveness of the object before she can see it as separate, therefore allowing her to benefit from the object as a separate good entity.

Whereas Caper's focus is on the analyst as 'proper object', Ogden's emphasis regarding the containing function, lies in the therapist's ability to use his reverie. He sees reverie as a crucial means of creating intersubjective dialogical narratives that form part of what he calls the 'analytic third' (2004a, p.167). In essence, containing is about finding ways of holding previously unarticulated experience (produced by the analytic third) in mind for long enough so as to gather new meaning. Following Bion, Ogden finds that reverie is essentially a state of acute receptivity and the conduit through which a new form of relatedness can emerge between analyst and analysand. In his words, it 'involves (a partial) giving over of one's separate individuality to a third subject, a subject that is neither analyst nor analysand but a third subjectivity unconsciously generated by the analytic pair' (p.9). Ogden goes on to emphasize the gravity of such an endeavour:

> To consistently offer oneself in this way is no small matter: it represents an emotionally draining undertaking in which analyst and analysand each to a degree 'loses his mind' (his capacity to think and create experience as a distinctly separate individual).
>
> (Ogden, 1997, p.9)

It is a state of mind that is attuned to fleeting experiences, apparently mundane, that occur throughout the session at various levels of consciousness. These are often dismissed or ignored because such experiences make little conscious sense and cannot be connected logically to the immediate content of the session. Through attending to these 'waking dream-thoughts' the analyst attempts to bring unassimilated experience into the realm of thought, thereby helping the patient contain previously split-off parts of the self.

Carl (revisited)

On one occasion while sitting with Carl it occurred to me that I had forgotten his name! I felt a sense of anxiety about this, it was not something that had occurred before with other patients. It started me thinking about how I would often feel unsure about whether Carl would forget about his sessions. He began the session by trying to recall where he had left off in our previous meeting. 'Forgetting' seemed to be between us now.

I noted the immense relief I felt in recalling his name a moment later. Somehow a sense of pride was the feeling that followed. I found myself thinking about an incident with my own son where I felt immense pride about his athletic achievements, but for some reason felt ashamed in expressing it. As a result, I said nothing of this to my son and it felt forgotten and was lost in other discussions about the event. During this short reverie I was aware of Carl's associations: he was telling me about a particular incident at work where he had grown close to another employee but was aware of a degree of idealization that he associated with his father. He felt as if he needed to please this friend and was aware that this often compromised his need to get on with his own work. Carl paused at this thought and said, 'I cannot think any further about this, it somehow disappears . . . he needs to "shine" in my eyes at all costs it seems.' The pace of the session seemed to shift at this point as he spoke about what his other working relationships were like. Listening to his thoughts on the subject, I found myself for some reason thinking about Dickens' novel, *Great Expectations*, that I had read to my children some time back. At the time this only occurred in the form of the phrase 'the promise of great expectations'. The words seemed to stick in my mind and I started to think about the central character, Pip, who feels ashamed of his 'common' life and takes up a life 'cold and proud'. It made me think back to my thoughts about pride earlier in the session. I said to Carl that I had found myself thinking about pride, and I wondered if he treated me much like his work colleague where the 'shine' he needed to see in me was a sense of pride.

Carl replied directly: 'pride of parents or pride of lions!' I was clearly surprised by his comments as it seemed to appear from nowhere with immense clarity. He was clearly upset and also surprised by what he had just said and seemed to cower away from me, expecting some kind of retaliation. I did not attend to this directly but together we began to understand more about the 'coldness' he feared finding in the transference. He began to associate this with the terror of being forgotten by me. He also linked this to a previously incomprehensible sense of idealizing his father 'but fearing his pride' (the pride of lions). This was complicated by a desperate search for a proud parental object in the transference.

I use the above case to briefly illustrate how themes around 'pride', 'shame' and 'forgetting' are conjoined in ways that give nuanced and specific meaning to occurrences in the analytic field. The themes are co-constructed while our intersubjective experience is unconsciously organized and only accessible to us through peripheral experiences, particularly dream thoughts or states of reverie. Through this process a detailed narrative emerges regarding Carl's need to split off 'proud' parts of himself because they are conjoined with a sense of 'coldness' and humiliation. Idealization appears to take on a dual function where it is used both to defend against the terror of being forgotten as well as being a way of holding out for a time when these 'paternal' objects might 'shine through'.

By emphasizing reverie as part of the clinical dialogue, Ogden, following Bion, is underscoring the importance of paying attention to conscious and preconscious products of alpha-function or dream-work-alpha, inchoate thoughts that reflect the immediacy of 'lived' experience. In the containing process the analyst's reverie comes to the aid of the patient's failing or disrupted alpha-function and their ability to contain their own experience. Reverie becomes a point of contact that tracks how unconscious waking thought reconfigures in ways that best articulate the emotional present while the analyst listens to the patient. Somewhat counter-intuitively then, taking Bion's position, reverie, or the waking dream, takes us to the coal-face of our experience, closer to 'truth', before it is ceased by rational conscious processes. I doubt that I could have arrived at the essence of what words like 'pride' and 'forgetting' meant in the above example unless I engaged with my own reverie, a process of understanding a preconscious commentary about how I was being transformed by Carl's presence. This can only occur through a kind of partial entanglement in the processes associated with projective identification.

Reverie may be conceptualized as a conduit between conscious rational thought and unprocessed unconscious experience. Importantly, however, this is not simply an intrapsychic process or strata of mind that might be taken to be similar to the way Freud described preconscious experience in his topographical model (Freud, 1900). Reverie is a very specific way of engaging that involves finding ways of tolerating emotional experience in order to relate in the intensity of the present moment. It allows two minds to connect, to attune at a preconscious level. In other words, as well as being the clinical manifestation of a preconscious process, the act of reverie also potentially opens up new ways of engaging and communicating with an object. It involves a process that places the analyst in a position of being present through being somewhat 'absent'; a mode of engaging I consider essential in maintaining a containing link with the patient. We shall return to this shortly.

Bion (1962b) understood reverie to represent the rudiments of a particular kind of mental connection between mother and infant: 'when the mother loves the infant what does she do it with? Leaving aside physical channels of communication my impression is that her love is expressed by reverie' (pp.35–36). But this is far from simply being the action of conveying one's care and love, it involves active curiosity, knowing (K) and immersion in the interaction. As Bion makes clear, reverie refers to the analyst being 'in a state of receptive observation . . . absorbed in my task of observation or I am absorbed in the facts' (1962b, p.95). In this process the mother or analyst pays special attention to images and thoughts that suddenly appear for no apparent reason and disappear in a similar way, almost eluding memory. Images, proto-thoughts and proto-emotions, appear and disappear 'as a single whole' (1967, p.127) as they act as a commentary on the evolution of experience (as opposed to the manipulation of experience) that cannot yet be articulated. This is where the analyst's mind is closest to 'O' or the 'ultimate reality' of the session (Bion, 1970).

To recapitulate, we have explored two opposing views of the therapist's container function. Caper emphasizes the role of the 'proper' analyst in detoxifying and neutralizing phantasies expressed through projective identification. Ogden, on the other hand, focuses on reverie and dream-like states in the analytic encounter as a way of identifying and holding in mind unassimilated experience. In the former, 'containing' focuses on the analyst having a mind of his own, separate from projected content. The latter focuses on the 'meaning-making' function of the analyst's mind brought about by the loosening of subjectivities. Caper's focus is on resisting identification with projections, whereas Ogden's places importance on the need to identify with the patient's experience in order to process them and find a way of putting thoughts and words to novel co-created experience.

One might argue that the problem here is simply one of emphasis. I doubt, for instance, that Ogden would disagree with the idea that some containment is achieved through the patient beginning to realize that their phantasies cannot damage their 'proper' objects. On the other hand, from these two opposing views we could extrapolate very different psychoanalytic epistemologies,[2] views on reality, therapeutic aims and techniques; but it is not necessary to do this here. While I retain the idea that these positions have an air of incompatibility about them, I take these two arguments to represent opposing ideals, irreconcilable extremes, different vertices that are always present in the clinical session to varying degrees. I adopt this position because my understanding is that the therapist's containing function necessarily exists somewhere between these two positions depending on the demands of the clinical situation.

The problem with Caper's argument is that it assumes that we know and can identify unconscious content, projections and so forth without going through a process of immersion, getting lost in the patient's experience. The 'essence' or 'feel' of how Carl and myself began to understand unconscious content would, I believe, reconfigure in very different ways with another patient. Caper acknowledges the importance of being receptive to projections but argues that this is demonstrated simply by interpreting the patient's projections rather than identifying with them. In my view this does not accurately reflect the struggle involved in getting to identify and 'know' unconscious communications in order to transform them into words or

2 Ogden's approach emerges from an intersubjective narrative tradition whereas Caper's assumes a more objectivist, classical stance.

images and make them part of the therapeutic dialogue. Earlier, I put forward the idea that not only is immersion necessary because counter-transference remains largely unconscious, but also because the struggle in which the therapist engages when coming into contact with split-off mental states has an essential mutative function. Here the patient's awareness of the therapist's attempts to imagine his internal world, as well as the therapist's limitations in doing so, constitutes an important part of the containing process (Lafarge, 2000). Bion's emphasis on the analyst's ability to operate from a position of uncertainty is important here. This takes seriously the idea that we cannot 'know' until the analyst is able to give himself over to the experience of the session in order to work with how this impacts his or her mind and the possible meanings this has for the analytic couple at that point in time.

Chapter 3

The analyst's containing mind

At the still point of the turning world. Neither flesh nor
  fleshless;
Neither from nor towards, at the still point, there the dance
  is

(T.S. Eliot, 'Burnt Norton', 1963)

My understanding of what constitutes the 'containing function' embraces both positions reviewed in the previous chapter. I see them as inextricably linked in that I take the essence of the 'containing stance' as being one of straddling, or bridging, different vertices of experience. The analyst's (and patient's) containing function offers a mental bridge between a number of opposing vertices: between analyst as 'dreamer' and analyst as a 'proper' object, between unassimilated internal experience and a focus on external reality, between the 'absence' and 'presence' of the analyst, between identifying and disidentifying with mental contents, and between 'not-knowing' and certainty. This is what I understand Bion to mean by the therapist's ability to maintain 'a balanced outlook' (1959, p.313): the ability to hold in mind multiple perspectives on an object in order to allow them to become something else or evolve new meaning. This position emphasizes the idea that the container function engages in a creative process of 'becoming' and resists being tied to categorical, factual, finite ways of thinking, endpoints. In considering the analyst's containing mind at work I apply Matte-Blanco's (1988) theory of symmetrical and asymmetrical principles to try and elucidate its transcendent, polar, dynamic qualities. Although my emphasis is on moving away from the notion of the container as overly schematic and static in its usage, it remains important that part of the analyst's containing function works as a 'limiting function' and I consider Caper's (1999) view on the analyst as 'proper' object as useful in this regard.

Between 'proper object' and 'dream object'

The scenario I have in mind regarding the therapist's containing function is as follows. As the therapist listens, he tries to adopt a state of mind that is receptive and resonates with the patient's projections. He does this by paying attention to his reverie and his 'speculative imaginings' that bring him closer to understanding the way unconscious experience is being organized between patient and therapist. In doing so, the therapist's reverie begins to metabolize unarticulated experience. This, however, can only happen if the analyst is able to demonstrate that part of their relationship is not overly influenced or overwhelmed by the patient's projections. In short, he remains in touch with a part of himself that approximates what Caper (1999) calls the 'proper object'.

The analyst's role as 'proper object' appears to me to be broader than simply attempting to maintain a relatively neutral and abstinent stance that demonstrates that the therapist has a mind of his own. More broadly I take it to signify a mental 'limiting function' that may emerge in the clinical setting in a number of ways. As well as the therapist working to demonstrate that he is not overly influenced by projections, I extend the therapist's role as 'proper object' to include his conscious decisions about what material to explore, interpret or leave untouched. This appears similar to Meltzer's proposal that part of the analyst's containing function includes the creation of psychic boundaries through selective attention (Meltzer, 1986). I would include here active interventions that serve to prevent the therapist and patient from being overwhelmed by the flow of dream-thoughts in the session that can shut down the patient's capacity to connect and think with the therapist. Also included are interventions that attend to aspects of the analytic frame which serve to regulate mental contact. In the previous chapter we discussed how actively exploring the reality of Carl's anxiety in the transference helped address the terror linked to this phantasy and got him on the way to engaging with it as part of his internal world (not overly flooding his external objects). In short, it served as a 'limiting function' between phantasy and his relationship with me. In most cases this 'limiting function' is expressed interpersonally, simply by the therapist's analytic attitude that demonstrates that he can go on thinking and remain receptive, but relatively unchanged by the patient's projections. There are times, however, where more active interventions are required that are related to preserving the therapist's and patient's ability to contain unassimilated experience. I give three brief examples below.

Paula

During the initial interview, Paula struggled to say much and was highly anxious. Apart from attempting to normalize her anxiety by reiterating that it was our first meeting, I had a sense that we were sitting too close for her to feel comfortably able to engage. I asked her if there was anything that could be changed between us that would put her more at ease. 'We are too close', she said immediately. In reply I suggested that she was able to move her chair if this made her better able to think while sitting with me.

Amelia

Amelia, a borderline patient, related to me in a particular way in her sessions. She would engage with me for approximately 15 to 20 minutes, then she would cut off and become increasingly anxious until she approached near panic. No amount of interpreting seemed to help but I noticed that if I worked actively to 'slow down' the sessions simply by intervening more often, she became more able to tolerate my presence and connect with me. It appears that she was being overwhelmed by dream-thoughts and proto-emotions that were acting against a mental connection that could contain them.

Christie

In a similar way, I noticed that Christie would often engage in particularly difficult analytic work for about half an hour but would then turn away from me and say very little till the end of the session. Christie was a patient who had been severely traumatised and abused as a child and was easily over-whelmed by sensory and mental experience. Instead of interpreting that she may be experiencing me as a persecutory object after her unburdening her 'abuse' on to me (perhaps the most obvious interpretation), I said to her that I thought that her turning away from me was a way of telling me that this was enough for one day: it was her way of ending the session with me, a way of placing limits on the containing function.

My point here is that the analyst's engagement with his role as 'proper' object steadies the analytic field sufficiently to enable the therapist to begin to pay attention to himself as 'dream object' using states of reverie. In contrast to the 'limiting function', I see states of reverie as imparting an analytic freedom, a creative capacity to 'name' unassimilated experience. I view the relationship between the 'proper' and 'dream' object as similar to André Green's (2005b) proposal regarding what constitutes 'clinical think-ing' and the formation of what he calls an 'active matrix' (p.25) between analyst and patient. It is worth quoting him at length here in what I would consider to be the patient's experience of the containing process:

> . . . there always comes a moment when the patient becomes aware of the extraordinary freedom that the situation offers him. He speaks about it differently, either deriving benefit from something he had been

unaware of hitherto or, on the contrary he realises that, although he now has the possibility of deriving benefit from it, he finds he is incapable of doing so. He experiences this freedom as at once tempting and frightening; but also the extent to which it can become creative. There is a possible misunderstanding that needs to be avoided here. This freedom can only yield its fruit if it is accompanied by a constraint. . . . For the same may be said of clinical thinking as of any other form of thinking. It needs affect to animate it, and yet it must keep this affect under control in order to avoid being overwhelmed. If this were to happen, thinking would soon be submerged, and clinical thinking would find itself in a perilous situation.

(p.28)

The analyst's engagement with his role as 'proper object' is containing in the sense that it not only imparts a sense of 'surviving' projections, but also serves the purpose of defining the constraints in which analytical thinking can be engaged. This level of engagement is synonymous with more conscious thinking, a reality-focused engagement with the 'rules' of analytic contact. Once these 'constraints' are in place the analyst is able to use preconscious and unconscious areas of mind to probe, explore and generate new experiences. Engaging with states of reverie introduces a form of relating whereby the analyst relates to himself as 'dream object'. Reverie, as a clinical manifestation of the containing function, is both an extremely private event and an intersubjective one. In other words, at the same time as being the analyst's personal creation, it is jointly co-created through a preconscious loosening of subjectivities between analyst and patient.

I use the simple analogy of a hiking party of two to illustrate the internal tension between the poles of the containing function that is reflected in relational terms. Let us imagine the journey of two hikers travelling through unknown terrain without previous knowledge of the trail, one more experienced than the other. In negotiating their journey they need to rely on each other's realistic appraisal of danger and difficulty. They need to remind each other of the real limits of their desires, ambitions and fantasies depending on the reality of the terrain. Importantly, this has to be jointly negotiated between two personalities. One would hope that the more experienced hiker could rely on what he had learnt from previous journeys, imparting a sense that he is able to engage with the challenges ahead and does not let the less experienced hiker's anxieties overly affect his judgement. On their journey we could imagine the two hikers placing limits on the paths they feel that they are able to take. These negotiated limits help them feel more secure in knowing that they are on the right track. All this I view as being analogous to the function of the analyst as 'proper' object, relying on what is 'known' about the analytic journey, tentatively interpreting unconscious phantasies so they impinge less on reality and demonstrating that he can 'survive' the patient's projections or anxiety. However, because the journey is unknown, and every journey has its own peculiarities, the experienced hiker-analyst has to rely on intuition and imagination to arrive at some understanding of what is on his colleague's mind and the path they are currently walking. Here he tries to make meaning out of cues from the current context and his colleague's state of mind, noting his abilities and difficulties. What is more, the assurance of being able to limit their joint ability to negotiate overly ambitious routes and difficult terrain makes it possible for them to dwell on, and notice, the details and intricacies of their journey, granting it particular personal meaning. This is about their appreciation of the quality of their experience, the essence of feeling, and their contribution towards sharing and building meaning as partners in relationship.

The 'between' position of the analyst's containing mind that I am emphasizing may be confused with Winnicott's (1975) term 'potential space', but they are very different. 'Potential space' refers to a neutral space between mother and child in which transitional objects can be used by the child as long as the mother's presence does not intrude on the child's experience. The 'in between' mental stance that is part of the containing function exists in the mind of the analyst or therapist. The containing function is also not a neutral space as it is constantly imbued with cycles of projective and introjective identification between patient and therapist (Segal, 1991). The tension or struggle here is best portrayed by the image of the therapist as a 'real contemplative object', constantly trying to grasp potential meanings in the analytic encounter.

The analyst's capacity to relate to himself as 'dream object' is in line with Bion's view that the analytic containing stance involves a 'partial severance' (1970, p.69) with reality. In containing and transforming the patient's experience Bion thought that the analyst needed to go through periods of 'patience' and 'security'. He meant 'patience' to stand for a non-pathological equivalent of paranoid-schizoid experience where fragments of experience are held in mind 'without reaching for fact and reason until a pattern evolves' (1970, p.124). This involves struggling with the persecutory experience that such a state of mind evokes in order to be able to value the confusion which this inevitably brings. Bion associates 'security' with the analyst's experience of disparate facts eventually finding temporary coherence that give rise to meaning. Here, 'patience' appears to be an apt way of describing a state of waiting that is involved in the analytic couple needing to find ways of tolerating and harnessing moments of confusion which are always part of engaging in states of reverie.

Both analyst and patient naturally move in and out of reverie throughout the session. It is the way it is used, or engaged with, that differs depending on the analyst's intention. The analyst's attention shifts between attending to 'external reality' and attending to more preconscious occurrences that

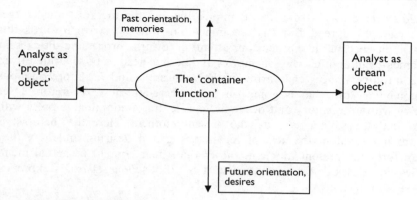

Figure 3.1 The containing function

present themselves in the analyst's mind as states of reverie. Although, at different points, the analytic process may call for the therapist to focus on either of these aspects of himself, it is probably more accurate to see the analyst's engagement with himself as 'proper' or 'dream' object as occurring alongside each other as unassimilated experience begins to gather new meaning. Put simply, the therapist's and patient's ability to use states of reverie as part of the therapeutic process, while also negotiating a sense of separateness in the analytic encounter, marks the place where the containing process begins. In this sense the analyst's containing stance operates between these poles as a means of regulating the exchange so as to find a way to tolerate and make sense of unassimilated experience as it occurs in the present moment.

This brings us to another polar conception that helps the therapist attend to and contain experience. The therapist attempts to stand between dwelling on what is 'known' or believed about the patient (past sessions, the patient's history, etc.) and what he hopes and desires (that the patient gets better, predicting outcomes, etc.). This shifts the therapist's attention on to the here-and-now of 'live' experience, experience that is currently being reformulated and communicated by the analytic couple. For the sake of clarity I represent the containing function as shown in Figure 3.1 and return to other polarities in the following chapter.

Although many psychotherapeutic approaches advocate working in the here-and-now as having greater therapeutic benefit, it should be made clear that this does mean that the therapist should attempt to dwell in the present constantly. Apart from being impossible, it would be too overwhelming to both patient and analyst. In theoretical terms, this would flood the analytic space with beta-elements, unprocessed sense impressions, and proto-thoughts (alpha-elements). It seems to me that Bion's (1970) recommendation about abstaining from memory and desire is often understood in very rigid extreme ways (from 'this is impossible', to 'the therapist must forget everything!'). I read Bion as recommending that we strive towards this possibility because it sharpens our attention towards processing the present moment. Put another way, memories and desires need to be separated from the intuitive images that arise in the analyst's mind as a preconscious commentary on what is going on in the here-and-now. Therefore I see being without memory and desire as representing unobtainable poles with the analyst 'moving towards' the present moment. Here the therapist is more interested in the acts of remembering and desiring and how they transform the present moment, rather than their content as actual memories and desires. A fragment from T.S. Eliot's *Four Quartets* expresses these sentiments:

> Go, go, go said the bird: human kind
> Cannot bear very much reality.
> Time past and time future
> What might have been and what has been
> Point to one end, which is always present.
> (T.S. Eliot, 'Burnt Norton', 1963)

Bion considered memory and desire the 'senses' of the past and the future respectively. He understood the mind's focus on past and future as being dependent on sensory impressions. The former is a sensory store of information that constitutes 'possessions' of the mind, while the latter involves the promise of sensually satisfying objects (Bion, 1970). With this in mind, Bion viewed them as distractions from the present moment in which elemental experience is being processed and lived.

Bion, particularly in his later writings and seminars, emphasizes the ephemeral nature of the psychoanalytic encounter (Bion, 1989, 2005a, 2005b). He draws our attention to the complexity of the personality. This is most clear in statements that depict the patient as being age 5, 14, 55, 74, etc., all at the same time. In addition, he emphasizes the fact that we can never return to what has been said or thought in precisely the same way again. It is also impossible to really know or replicate what we might want to say or think. In Bion's terms, we are always in a state of 'becoming'. Beneath this is an optimism that relates to the containing mind waiting to be surprised by peculiarities and details, occurrences that never repeat themselves in quite the same way (which have yet to be held in mind). It offers a chance to look past repetitions, stale conceptions or constant conjunctions, and consider experience in its unique context (internal and external). These peculiarities draw the analytic couple into the present moment, giving us a sense that experience is always in flux. In a similar way we could understand memories and desires to represent 'known' repetitions that obscure connecting with parts of the patient's personality which hitherto remain uncontained.

To use a simple example, as long as I allow my memory of a patient's aggressive tendencies to hold too much weight in my mind, I will miss moments of tenderness, possibilities of kindness or reparation, that remain uncontained and too difficult to think about in the existing analytic field. Likewise, as long as I predict that this patient is going to be aggressive in the session or at school, the less chance I have of attending to what is happening in the present moment. This is particularly difficult to do when elements of trauma are evident in the patient's dynamics. Here a focus on the future and past more easily takes on a defensive quality in the analyst's mind, obscuring his containing function.

James

James, an 18-year-old man in his final year of school, comes to see me complaining of depression and thoughts of suicide. He tells me that he has been feeling this way for three years, ever since he was caught sexually abusing his six-year-old sister. He says this with little affect and indicates that he doesn't want to talk about it further. We spend the best part of three months essentially considering how he feels shamed by others who had heard about what he had done, making school very difficult to attend. During this time, however, whatever he talks about, I am aware of my mind being filled with images of him abusing his little sister. I am repulsed and try to put them out of my mind. I am aware of finding it difficult to listen to him but feel assured that his 'shame' is a good 'starting point' to help him with his depression. A few weeks later he ends his therapy furious that I cannot stop his angry displays at home or his suicidal intentions. As he leaves he says, 'You're just like them, you look at me with wide eyes and suspicion'.

I think if I had better attended to the numbing impact that these flashback images (or my 'memories' of abuse) had on me, I may have been in a better position to listen to James. It seems that the trauma of the past event lay waiting to be processed – projected into me – but I failed to get past its mind-numbing effects. As a result, my 'memories' of what he said about the abuse determined how I listened and prevented me from working with what it might have meant in the present moment. In retrospect it appears that his projections were alerting me to the fact that he too was traumatized by these images and had split them off. Perhaps because of the immense mental pain related to this issue, I avoided giving due thought to it and enacted a shaming dynamic where I was 'just like everybody'. It is difficult to say if I could have dealt with these 'flashbacks' differently within the given context and if my actions were related to not being able to help him. I do feel, however, that there could have been better ways of beginning to attend to these images so that they did not appear like uncontrollable 'flashbacks' keeping me off guard. For instance, I think it would have been better to try and find a way to use my countertransference as a reflection of his own feeling state, conveying to him how often this situation stops him dead in his tracks, preventing him from knowing what he feels. This could be one possible way of trying to connect with, and contain, the effect of such powerful projections.

In *Learning From Experience* Bion (1962b) argues that learning is only possible if the analyst's mind acts as a container that remains integrated but flexible. This is a state of mind where the analyst 'can retain his knowledge and experience and yet be prepared to reconstrue past experiences in a manner that enables him to be receptive of a new idea' (p.93). To re-engage with the nearness of experience and its real-time impacts on psychic reality, one has to attempt to obscure the intrusions of memory and desire. It is a process that encourages spontaneity and 'aliveness', a case of not thinking in order to think anew in the real-time of interaction. Bion adopts a similar approach when thinking about how one should read his work:

> An analyst reading this paper must be able to forget it, to dismiss it from his mind, unless something is said by the analysand which calls it into his consciousness and causes him then to formulate it in such language as he is able to use.
>
> (1989, p.55)

This is a state of mind that attempts to tolerate and value confusion in the present moment, allowing aspects of the analyst's mind to represent 'variables' to be replaced by outside elements.

'Being between and on the way to something'

Theoretical underpinnings

My starting point for exploring the theoretical underpinnings of the containing process, the ongoing tensions between 'proper' and 'dream' object, is the work of Ingacio Matte-Blanco (1975, 1988). In *The Unconscious as Infinite Sets*, Matte-Blanco (1975) argues that Freud's main discovery was not the unconscious as such, but a particular form of logic. Using mathematical set theory, Matte-Blanco proposed that the unconscious be understood as primarily governed by principles of symmetry, whereas conscious experience, or secondary processes thinking, abides mostly by principles of asymmetry. These two forms of logic exist in mixed forms at different levels or strata of the psyche. In this way the psyche functions as a bi-logical system comprising two antinomous modes of making sense of the world.

The asymmetrical mode makes use of what Matte-Blanco calls 'bi-valent logic' where one object cannot be equated with another and objects are seen as discrete entities (either you are making statement A or statement B). By implication, two contradictory statements cannot both be true at the same point in time. The principle of symmetry, on the other hand, is upheld by an absence of mutual contradiction and in the depths of the unconscious all objects are treated as similar or identical, leading to an experience of unity. For this reason Matte-Blanco calls it the 'indivisible mode' and sees it as representing the qualities of infinity. When the principle of symmetry applies, objects lose their place in time and space and the principles of movement (moving A to B) do not apply because at this level of mind all objects merge and are experienced as being 'everywhere'. Given this, the ideas of 'inside' and 'outside', 'external' and 'internal', do not exist. Furthermore, because objects cannot be easily separated from one another they cannot be held in mind or made conscious.

Put another way, the symmetrical mode draws on qualities of the object that can be perceived as equitable across a group of objects (the propositional function of the group). To use an example, 'my mother is angry with my father' is a statement understood in terms of bi-valent logic to define a relationship between mother and father as discrete objects with anger 'moving' in a particular direction. When the principle of symmetry is applied, on the other hand, all objects begin to verge toward the same point. This level of mind would treat all mothers the same; it is the 'motherness' of all objects that is related to. This leads to slippages in meanings and confusions in reasoning where all 'mothers' are seen as aggressive, or where motherly qualities as confused with anger. Due to these equivalences, the anger expressed in this example would also be generalized to other objects. These forms of symmetrical 'slippages' differ from ordinary secondary process thinking which rejects generalization across categories or subsets.

Using these principles Matte-Blanco contributes a great deal to understanding the logic of the unconscious and affect. The slippages that occur at a more unconscious level, for instance, explain how displacement occurs in dreams. Through symmetrical logic, and to satisfy the unconscious, many objects can be acceptable recipients of a particular projection. We can also use his theory to explain how the experience of intense affect quickly breaks down discrepancies and differences between objects, causing all things to appear imbued with the same affect. Further, when the principle of symmetry is in ascendance, part of an object easily becomes equated with the whole. For instance, greed, sexuality, race or some other physical quality, all part-objects, might be generalized to the whole object in specific ways making the person seem 'devouring', 'perverse', 'hated', 'all bad', and so forth.

It is important to make clear that symmetrical and asymmetrical logic are not synonymous with the unconscious and conscious respectively. It is the case that each mode is over-represented in the above respective states of mind, but these different modes of logic are better understood as representing different vertices, points of view, on the object at hand. They are incompatible with each other, antinomous modes, that resist merger and translation.

Projective identification also represents a bi-logical organization of a particular kind. Matte-Blanco (1988) goes to great lengths to illustrate how the phantasy of projective identification can only be successful if understood as a bi-logical structure. In his words, projective identification is a process which 'starts with two separate entities, self and object, and ends in the latter becoming an extension of the first, like a colony. It seems that in both the initial and the final state one must distinguish between self and object as one does between 'mother country' and colony' (p.147).

For split-off parts of the self to be located in another object, projective identification needs to contain 'the concepts of indivision and also that of distinction' (p.149). With this come particular anxieties, notably the fear of losing one's identity (a product of symmetrical logic) due to a sense of being lost in indivision which approximates a sense of annihilation.

What implication does this have for the containing function? In what is to come, I want to put forward the idea that the analyst's containing mind emerges in his attempts to meet and complement the bi-logical nature of projective identification. In my understanding the container function occurs at the cusp between asymmetrical and symmetrical modes. In this way 'containing' attempts to unite two incompatible systems, always failing to some degree due to their antinomous nature. How would we apply this to Bion's schematic example quoted earlier?

> Normal development follows if the relationship between infant and breast permits the infant to project a feeling, say, that it is dying, into the mother and to reintroject it after its sojourn in the breast has made it tolerable to the infant psyche. If the projection is not accepted by the mother the infant feels that its feeling that it is dying is stripped of such meaning as it has. It therefore reintrojects, not a fear of dying made tolerable, but a nameless dread.
>
> (Bion, 1962a, p.306)

Using this example, I imagine that the feeling of dying is apprehended in the infant's inchoate mind at two different levels. The infant's fledgling alpha-function begins to produce experiences that he cannot manage or give meaning to. As a result, feelings of dying overwhelm every part of his mind. Here, the symmetrical mode works to unite 'sameness' or the qualities of these feelings that make them feel timeless, terrifying, infinite. As a result, the infant begins to signal for an object, say by crying, 'pushing' until a response is felt. Bion used the word 'hyperbole' to express the move towards exaggeration as a means of signalling the object. I am suggesting that hyperbole also acts as a probe in search of a 'different' object that 'defies' the principles of symmetry. The mother at this level is felt as different, discrete and as a result the feeling of dying can be apprehended as a 'thing' that cannot yet be named. In other words, this is a part of mind where the infant's inchoate asymmetrical mode is at work. If we could imagine these processes as separate for a moment, in the symmetrical mode there is no conception of inside and outside, at its ultimate extreme everything is the same. In this mode the concept of projection, introjection, external, internal make little sense. From the vantage point of the asymmetrical mode, however, this fear can in fantasy be located 'outside' the self through projection (from one point to another), a conception dependent on differences between objects.

I use the words 'forced asymmetry' to emphasize that it is the escalation of feeling and intensity (the symmetrical mode) that leads to a 'pushing up' against the object, signalling difference and therefore asymmetry that brings relief but also creates difficulty. To be sure, I am not assuming that asymmetrical capacities are absent in infancy. Infants appear to have a remarkable capacity for differentiation from birth (Kernberg, 2003; Matte-Blanco, 1988; Stern, 2000). These capacities, however, are easily overwhelmed by peak affective experiences which flood the ability to distinguish between objects. Containment of such feelings requires that it is felt to be limited; 'a thing' that can be located. On the other hand, and this is the difficulty, too much asymmetry leads to a sense that the containing object is so different, discrete, bounded, that no meeting of minds can take place.

Applying bi-logical theory suggests that unassimilated experience remains uncontained, unable to be held in mind for two reasons. First, intense affective states lead to psychic capacities being loaded with symmetrical qualities, leading to confusions between self and other. At extremes this leads to psychotic-like projections, a sense of being everywhere, occupying many objects, leaving the individual with a fragile sense of self. This, in my experience, is accompanied by understandable anxieties of 'disappearing' or being 'infinitized'. The second version of 'uncontained mental states' occurs when asymmetrical logic is applied so stringently that the patient fails to sense or use the relationship between objects. Often this occurs when emotion and cognition are treated as discrete unrelated mediums. It creates the impression that such patients are able to think reasonably and 'hold things in mind', but soon the therapist gets the sense that the patient's over-formulated ideas, reasons, appear meaningless and do not develop as treatment progresses. Behind this veiled form of reasoning lies immense anxiety related to either feeling trapped in an object (claustrophobic anxieties) or feeling flooded by unbearable meaningless affect. This seems very similar to the core dilemmas and anxieties found to exist in schizoid personality organizations (Fairbairn, 1952; Rey, 1979).

Reformulated from a bi-logical perspective, the containing process is about bringing both asymmetrical and symmetrical logic to bear on the experience at hand, a way of wrestling with certainty and infinity, knowns and unknowns, differences and similarities; all are representatives of the asymmetrical and symmetrical mode respectively. The containing process emerges from the experience of being able to locate particular experiences inside one's self whilst acknowledging their 'infinite' qualities that give these experiences meaning (symmetrical qualities), allowing commerce with different parts of self and others. To return to Bion's example, I imagine the mother's containing response works to complement the symmetrical and asymmetrical tracks of experience outlined earlier. The mother responds by communicating that she is aware of a 'thing', a discrete object linked to her infant's sense of distress and dying. But the mother also communicates that this hitherto be found discriminate object is joined to a network of possible other 'things', that she knows about similar experiences, as she stumbles and intuits what this cry might be about. In short, she draws on the symmetrical qualities of her mind. As their minds meet, so do their bi-logical qualities. The baby's engulfing distress is limited by the mother's awareness of treating it as a 'thing', 'symmetrical' intrusion is checked, limited, by bringing the mother's asymmetrical mode to bear on the baby's mind. Conversely, the mother treats the 'thing' as belonging to a group of possibilities and brings symmetrical qualities to the baby's bi-valent logic, his awareness of the feeling that he is dying.

I would argue that a similar process occurs in clinical practice as part of the therapist's attempt to engage in the interpenetrating dialogue between projective and introjective identifications (Schafer, 2000). This occurs through the therapist's attempts to maintain a 'balanced outlook' by drawing on peculiarities and unique qualities, on the one hand, and the similarities and resonances, on the other. In meeting the asymmetrical and symmetrical qualities of projective identification, the containing function attempts to balance or titrate these two vertices in a way that allows for meaning to cohere and in a way that eventually finds transient existence in symbols. For instance, the infant's fear that he is dying might eventually emerge in symbolic communications like 'I'm starving to death' or 'I'm sick to death of you' (see commensal mode, Chapter 7).

So far I have attempted to illustrate how the mechanism or phantasy of projective identification needs to draw on both symmetrical and asymmetrical principles to exist. For projection into another object to be possible, the object has to be experienced as somewhat separate (asymmetrical). But if it is to succeed in being a receptacle for part of the self, symmetrical qualities of the containing object also need to be evident. In this way projective identification might be understood as a primitive attempt to bring both modes into the same proximity. We might say then that projective identification represents the infant's best attempt to 'make meaning'. As Matte-

Blanco (1988) puts it, projective identification 'is felt as so fundamental because it points to, and implicitly gives place to, the indivisible' (p.147). This seems in keeping with Bion's emphasis on projective identification as a form of communication. More importantly, it seems in keeping with his ideas that projective identification acts as a means of conveying proto-thoughts or emotions 'on the way to being something else' (Bion, 2005b). Using Matte-Blanco's reasoning, I see projective identification as one way in which the individual attempts to deal with the fundamental antimonies of psychic experience. In my view, the therapist's containing function also represents a bi-logical structure that strives to 'take on' or complement the bi-logical qualities of projective identification so as to carry on the process, representing its meaning in more modified forms through symbols and symbolic communications.

Does this mean that the therapist's containing function, in theory, attempts to transform symmetrical, unconscious features into thinkable more discrete manageable objects? Although this appears more consistent with Bion using the word 'transformation' in the context of the therapist's containing function, it appears only partially accurate. There is another way of thinking about this that seems more consistent with the clinical reality of what the containing analyst attempts to do. Matte-Blanco (1988) makes it clear that the two modes of apprehending an object are anti-nomous, incompatible, it is not possible then within this theoretical system to transform one mode into the other. This is not to say that we do not attempt to do this. Matte-Blanco (1983) calls this 'thinkating', an attempt to think the symmetical mode, something impossible due to differences in logic. But these attempts amount to what he called 'fertile failures' (p.513). We come up against this experience, for instance, when we try to think about infinity itself. We give it a name that helps us think about it but it cannot be grasped; it is a 'fertile failure' in that we get a sense of how incomprehensible it is to think about infinity. This represents our best attempt to think about the symmetrical mode.

In terms of the containing function, we could say that the translations of unassimilated experience into more meaningful experiences are clinical representations of 'fertile failures'. The word 'transformation' is proble-matic because it tends to imply movement of an object from one system to another. This is not how I see the therapist's containing mind operating. While the therapist attempts to 'name' or hold in mind unassimilated experience he does this by drawing on his own bi-logical potential, his own abilities to bring these two incompatible systems together in a way that gives rise to useful, but transient meanings; meanings that can never be fixed or precise, but are nevertheless useful in building a sense of self. In this way I emphasize the therapist's containing function as conveying a sense of working with the antinomies of experience that respects the fragility of genuine thought, symbols and meaning systems. I see the therapist's ability to bear these antinomies, not lapsing into omniscience (symmetrical) or states of mindlessness (asymmetrical), as the ultimate aim of the therapist's containing function. In the clinical setting we see this version of the containing function most evident in the therapist's struggles and fumblings as he tries to maintain a mental connection that takes on the unarticulated transference pressure of the patient's communication while trying to give it some form of meaningful representation. It requires that the therapist take on the patient's terror of 'slippage', the fear of everything meaning the same thing, in order to find a way of making it more bearable. This is compatible with Bion's (1970) idea that the analyst moves from 'patience' to 'security' in making the analytical material more meaningful. Here the analyst struggles with disparate thoughts, encountering a state of mind similar to the paranoid-schizoid position. If he can tolerate this state for long enough his thoughts begin to cohere and gather new meaning and he reaches a position of 'security' that shares features of the depressive position. Using bi-logical theory perhaps we could say it is also possible that this sense of depression emerges due to some peripheral sense of the ambivalence created in the analyst in producing 'fertile failures', transient imprecise meanings that he must let go of. In this he communicates the fallible, imperfect nature of containment.

In case of misunderstanding, I am not suggesting that the containing process involves simply transforming primary process thinking into secondary process thinking or more adaptive cognitive abilities. Nor does it just involve working with largely unconscious mental states in order to make them more conscious. It is not the case that the therapist simply attempts to translate symmetrical logic into ordinary secondary process thinking. In other words, it is not the case that the therapist attempts to complement the patient's symmetrical reasoning with more asymmetrical logic that is more reality based. I am suggesting that the containment process involves bearing the antinomy of bi-logical processes which allow transient meanings to form and expand the patient's capacity to think. If we return to the idea of a psychic field, this requires that the therapist connect with the patient so both the symmetrical and asymmetrical mode are enjoined, creating different tracks or modes of generating experience. The process of containing is represented in the capacity for the therapeutic couple to allow a process of titration to occur between these two incompatible systems.

Kernberg (2003) provides an excellent example of what I am referring to in his suggestions regarding managing affect storms with borderline patients. These are situations where affect begins to escalate and countertransference becomes more difficult to manage. Often the therapist responds to such states with overly interpretative, reasoned, soft-spoken analysis in attempts to calm the patient down, but this only serves to escalate the situation. Kernberg argues that in order to maintain mental contact with the patient, the analyst has to meet him in this experience matching some of its intensity. Using bi-logical theory Kernberg understands this to be a situation where meeting the patient in his experience is enhanced by 'the therapist's tolerance and use of partial symmetrization of his affective experience in the countertransference and in communicating counter-transference' (p.523). In terms of his containing function, meeting the affective tone of the session signals a receptivity and responsiveness, on the one hand, and a sense of surviving the patient's projections and not being entirely contaminated by them, on the other. In clinical reality it means negotiating a tension whereby the 'therapist must attempt to stay in role, even when responding with corresponding intensity to the intensity of the patient's affect' (p.527). In this way the therapist attempts to expand the patient's ability to contain affect by demonstrating that he can carry on thinking (asymmetrical capacities) about the issue at hand while tolerating and maintaining mental contact (symmetrical capacities) with the patient.

Attempts to titrate these two forms of logic in the containing process appear to be a version of what Bion called 'binocular vision' where con-sciousness (mainly asymmetrical) and unconscious (mainly symmetrical) perspectives verge towards one point to form the 'psychoanalytic object'. His ideas here are based on the model of ocular coordination where 'two eyes operate in binocular vision to correlate two views of the same object' (1962b, p.86). The challenge, as I see it, in relation to the therapist's con-taining function, is connecting with both of these perspectives and upholding their different viewpoints so as to attain a 'balanced outlook'. Using Bion's model, collapse of these two vertices, when psychic elements are overwhelmed by symmetrical or asymmetrical logic, is analogous to losing perspective on the full dimensionality of the object.

As a process that focuses on 'meaning-making', containing brings sym-metrical and asymmetrical logic to bear on an object creating new meaning which, in turn, adds or is fed back into both unconscious and conscious processes. It is not a matter of simply making the unconscious more conscious. Transformation, in other words, occurs in both directions. Bion refers to this dynamic process as follows:

> In the psycho-analytic experience we are concerned both with the translation in the direction of what we do not know into something which we do know or which we can communicate, and also from what we do know and can communicate to what we do not know and are not aware of because it is unconscious and which may even be pre-natal, or pre-birth of a psyche or a mental life, but is part of a physical life.
>
> (1989, p.54)

Returning to the clinical situation, I would propose that the above reformu-lation of the containing function maps on to the clinical concepts of 'dream object' and 'proper object'. In terms of the former, reverie appears to be the clinical representation of a loosening of symmetrical bi-valent logic and the emergence of elements of symmetrical logic in its most accessible form. Here reverie appears to be the medium through which the analyst relates to himself as 'dream object'. The latter, the analyst's relationship with himself as 'proper' object, more readily represents asymmetrical, categorical logic that attempts to orientate and circumscribe the emotional area of enquiry.

Chapter 4

Polarities of the containing connection

There are a number of other related vertices apparent in Bion's thinking that might be understood in polar terms underlying the analyst's internal potential as 'proper object' and 'dream object'. I use these polarities in an attempt to further explore what constitutes a containing stance or attitude. Conceptualizing the containing mind as straddling a number of polarities that represent inherent and inevitable tensions also constitutes an attempt to move it away from the image of the containing mind as a near-physical 'thing' or discrete entity. I view these polarities as representing ideals. As representations of psychic aspects of the 'proper' and 'dream' object, they also, by implication, uphold the ideal division between asymmetrical and symmetrical logic that always exist in varying mixed states. The outcome is a transient state of mind that resists certainties and attempts to find a way of representing preconscious experience that also conveys the limitations and fragility of the analyst's containing function. To add to Figure 3.1 (p.51), the polarities to be discussed in this chapter can be represented as shown in Figure 4.1.

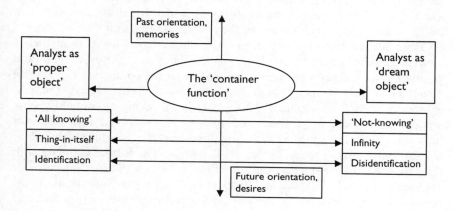

Figure 4.1 The polarities of the containing function

Between 'knowing' and 'not-knowing': Heeding the negative

> . . . so that there will be a chance of hearing these very faint sounds that are buried in this mass of noise. I imagine that even a newborn infant has to do this: when it opens its eyes and is suddenly presented with masses of facts by its optic apparatus, then there has to be some sort of selection.
>
> (Bion 2005b, p.17)

Bott Spillius (1988) points out that Bion essentially presents three theories of thinking. The first asserts that conceptions are formed through the mating of innate preconceptions with realizations. A preconception represents a 'state of expectation' (1963, p.23) and in this model thoughts, conceptions, are based on the presence of an object. As opposed to other forms of thought, conceptions appear to be tinged with a sensual satisfying quality (Grinberg *et al.*, 1993). We might assume that the infant has a set of innate preconceptions about feeding and the breast. If the infant's need (preconceptions) for the breast is met with the mother producing milk (realization), inchoate thoughts about a warm caring object can begin to form.

The second model is based on 'negative realization' when preconceptions are not met with realization. This evokes frustration and, if tolerated, leads to searching mental activity and the creation of thoughts to either alleviate frustration or provide a means of moving toward rewarding satisfying objects. His final attempt involved his notion of alpha-function, an 'unknowable' function that acts on sense impressions in order to convert them into the components of thought, dream thoughts, crude thoughts available for dreaming and thinking. Through maintaining a state of reverie the mother assists the infant in developing his fledgling alpha-function capacity which overlaps with the internalization of the containing function.

'Thoughts' that emerge as a result of alpha-function are perhaps better viewed as subordinate to thinking proper. They are proto-thoughts and proto-emotions, flashes of experience, that await the containing function to be elaborated as proper thoughts (Ferro, 2002, 2005a, 2006). I am in agreement with Bott Spillius (1988) in viewing thinking as probably being an alternating mix of positive and negative realizations. But there are important differences in the psychic qualities of these realizations that Bion (1962a) only hints at in 'A Theory of Thinking'. The former is linked with the experience of satisfaction that, in effect, saturates the need to know or explore; there is little need to attend to such thoughts but the thoughts remain at some level of awareness. Our preconceptions of a chair, for instance, are satisfied by the arrival of a four-legged object with a seat and a back, there is no need to think further, the thought exists somewhere in the background. If, however, a chair without some of these characteristics is presented, our preconceptions are met with a degree of 'absence' prompting new ways to think about a chair. This represents a negative realization, the emergence of new experience out of the ability to tolerate frustration and generate new thoughts and meaning out of absent aspects of the object.

Because positive realizations are met with satisfaction, it appears that these kind of thoughts are in less need of the containing function offered by the analyst or by the patient themselves. Indeed, in a number of ways the 'certainty' inherent in this kind of thinking acts against the containing function. We shall return to this shortly. Negative realizations, on the other hand, require a kind of engagement that involves connecting with this 'negative capacity', an interest in the unknown, while at the same time helping the patient to tolerate frustration for long enough to bear the 'fruits' of this process.

In this way the analyst's containing function is linked to his adopting a therapeutic stance that embraces what Bion called 'negative capability'. Drawing on the work of the poet John Keats, Bion described this as a state of mind where 'man is capable of being in uncertainties, mysteries, doubts, without any irritable reaching after fact or reason' (1970, p.125). Adopting a position of negative capability ushers in a mode of engagement that embraces the idea that we cannot know an object as a 'thing-in-itself'. Put another way, it embraces the inevitable 'absence' of the object in thought and takes seriously the idea that new thoughts and meaning are created in the absence of the object. Such an approach involves considering the generative power of 'the negative' in the development of psychic states (Green, 1999). We can understand this best by considering Bion's use of the term 'no-breast' or 'the place where the breast was'. Following Klein, he thought that absence of the breast (or object) evokes negative emotional states that make up the initial psychic representations that become the 'bad breast' (via projective identification). Based on this model, thought is always formed in the absence of the object and associated with lack and suffering. To use Bion's phrase, words and thoughts are representations of 'no thing'.

In part then, the therapist does not strive to satisfy desires, needs of the patient and so forth. This is no different from the analyst's attitude based on free floating attention, abstinence and relative neutrality. However, in the context of understanding it as part of the containing function I am emphasizing its role in triggering states of mind in the patient, unborn thoughts, that seek containment. Second, in line with the theory of negative realizations, 'absence' in the analyst's mind, if it can be tolerated, gives rise to meaningful thoughts that help 'name' previously unarticulated experience. In short, 'absence' triggers the analyst's reverie. We might say that attempts at negative capability, or maintaining a 'not-knowing stance' as part of the containing function, works to obscure the full presence or 'known' presence of the object in order to create a space in which new meaning can be contained.

Melissa

Melissa talks to me about her father's criticism of her and how difficult this is. We explore how evident this is in many of her relationships with men including myself, leaving her feeling very anxious and inadequate. I was indeed aware of thinking about her in a critical manner, wishing she would move on to something that felt more meaningful to me. In a similar way to other sessions, she tells me about an old boyfriend and how much he has let her down. As she talks I begin to think about another patient who kept on reminding me of how 'special' her therapy was. I was aware of being very gentle with her sensing that her idealization protected her from immense fragility. While listening to Melissa I recalled the chorus lines of an old song: 'The ballad of Lucy Jordon' by Marianne Faithful: 'At the age of thirty-seven she realized she would never ride through Paris in a sports car with the warm wind in her hair. So she let the phone keep ringing and she sat there softly singing reading nursery rhymes she'd memorized in her daddy's easy chair.' This is a song about lost paternal idealizations. It seemed to shift my way of thinking and the way I felt about Melissa. I began to see her 'critical object' as representing a painful loss of hope and I found myself attending more to her anxiousness as a response to 'sudden loss'. This appeared to change the analytic field in the sense that I felt myself able to listen with a sense of compassion.

The above brief vignette illustrates how my reverie started to change the way I thought and felt about Melissa. I understand this to have occurred in moments in the session where I felt less wedded to listening intently for meaning, unconscious derivatives, transference manifestations, what to interpret, while having a background sense of trying not to enact the role of her 'critical object' (relating to myself as a 'proper object'). In effect, this 'gentle withdrawal' served to obscure the full presence of Melissa's conscious narrative about criticism (the way she typically engages her object at a conscious level), leaving space for the emergence of thoughts and feelings that help shift my way of listening and the way I hold her in mind. The quality of these thoughts is different to thoughts constantly apparent to me when I listen attentively. In Bion's terms, they represent 'no things', thoughts that appear in the absence of the object. There is a sense here that my engagement through reverie has a scanning function, preconsciously searching for 'essences' or qualities in the analytic field that mark the place where 'something was'. This state of 'absence' in the therapist's mind appears to set up a particular state of awareness that is linked to the analyst's containing function. In Bion's words:

This 'consciousness' is an awareness of a lack of existence that demands an existence, a thought in search of a meaning . . . A psyche seeking for a physical habitation to give it existence, ♀ seeking ♂.

(1965, p.109)

The 'awareness of a lack of existence' appears to reflect the tensions discussed earlier between reverie, the analyst's private thoughts, and their need to be founded or confirmed in some physical reality. The container seeks some link with the physical world to create meaning. If however, this need becomes excessive because the sense of 'absence' cannot be tolerated, analyst and patient begin to act in ways that reduce the containing function to a near-physical object or act. In such cases, physical touch might be used as a substitute for 'mental' containing. Alternatively, thoughts and interventions tend to become associated with physical qualities to obscure the inevitable 'negative' nature of thoughts and the idea that authentic thoughts emerge from the capacity to 'not know'.

It perhaps goes without saying that our attempt to hold things in mind without them being obscured by preconceptions is always somewhat relative. For this reason I see 'not-knowing' as representing an ideal extreme. In reality we are never without some knowledge of the patient (the other polar extreme). In my view if this were not the case, the therapist's striving toward negative capability becomes too difficult to tolerate. In other words, what is known acts as an anchor in the session from which the therapist can stray. Returning to bi-logical theory, 'striving towards' negative capacities appears to represent a state of mind attempting to draw more on symmetrical logic to broaden what is 'known' by analyst and patient, their existing preconceptions. On the other hand, what is 'known' tends towards the bi-valent logic of the asymmetrical mode where it is taken to be the ultimate and only 'truth'.

In striving towards a 'not-knowing stance' the therapist reiterates a very different view of the container that is often implicit in clinical use where it is conceptualized as being boldly present, stable, all-knowing, in its attempts to 'absorb' the impact of affects that cannot be tolerated by the patient. In Chapter 8, I explore some of the reasons why the container begins to take on near-physical and idealized qualities in clinical practice.

Between infinity and the 'thing-in-itself': 'representation' and loss

While we are trying to elaborate a system of thought. . . . We have to be aware that we are also excreting a kind of calcification which is going to make those thoughts become more a prison than a liberating force.

(Bion, 2005a, p.12)

Bion's words capture the essence of a core dilemma that occurs to some degree in all thinking. All attempts to hold something in mind in a meaningful way also confine expression or place limits on other perspectives or ways of thinking about the object. It often happens that we are very quickly drawn into a way of thinking about a patient that we feel so certain about but it shuts down reflection on the fact that it is only one possible view that has its own limits and restrictions. It is the difference between thoughts and interpretations that become 'overvalued ideas' (Britton and Steiner, 1994) and those that become probes or ways of meeting the patient's mind in a way that is bearable and meaningful.

As Bion suggests, there is only one way out of this dilemma and that is to treat this fact with acceptance and awareness. This translates into an analytic attitude that strives to consider multiple viewpoints of a situation, always open to suggestions and cues from the patient or the analytic field. In doing so, there is tacit acknowledgement that meaningful probes, interpretations, ways of thinking, have a limited lifespan and are always in transition. In a similar way, I view the containing function as working to transcend 'impressive caesuras', points of calcification, that obstruct continuities, so as to draw on different perspectives that hitherto had no apparent relation to what patient and analyst were attempting to hold in mind. I am suggesting that this state of mind is represented by tensions between relating to the object as a discrete 'thing-in-itself' (an ultimate representation of bi-valent logic) and a sense that the object has infinite meanings (as apprehended by the symmetrical mode).

Bion links the idea of infinity to his concept of 'O', ultimate reality. In *Attention and Interpretation* he begins to emphasize the limiting and deceptive nature of the senses in understanding the internal world (Bion, 1970). His model of mind, although never rejecting previous notions, moves away from definitive exchanges based on sensory input, definitive objects, to the notion of O, ultimate unknowable reality and the infinite. In shifting towards understanding the implications of O, Bion never fully explores the relationship between O and the container. How does the therapist approach O? Does this alter previous notions of the container? In terms of the container–contained configuration, does O represent the ultimate container (Grotstein, 2000) or a containerless ineffable space? An argument could be made for both of these possibilities. This appears typical of Bion's writings where there is little compulsion to systematically link some of his theoretical ideas and he deliberately leaves this up to the reader to develop. However, a case may also be made for arguing that Bion drew less on ideas related to his container model in his later work because it was too rigid a concept, too tied to sensory objects, to fit his ideas related to 'becoming' and evolving in O. In my reading of Bion, his emphasis on encounters with O bring into sharp focus the dilemmas inherent in the clinical encounter in trying to bear the thrust of 'ultimate reality' while having to deal with the fact that it will always remain ultimately unknowable.

We have already considered Bion's (1970) proposition that the analyst needs to 'abandon memory and desire' in order to make himself available to connecting with the analysand's mind in the present moment as part of analytic containment. This practice was driven by his argument that the analyst should focus his attention on O, ultimate non-sensuous reality, a reality beyond concepts like good or bad; O is the place of constantly emerging essences and is ultimately ineffable. In Bion's words: 'its presence can be recognized and felt but it cannot be known' (1970. p.30). Without a grounding in sensual reality and sensory gratification, approaching O requires what Bion calls 'an act of faith' (1970, p.34). 'Faith' might be understood to mean belief in the possibility that out of 'suffering' experience, without escape into defensive thought, comes the birth of new meaning that is never rid of pain or struggle, but can be made more bearable. This translates into an analytic goal that strives to expand the analytical couple's capacity for containment by increasing one's exposure to O and to making creative use of the emotional storm that ensues. In sum, the containing function of the mother, father or even family is one of transforming experience from the 'deep and formless infinite', infinity, into basic concepts that make the ineffability of O more bearable (Grotstein, 2000).

In thinking about the analyst's containing function as existing between 'proper' and 'dream' object, the analyst is in effect attempting to find a way of surviving such situations. At extremes, I understand the analyst's mind to offer two irreconcilable 'ideal solutions', two phantasies that reflect Matte-Blanco's (1988) bi-logical theory. The first constitutes an attempt to know the object as a 'thing-in-itself'; the second relates to the analyst identifying with O as an infinite and indivisible entity. The former occurs when mental objects are reduced to the world of 'things' and treated as if they possess the same properties as a physical object. At this extreme there is no difference between thought and object and therefore we succumb to the phantasy that we have direct contact with the object itself, the 'thing-in-itself'. In this way each object assumes a discrete meaning, not replaceable by any other object, it constitutes a fixed relationship that ceases to evolve in the passing of experience. Because thoughts are treated like objects they are also assumed to exist within a network of simple causal linear relationships. The thought 'his sister always treats him like a child' becomes the only way of thinking about the patient and his sister; two discrete objects in a rigidly defined linear relationship.

The second solution involves phantasies that the analyst can become O in all its infinite possibilities. It is best understood to involve a process where the analyst attempts to 'become infinite' (Bion, 1970, p.46). Although O could evolve to the point where it presents itself in a way that finds understanding (K), Bion thought it could also be accessed more directly through the analyst's intuition. In its extreme form, however, these intuitions are felt to be ultimate truths governed by omniscient phantasies that are felt to unify all objects. I understand this to map on to Matte-Blanco's movement toward a way of thinking that is dominated by the symmetrical mode.

To reiterate, I am suggesting that the analyst's containing function emerges in his ability to maintain the tension between the object as 'thing-in-itself' and a sense of infinity. An inability to do so results in ways of engaging represented by falling into the above two extremes: either the analyst's thinking becomes overly defined, precise, causal, or it becomes tinged with an omnipotent sense of possessing ultimate truths that unite all objects, but struggle to contain or articulate them in an understandable way. From this perspective the containing process involves tolerating 'a sense of infinity' where emotions function as constants that can be replaced, thereby setting in motion an ongoing process of receptivity and recombination, releasing oneself from simple causal relationships.

In struggling with these polar dimensions the analyst's thinking and manner of communicating takes on a particular quality inherent in attempts to 're-present' experience. As Baranger et al. (1983) point out, in terms of the analytic field the analyst and patient can only begin to understand the analytic field through taking a 'second look'. Through this process the therapist encourages a process of 're-presenting' analytic experience. The analytic field acts like a screen on which analyst and patient re-present their ideas, conflict, feelings, in search of a different point of view. But also implicit in the analyst's attempt's to take a 'second look' is acknowledgement that we cannot have a 'first look'. We might say that the ineffability of O and the impossibility of possessing the 'thing-in-itself' is a constant unconscious reminder of our limitations and ultimate aloneness. A mother, in using reverie, can intuit and approximate her child's emotional needs, but can never be that reality for her baby. The quality I am referring to is best described as a sense of loss.

Links between representation and loss have been studied a great deal in psychoanalysis and philosophy. My focus here is on how the mental action of 're-presentation' portrays a sense of impermanence, otherness, separateness and fallibility. In my view such qualities usher in a process of mourning and a movement towards a more realistic appraisal of one's objects. This is consistent with Klein's (1940) view that mourning forms part of the psychological work needed to work through the depressive position. Here the loss of external objects threatens nourishing, good internal objects and as the infant moves towards whole-object relating he becomes more concerned about the status of his loving objects and how he may have damaged them. 'Loss' refers to any occurrence that challenges idealistic conceptions of good objects and the splitting of good and bad objects: absence, vulnerability, inattention or actual bereavement all involve a process of mourning. My contention is that in the containing process the therapist presents himself as a real object, affected by the emotional climate of the session ('dream object'), struggling to understand and put into his own words its possible meanings ('proper object'), succeeding, but inevitably failing to meet the patient's idealized unrealistic expectations. If the patient is to make use of such 'fertile failures' he has to mourn idealized conceptions of his object and related phantasies about why the containing object is fallible, vulnerable, and so forth.

As mentioned in Chapter 1, Steiner (1993) has made the important point that the containing process remains incomplete if a process of mourning is not achieved alongside the analyst's ability to make 'unthinkable' psychological states more bearable. In essence, he argues that while helping the patient think about unbearable mental states is useful in the short term, this does not lead to the withdrawal of projections from internal objects. If structural change is to occur the patient has to come to terms with the fact that his external objects are changed and damaged by his projections. This instigates a process of mourning and the internalization of a more realistic object in the form of a 'containing' therapist. Without this the patient cannot internalize more realistic ways of exploring and understanding internal experience (the internalization of the container function) and constantly relies on external objects to bear his projections. In focusing on the minutiae of the therapist's thinking processes (the moment-to-moment struggles to 're-present' experience), I am making the point that he gently instigates an invaluable move towards the patient beginning to mourn omnipotent and idealized phantasies of their containing object.

Between identifying and disidentifying: 'becoming something'

The analyst's role as 'proper object' is aligned with active attempts to disidentify with the patient's projective identifications. Here, there is a moving away from conscious and preconscious identifications with the patient. This constitutes one of the intrapychic routes through which the therapist carries out the limiting function of the 'proper object'. Identification, on the other hand, marks the therapist's psychic attempts to 'know' what is being projected. This requires that the therapist be partly immersed in the patient's psychic reality and the interpenetrating dialogue between projection and introjection. In this process the therapist is drawn into either identifying with the patient or with what has been disowned and projected into him, otherwise known as concordant and complementary identification respectively (Racker, 1957). The process of identification is mainly unconscious and permits the therapist access to aspects of the patient's internal world aiding further understanding of the transference and interpretative possibilities. Through engaging his own dream thoughts and emotional states (that have passed through alpha-function) the therapist attempts to give some form to how he is being used in the transference. More importantly, however, identification might be seen as a process en route to the transformation of unassimilated experience in that it initiates a process whereby the therapist has to begin to think about experiences evoked by the process.

Bion (1965) writes about the importance of 'becoming the analysand' (p.146). We could understand this to be the therapist's attempts to 'become' unconscious aspects of himself that are evoked by the patient through identification. Containing thus involves an internal sense of 'becoming' as the therapist is 'awakened' or exposed to derivatives of his own unconscious. From this point of view he is also inevitably involved in a process of 'becoming himself', getting to know parts of himself that have never been experienced in quite the same way. In my view it is the therapist's interest and curiosity in the novelty of this experience that signifies his attempts to contain something that is 'alive', evolving, on the way to being meaningful. I have often found this to be a useful point of departure when it has been difficult to reach a patient or there appears to be an impasse in the way we relate. Here, orientating one's awareness to the novel aspects of what is otherwise routine and expected opens up a different way of listening to the patient. In the vignette concerning Melissa (p.66), my dream-thoughts appear to connect with something beyond the repetition of her narrative about being a victim of critical men. These thoughts transform the way I feel when I sit listening to her. The way I listen and attend seems changed as I engage in a sense of 'becoming', experiencing the session in a new way. I see this as similar to Bion's (2005b) notion of trying to connect with what shines through the resistance, as opposed to attempting to interpret the defensiveness or impasse head on.

The containing attitude, however, appears to involve more than the analyst's attempts to identify with the patient. Freud (1923) taught us that secondary identifications are primarily based on a sense of loss: I identify with the object because I cannot be, or have, the object. We might say 'being like' is a substitute for the fact that we can't 'have' the experience of the object. Further, the process of identification tends to circumvent the emergent aspects of experience which constantly evolve in the analytic encounter. Bion is clear that identification can stand in the way of real growth of the personality where 'how to be *just like* a loving or affectionate person takes the place of *becoming* one' (Bion, 2005b, p.9). In this sense identification, as part of the containing process, retains static qualities that can stand in the way of broadening what we are able to hold in mind. In short, although always evident to some degree in the analytic encounter, it is never an end in itself. 'Becoming' seems also to involve moving away from simply identifying with the object so as to allow oneself to be partially transformed by it: this is the difference between 'being or feeling like' the other's mind and 'becoming'. In the case of Melissa, I move somewhat away from simply identifying with her as a victim of critical men as I notice how I am transformed by my own experience.

Negotiating this tension is inevitably painful and turbulent and has to be endured for long enough to approximate some sense of 'truth' about emerging parts of the personality (the patient's and the therapist's) that enter the containing process. Perhaps for this reason we easily fall back on more primitive forms of identification and mimicry. It is easier to 'identify with' than it is to work out how one is transformed by the identification. Bion suggests that this is often a default position that has no place in real mental growth of which 'containing' is such an important part. In his words: 'it is possible that our simian ancestry is much too powerful for us, our simian capacity for learning tricks far exceeds our capacity for acquiring wisdom' (Bion, 2005b, p.33). We could say, following Bion, that 'becoming' involves attempts to attune to the constantly evolving nature of experience as it emerges in waking dream thought. As a running commentary, it is as much about tracking the patient's narratives, non-verbal communications and so forth, as it is about the therapist developing an astute awareness of how he is 'reinvented' anew in the analytic field during each session.

A sense of 'becoming' involves a deeply introspective and creative process where the analyst opens himself up to evolving aspects of the self that respond to initial identifications. In the vignette below I attempt to illustrate this process as it emerged in a rather dramatic way with a patient. The case also illustrates another important point: the therapist's sense of 'becoming' is not confined to the limits of the session. Because the containing function is an intrapsychic process, how one is being transformed by the experience of each session is not bound by time or interpersonal space. Indeed, there is often a great deal that we are left with to process at a preconscious level after each session. It is probable that this occurs more often when the therapist finds it difficult to have his own thoughts while sitting with the patient. Because our states of reverie do not necessarily finish at the end of the session it is often easy to miss some of these references as they occur in the analyst's daily life.

Matthew

Matthew cannot keep a job. He always seems to be unable to deal with mundane activities and prefers to aim high. He regularly goes through hypermanic episodes where he tries to change everything that feels wrong at work but nothing seems sufficient. He resigns from his job because he feels he should have been promoted due to all his hard work. When he sits with me he shakes, he is full of stories of woe about how he has tried so hard but people fail him. He says he cannot continue and has suicidal thoughts because he feels ashamed of past failures. I cannot think when I'm with him, I can hardly talk and feel hopeless and threatened. I make some comments trying to simply reflect his situation. He bristles and seems irritated that I am inter-rupting him. It seems that if I say two words he feels controlled by me. I attempt to show him how difficult some of his shaming experiences have been, particularly with his father. He often attacks and laughs at me for the 'psychological crap' I infer. At times I feel as though I have nothing to say that will be of use to him which leaves me feeling both irritated and vulnerable. Among all this, there are times when he idealizes my position as a therapist saying he would only see someone with a PhD.

Later I learn that Matthew loves to talk about his conservative political views and takes great pleasure in engaging in arguments with 'lefties'. He says he feels like he could be a 'serial bomber' when people brush him off. I am aware of feeling intimidated by this man when he is with me.

After another difficult session, I go for coffee over the road from my office. As the lady gives me my coffee, she doesn't ask for payment. I am surprised by my reaction: I think about walking away, having a free coffee, stealing the coffee. These are strange thoughts to me (I do not make a habit out of stealing my coffee!). I began to think about Matthew: Why am I a thief? Is this his antisocial side projected? Is this an antisocial expression of me wanting to somehow get him back for his attacks on me? Is this a part of me identified with him stealing others' experiences without really engaging? Perhaps it goes without saying that I mention nothing about this to Matthew but am relieved that I'm able to think about him properly for the first time – albeit out of the session.

In time, I seemed to become more astutely aware of how he engages with me by trying to 'steal' my experience and abandon his own. He adopts a parasitic mode (see pp.143–144) that I start to be able to think about and contain. During the sessions I begin to draw his attention to this observation as it emerges in the transference. In essence I begin to suggest that he so desperately wants to learn something from me but ends up feeling so frustrated he wishes he could just 'take it' from me. He seems to accept these simple interjections and does not retaliate in his usual fashion.

Six months down the line we get to a point where Matthew does not physically shake or appear so anxious as he sits with me. He starts talking about how it troubles him that he goes from woman to woman because he feels he needs greater and greater stimulation. I say to him that I feel like he is always rushing around trying to build himself up to cover up how vulnerable he feels. I tell him that I sometimes feel he rushes round the session trying to build himself up in front of me in the hope of some excitement and release. In response he breaks down, punches the table in anger and then becomes tearful. He begins to sound a little more real to me and starts talking about how he feels he has to constantly copy everyone else, imitate what they do and pretend it is himself. He cannot create anything he says, he 'just moves other people's things around and takes their ideas. That's why it's good talking politics, you can play a role, you don't have to be original.'

The following session he makes no reference to this important event but reports a dream: *He is at his old workplace and feels he has all the time in the world. He is a police officer investigating a suicide. The 'jumper' is outside on the pavement. He is told that the victim jumped because he had got 'sick of the rush and hype of work'. His boss is in the background not intruding, allowing him time to think and go about his work.*

My work with Matthew is a good example of a patient who constantly 'attacks the link' (Bion, 1959) between two objects in order to prevent psychological growth. Any attempt by me to understand (K) his vulnerability is omnipotently attacked leading to phantasies that I would attack back. I am unable to think and am not, in essence, allowed to have my own thoughts when I sit with him. The coffee experience helped me begin thinking about him outside of the session. It seemed to me to signify the start of a process where I was better able to contain unformulated experiences. By engaging in my own sense of 'becoming' something different, I began to understand how I was being transformed by my experience with Matthew. This initiates a shift in me that later becomes part of the analytic field in such a way that he begins to think about similar possibilities. With this he is better able to tolerate and contain his 'stealing' thoughts himself. The dream, as we understood it, represented the new 'thinking part' of him that was better able to tolerate thinking about the suicidal, shame-filled, vulnerable parts of himself. In short, the dream elements appeared to represent the possibility of him being able to access split-off parts of himself.

In terms of conceptualizing the analytic space as a bi-directional field. The process of 'becoming' does not only involve the analyst as an evolving 'container'. It is more a case of both parties feeling able to engage experience in the here-and-now and sharpen their sensitively to how they are changed by thought, the analyst's suggestions, interpretative and non-interpretative interventions, symbols or non-verbal movements in the analytic field. This process occurs more when therapist and patient are commensally linked (see pp.145–151) where both parties feel better able to 'give themselves over to the process'. As I will explore shortly my sense is that this is only possible if the psychic field is supported by proto-containing experiences, a field of intensities and essences that cannot be made psychical.

Pathways of return and withdrawal?

In this chapter we have been considering the nature of the containing function, locating it in a particular state of mind that deliberately remains fluid in order to hold projected experience in mind long enough for it to start to gather meaning. In this the essence of the containing function is about maintaining and regulating a mental connection with the patient's mind that allows new thoughts and perspectives to emerge in the analyst's experience (and to varying degrees the patient's mind) that make phantasies and unbearable aspects of psychic life more tolerable. I have put forward the idea that it is a 'balanced' internal tension between himself as 'proper object' and 'dream object' that represents the containing function at work. The 'detoxification' process occurs through the analyst 'surviving' what is projected into him, tolerating and managing conscious, but undeveloped thoughts and feelings that appear to be related to his countertransference. It also may involve managing aspects of the frame that are under threat, thereby placing limitations on the effects of core phantasies (emanating from identification with the 'proper object'). This effectively demonstrates to the patient that aspects of the analyst's mind and the analytic space are not overwhelmed by what, to the patient, feel like uncontrollable and unbearable aspects of himself. At the same time, in order to get a sense of the real essence of what the analyst is containing, he in part becomes a player in the core organizing phantasy. In terms of field theory and Matte-Blanco's principle of symmetry that hold sway over the unconscious, the analyst and patient become players on the same unconscious field, it is not a matter of choice. In other words, it is not a matter of 'whether I'm being affected' but 'how am I being affected' that the analyst attempts to engage with. I have suggested that through reverie the analyst is able to engage with himself as 'dream object'. This involves engaging with a preconscious narrative that represents our best chance of understanding countertransference states that are, by definition, unconscious. This process of struggling to think about and understand derivatives that emerge at the fringes of consciousness constitutes the other pole of the therapist's role in 'detoxifying' projected contents. In sum, we could say that while the 'proper object' conveys a limiting function, the 'dream object' gives it meaning: both make unbearable experience more tolerable.

With this model in mind, how are we to understand how such projections are returned or withdrawn? In understanding the containing process, I am focused on aspects of the analytic field that make up an interpenetrating mix of projective identifications and introjective identifications. Within this theoretical framework, containment is often associated with ideas about 'returning' and 'withdrawing' projections. Behind this lies the clinical idea that the analyst needs to transform projections into more bearable forms so that they can be returned or withdrawn. While I find great value in understanding the container as being the receptacle of projective identi-fications, I do not find the idea of 'return' or 'withdrawal' useful in the clinical setting. In my experience this way of thinking causes the therapist to make interpretations that supposedly 'return projections' but usually have the opposite effect of increasing anxiety about split-off parts of the self. Such interpretations often take the form of trying to tell the patient about split-off feelings: 'I get the sense you are avoiding feeling vulnerable' or 'I have come to represent an angry part of you'. Interpretations of this nature amount to telling the patient that he feels something that he does not feel. Instead of feeling understood, the patient experiences these kind of 'returning' interpretations as if something frightening is being pushed into him (Carpy, 1989). Alternatively, such interpretations are simply accepted at an intellectual level, leaving the patient feeling that he cannot talk about related issues and should 'contain' them. The idea of 'return' seems to be linked to the tendency to treat the container as if it were a concrete three-dimensional object with near-physical properties.

I would argue that it better reflects the clinical reality of the analytic process, at least in terms of what I have found useful, to think about the internalization process as occurring via what might be called a 'collabora-tive elaborating' process. Here the analyst and patient focus on the analytic field and what is co-created between them to try and arrive at meaningful ways of apprehending projected experience. It is the combination of a mutative struggle between patient and analyst to try and engage split-off experience and the meaningful elaboration of unassimilated experience that is eventually internalized, making the patient's phantasies more bearable. Through locating the container function within the tensions between incompatible poles or vertices, I have emphasized its part in generating 'fertile failures', always communicating the precarious nature of meaning-making. In this sense the container function is always imparting a sense of loss, a sense of not being able to contain the patient's phantasies in immutable ways. We could say that the container function, in part, also ushers in a process of mourning ideals related to containment, the idea that the therapist will invariably contain split-off parts of the self without consequence.

Put simply, the projection is not actually returned, even a more bearable version of it. Rather, the patient internalizes a new 'collaborative elabor-ating couple' that helps him access and think about the phantasy of projective identification in more adaptive ways. I see this as being consistent with Bion's ideas regarding the commensal mode where a third object is created to the benefit of patient and therapist (see p.145). Here the con-taining process gives rise to narratives and symbols that become containers themselves. From this point of view, the idea of 'return' makes little sense. It also challenges the idea that the analytic containing process occurs as a simple linear process of reception–detoxification–return. We will return to various aspects of this process in discussing interpretation in the next chapter. For now, I simply want to demonstrate this process, particularly the role that narratives and symbols play in elaborating the containment system.

Nirvana

Nirvana came to see me after her best friend had left town and was distressed about not being able to cope without her. She had begun to have thoughts about whether she wanted to continue her studies in medicine, something she and her friend had done together. Nirvana started coming to see me twice a week with the aim of trying to understand why she might be 'overly' distressed about her friend leaving. However, it soon became apparent that she had spent long periods of her childhood and adolescence feeling depressed, causing her to spend long periods away from school.

Much of the first four months of therapy were taken up by work problems she was encountering. We began to understand how easily she felt others perceived inadequacy in her. While the 'work issues' seemed to engage the therapeutic process, I was aware of her resistance to talking in any depth about her family. When I pointed this out to her she responded by telling me that she would agree to talk about her family only if I would agree not to try and change anything about her family situation. Taken somewhat by surprise, and with no understanding regarding what this may be about, I agreed, saying that I felt I could not change anything in a direct way but that perhaps simply 'seeing in' would help her in understanding things 'outside her family'. She started to tell me about her experience at home. Her father was an alcoholic and drank vast amounts after a retrenchment. Although he worked again, his alcohol abuse continued. He had never been confronted on the matter and Nirvana's mother, a pharmacist, constantly behaved in ways that would keep it a family secret. It seemed a reality that they very rarely socialized or visited friends in order to avoid the risk of her father becoming aggressive in front of others once he started drinking. There were also a number of examples where Nirvana was clearly prevented from having contact with others: when a relative died her father deliberately withheld information so she could not attend the funeral.

Nirvana was extremely introverted and hardly maintained eye contact in our sessions together. I felt like a towering presence as I sat with her, conscious that I may say something that would frighten her. She constantly made reference to the fact that others found her boring and felt that she had no need for contact with other people. Nirvana regularly spoke about her perceived shortcomings and said that she found comfort in thinking this way because this was something she knew and could hold on to with certainty.

At some point I noted how difficult it was for me to use the word 'alcoholic'. I deliberately avoided it for some time. There were other words too that took on a particular kind of 'feel': her 'house' had a dark, musty feel, isolated and abandoned. At one stage I wondered out loud why I had such difficulty saying the word 'alcoholic'. She responded by saying that she was feeling anxious and associated it with me 'forcing' her to think about 'alcoholic'. I replied, saying that she seemed to have started experiencing me as dangerous, somehow trapping her. She agreed, saying the room seemed to get smaller and she wanted the session to end. Nirvana remained anxious for rest of the session to which I found myself trying to respond in a caring maternal way.

My response to her drew my attention to the fact that during this initial phase of therapy I had been relating to Nirvana in this way. 'You've had a really hard life haven't you'. I would often say to myself. This was interspersed with a deep sense of boredom, hopelessness and no real sense of direction. I started thinking about her relationship with her hostile father and how much this must have isolated her, imprisoned her and her mother. Was her self-criticism related to an internalized brutalizing father? Was there a process of identification with her mother influenced by her mother's passive-aggressive and pathetic stand against him, or had she made herself invisible to her parents and adopted a caretaking role towards others? Still further, was she unable to feel because she lacked a tolerant containing object and thus had never been able to work though her own hostility? Was she projecting this state of mind on to others providing a rationale for her withdrawing tendencies?

All this made some sense but none of it was useful in coming to know her experience while she was sitting with me. In response, I suspended trying to think too hard about a way forward. Shortly after this, I found myself thinking about an event in my life where I had tried to help a friend out by attending a function with her after she had asked me. It was clear to me at the time that I had no interest in going but accepted mainly out of courtesy but also out of pity because I was aware that she had no one else to go with. All along there was a real sense of awkwardness and lack of authenticity about the outing. We had gone along with it but there was a sense of something unfinished between us that was never addressed and it was never mentioned again. I found myself thinking about how my actions must have felt quite patronizing at the time. After some consideration I went back to my initial feelings in relation to Nirvana and wondered if my displays of concern about her situation were being experienced by her as having a patronizing, gratuitous ring to them.

With these thoughts in mind, and in the context of her saying that she felt awkward when others seemed to care for her and wondered whether she could trust them, I suggested that perhaps she felt awkward about how to deal with the way I listened to her. I went on to say that I had a sense that she sometimes felt it to be patronizing, but she was used to it so went along with it. She said she doubted that I really cared but was terrified to find out or believe that I might. Nirvana sat in silence for a while and then said that her mother always talked about pitying others and for the first time she sensed that she could feel what that was really like. She felt too that she could now see it in the eyes of some people she knew and wondered if that was why she sought their contact. Nirvana said she wanted to move past that feeling as it was an image of her inside her family. The session changed track at this point and she told me that last week she had been at a social occasion and had unusually voiced her opinion on something and was surprised to have felt understood, instead of simply being ignored. I suggested to her that something important seemed to have happened when we talked about her feelings of being patronized that had led to her feeling a sense of understanding instead of us ignoring the matter.

After approximately three years of psychotherapy the therapeutic relationship appeared to change track when our sessions took the form of Nirvana relaying to me what she thought she had achieved. Some of these accomplishments were impressive. She had started dating. She was better able to initiate contact with others and had started to think about moving out of home. My interest in these changes was considerable and in many ways I had never expected such gains. But Nirvana was also conscious of the fact that she was able to 'do' a lot but could not 'feel' these changes. In response to this I made a number of different interpretations, some related to her sense of self still being behind 'closed doors', while she secretly moves on. Other interpretations concerned her fear that her 'doing' version of herself felt isolated as it had no 'parents' to approve of her actions. Nirvana would agree with these possibilities but there seemed to be no real new material evoked, nothing seemed to shift. Only on reflection did I realize that my suggestions all avoided material related to her father's perceived terrorizing response.

The following session I listened to her latest achievements about her being able to stand up to a particular colleague who had done something questionable. She was surprised that instead of being belittled, or singled out, by those who knew about this, she was commended for her actions. While listening to Nirvana I found myself considering if this would be an event that she could really experience and feel. At about this point, apparently unconnected with anything else, I was flooded with intense fear and a sudden thought that I had left my son, then about a year old, in the back of my car. In that second, I thought I had abandoned him, forgetting to drop him off at home. The feelings, the sensations in my chest, were overwhelming but remained undetected by Nirvana as she continued. Having recovered somewhat I began to consider my thoughts and was struck by how disparate this experience felt. I wondered what this could be about. In reality I had no reason to drop my son off and he had not been in the car that morning. I began thinking about myself as a neglectful parent. My fear seemed connected to the sudden awareness of neglect as well as the suffering of a trapped one-year-old. I turned to considering the possibility that this experience had somehow been generated between us in the session.

During this time Nirvana was still wondering about why she couldn't feel a sense of achievement and had settled for the thought that it was more comfortable not to feel. I agreed with her but added that perhaps there was something else. I said for some time now the sessions had taken a form where she would report her progress, telling me how well she was getting on, and I wondered if that was due to some awareness that it held my interest. She agreed. I said these achievements were very positive things, but perhaps she felt that if she did not remind me I would forget about her. I said I had a sense that she worried that she was not making an impression on me. She looked pale in response, saying that she had just seen her father's 'stony face', up close, terrifying her. Nirvana changed the subject and said that she had worried for some time about a 'weird sense of not feeling real' when she sat with me. She reported a sense that sometimes she felt that the sessions existed only in her imagination and had not really happened. I asked her if she thought it was possible that what I had said about her fear that I would forget her was too difficult to think about, so it was easier to think that it was all imagined. She sat in silence for a while then became tearful and angry about her father never once attending her hockey matches at school. She tried to help him, she said, but she was angered by the fact that he did not even attend one match.

Nirvana reported a dream: *She felt terrified and was trapped in a room with an intrusive colleague who kept on saying he wanted to get to know her. While he repeated these words, he kicked the wall, terrifying her. The dream suddenly shifted, she said, and she felt like she must have 'died and gone to heaven' because the next scene depicted her as an angel, reading a book, and the object of attentive worship.*

On discussing the dream we began trying to understand the 'terrorizing presence' in the dream. We understood the dream to be about how difficult it was to tolerate allowing me to get to know her without feeling that it was unreal. It would be easier, we surmised, if we could meet in a place of 'heavenly good' where there was no sense of terror and she would receive an ideal kind of care and loving. Reading seemed to be a clear symbol of how she achieved this by burying herself in novels as a child.

After this session we began to talk more openly about 'a terrorizing presence' in the room and she was better able to mention when she felt this was beginning to escalate. With this she grew more open to thoughts and memories about her father that had previously not occurred to her. She had forgotten the gun her father would ominously place behind the kitchen door at mealtimes. She also came to realize how much her present dilemma about leaving home was less about her own insecurities as it was about staying at home to protect her mother.

I think this case illustrates the gradual emergence of Nirvana's 'terrorizing presence'. It is projected in many forms, split off from thought, having a paralyzing effect on her ability to feel and benefit from 'good' experience. For some of the time I am drawn into a symbiotic avoidance (the configuration is symbiotic) of the terrorizing object. For instance, while I remind her that I cannot actually change anything in her family (the presence of the 'proper object' implicitly reassuring her about the limitations of her 'invasive phantasy'), I begin to be drawn into a sense of needing to appease her by sensing fear and saying that we will just 'look in' and always remain 'outside the family'. I am drawn into the role of 'dream object' as I start to unconsciously identify with the emotional current of the session. Later on, I adopt a patronizing maternal way of relating which also serves to dance around the unbearable fear that occupies the room.

Gradually, however, through attending to states of reverie, our defensive symbiosis can be thought about and it gains symbolic meaning and a sense of understanding. With this, the paralyzing fear associated with her father begins to gather narrative meaning and can be held in mind for longer periods of time. This begins with my attempts to understand my awkwardness around the word 'alcoholic' and aggregates new feeling and meaning when I stumble on my intrusive fears about fatherhood and neglect. The unassimilated 'terrorizing presence' becomes more tolerable and meaningful through a collaborative process which involved curiously exploring and putting into words previously unexplored experience. There are no interventions here that aim to give back or 'return' her projected terror, only the building of narrative derivatives (Ferro, 2005a, 2006) that make split-off parts of the personality more bearable. They build symbolic, verbal, thinkable options that diminish the need to disown or communicate through the use of projective identification. Together, and through tolerating the countertransference, we struggle to take a 'second look' (Baranger *et al.*, 1983) at the experience generated between us.

Conclusion

In conceptualizing the containing function in terms of 'ideal' polar dimensions, it can be conceptualized as a process, a wavering mental connection, always in a state of becoming. To be able to hold the patient in mind in a way that is experienced as sustained meaningful contact, we have to embrace the idea that 'the patient has gone on living and thinking and will not be the same patient tomorrow as today – or at the end of the session as at the beginning' (Bion, 2005b, p.16). In exploring polar dimensions of the containing process I have argued that the container cannot be located as an overly discrete mental entity although it does have limits. Nor can it simply be located in the therapist's mind. It exists in the mental connection between patient and therapist and is better conceptualized as existing in a system or field between patient and analyst.

Perhaps the inability to locate the container as a clear-cut, defined entity has an element of dissatisfaction to it. I have a sense that this mirrors the limited, transitory, opaque, ineffable, but invaluable nature of the containing process. In fact, from the perspective of container pathology, the emphatic or concrete location of the container (or its functions) contributes to the emergence of various pathological states which we will consider in later sections.

Chapter 5

Notes on interpretation

I allow the analytic situation to evolve; then interpret the evolution. It is essential for the psycho-analyst and his analysand that the operation of curiosity itself should be demonstrated and not its name.

(Bion, 1967, p.161)

The problem is how to let the germ of an idea, or the germ of an interpretation, have a chance of developing.

(Bion, 2005a, p.12)

The act of interpretation cannot be separated from the containment process. Although it is often implied that the therapist 'silently' contains the patient's projections until they can be 'given back' in the form of a brilliant incisive interpretation, this is not my clinical experience. There are a number of problems with this assumption. It depicts a model that implies that projections are somehow held at bay or 'removed', processed, and then returned in a more tolerable form via interpretation. Although a 'neat' model, it does not reflect the clinical complexities involved in the process of 'containing' and interpretation. I hope to have shown that the containing function involves tolerating a number of internal tensions constantly being communicated in a bi-directional analytic field where meaning is co-constructed. From this position overly formulated interpretations are understood to come from an isolated mind, not the moment-to-moment interaction between two minds. In keeping with the idea that the analyst's containing function is part of an ongoing dialogical and reciprocal process, containing is constantly being communicated verbally and non-verbally. The need to act from within affective links between patient and therapist also implies that interpretations need to convey containing qualities. As Lafarge puts it:

Interpretation always rests in part on containment, for in good analytic work the analyst is informed by his affective responses to his patient's non-verbal communications as well as verbal associations. Interpretation is also an act of containment.

(Lafarge, 2000, p.68)

Lafarge appears to be making two points here. First, interpretation relies on a containment process, metabolizing experience so that it can be better thought about. Second, the act of interpretation itself conveys aspects of containment. The way the analyst makes an interpretation, how he positions himself in the analytic field in order to allow it to be containing for the patient, forms part of this process. It is this latter point that I am interested in pursuing in this chapter.

What then comprises 'containing' interpretations? If 'containing' is constantly being conveyed in moment-to-moment interactive sequences, then what specific value do interpretations have? Bion added a unique perspective to understanding the role of interpretation that emphasizes the analyst's engagement with intense emotions while still holding on to some capacity to think about them. From this perspective, interpretations can be understood as the analyst's best attempts at demonstrating and commenting on the evolution and broadening of experience between them. It is more about creating an experience conducive to the emergence of new thoughts than it is about directly conveying understanding; more about the act of interpretation, than its content. I want to consider what it is that constitutes the qualities of 'containing' interpretations.

The 'containing' process emerges out of the analyst's engagement with internal tensions between the 'proper object' and 'dream object', between limiting the impact of the patient's internal world and taking it on. Once the therapist finds it difficult to engage with this ongoing tension, he is at risk of interpreting in ways that are not experienced as containing. Such interpretations usually reflect the therapist's 'over-valued' ideas (Britton and Steiner, 1994) or simply convey an internal confusion while the therapist is in the throes of unbearable emotion; both might be considered defensive enactments against 'containing'. My understanding is that interpretations convey the therapist's containing function if they stay close to the evolution of experience in the here-and-now, creating the conditions that allow the patient to have an emotional, but tolerable, encounter that changes him somehow or shifts his way of experiencing things. Symington and Symington (1996) ask the following questions:

When we make an interpretation are we just exchanging concepts or is there a realization that applies; are we doing anything more than just ingeniously manipulating symbols? Does the patient really get in touch with something so that light dawns, does he have an emotional experience that changes him, or does he merely learn a new vocabulary so that he can talk about himself in a different way but has had no real emotional experience in the analysis?

(p.91)

These are important questions. I consider 'containing' aspects of interpretation to include elements of an intervention that aims towards helping the patient tolerate being changed by experience. I am not referring to single climactic experiences so much as partial interpretations that help the patient connect with split-off experience in a tolerable and stepwise way. As a general rule of thumb, 'containing' interpretations aim to meet the patient in their experience and make them feel understood so as to expand their capacity to tolerate emotional experience and be transformed by it.

I will focus on three areas that I consider important in conveying a 'containing' stance within the analyst's interpretative approach. These include:

- a focus on analyst-centred interpretations
- the use of 'unsaturated' interpretations
- the role of the analyst's 'passion' and subjectivity in conveying interpretations.

Although not intended, these three elements appear to have some bearing on Bion's (1963) statements that 'usable' interpretations must make tangible the nature of the psychoanalytic object and to do this they must possess dimensions of sense, myth and passion. By this he means that interpretations have to rely somewhat on sense impressions so patient and analyst know that they are referring to the same 'thing', they need to extend or use the personal metaphors, myths, language of the patient, and they require the emotional participation of the analyst. The approach I discuss below appears to convey some of these features in particular ways.

Analyst-centred interpretations

Steiner (1993) proposes a distinction between 'analyst-centred' and 'patient-centred' interpretations as a means of helping the patient and therapist begin to think about and contain what is being projected. He suggests that the analyst begins with interpretations that focus on spelling out the patient's perceptions of the analyst in a way that does not question such perceptions. He calls these 'analyst-centred' interpretations. This gives the patient the 'distance' to consider that these perceptions might have some meaning or mental currency between them. In turn, it conveys a sense of feeling understood. Only once this has been achieved, he contends, are we able to use 'patient-centred' interpretations that focus on interpreting projections as split-off parts of the self in a way that generates understanding and enables the patient to begin to 'take back' split-off parts of the self. These kinds of interpretations depend on sufficient mental capacity to contain them and might be called 'weaning' interpretations when less containment is required (Mitrani, 2001). In Steiner's (1993) view:

> . . . containment is weakened if the analyst perseveres in interpreting or explaining to the patient what he is thinking, feeling, or doing. The patient experiences such interpretations as a lack of containment and feels that the analyst is pushing the projected elements back into him.
> (p.407)

I turn now to a case, Susan, to illustrate some of these points.

Susan

Susan came to see me after a relationship breakup. Her ex-lover had walked out on her without any explanation and she was struggling to understand what had gone wrong. She was worried that she was unable to form long-term relationships because she thought that men found her threatening as she had a good job and had no need to depend on them. Although Susan had a close relationship with her younger sister she had distanced herself from her brother because she felt he was always trying to compete for their parents' affection. She also felt emotionally distant from her parents. Susan sensed that her father had instigated this difficulty because she had grown up witnessing him being physically abusive towards her mother. She felt her mother was a 'senseless person' staying married to her father and Susan spent a great deal of time blaming her parents for being 'bad role models for relationships'.

Susan had a very particular way of relating: it felt as though I would be invited to attend to some apparent happening or insight which would then be abruptly cut short so as to move on to another subject. She would often come across as quite excited in a way that seemed to communicate that she had made some sort of important discovery. But then Susan would suddenly shift to other matters, leaving me disorientated and in mid-sentence. When I drew her attention to this she would say something like: 'That's all there is, there is nothing else to say about that'. I seemed to be playing out some kind of 'find the treasure' game with her, only to find that the map was quickly whipped away from under my nose.

In one particular session she started telling me about a party she had gone to where her ex-boyfriend constantly avoided her. Susan said this made her drink more and pursue another man who seemed to keep on cutting the conversation short in an attempt to escape her, she suspected. She recalled how her younger brother would often get angry with her for always winning family games. She was also reminded of a particular time when he refused to share his friends with her because she 'always wanted to have all the fun'. I had an image of her in the school playground shouting 'Look at me, look at me!' so loudly that it made me cringe and I was aware of a kind of irritability attached to this. It was an image of people moving away, not towards her appeal for greater attention. At this point I interpreted that it seemed to me that she was often trying to put herself in a position with me where she was trying to get my attention, but once she had it she cut me off because she was worried I may become irritated like her brother. At the time I had a sense that her brother had become a repository for her split-off irritable 'bad' feelings that emerged as a result of rivalry for her parents' affections.

Susan replied, 'You could see it that way, yes'. She went on to recall a situation where she was playing a game of netball at school and no one wanted to be on her side. She fell silent for a while, then said she felt tired and had sustained an injury to her back and felt she needed to go for a massage immediately after the session. At the time I seemed to have little awareness that her statements here may have been transference references to her experience of my interpretation.

The following session Susan started by telling me she did not feel like coming to the session because she had a headache. She reported a dream: *A local member of government stood on a distant podium that somehow floated above a crowd. He was becoming irritable and started threatening violence if they did not vote for his political party. Susan felt like she had to vote for him and there was no way out of his propaganda.* Susan felt the dream was about her mistrust of politicians who always 'preach at a distance and get angry when they don't get their own way'. I said I was aware of something changing between us since our last session and that she was not her usual jovial self. I wondered if since I spoke to her about her position in relationships she had started experiencing me as distant and perhaps angry. She said she had taken what I had said to mean that she was being manipulative and 'attention-seeking' and she felt there was no room to disagree. I replied by saying that perhaps I had stated things wrongly, or we had misunderstood each other, but it felt important to me that she experienced me as being hostile and not giving her the room to be herself. Susan said that she was aware that she avoids hostility as it reminded her of her father. She recalled a time when he had angrily chased her out of her parents' room while she was trying to show her mother her new reading book. 'It was either fighting for attention or getting growled at in our house', she said.

After establishing this line of communication, it seemed more possible to talk about her experience of me as distant and hostile and it became more easily identifiable to me. Through drawing her attention to how this fluctuated in her experience we began to identify, in the real-time experience of the session, that her experiences of hostility escalated when she feared she could no longer hold my attention.

Although not an entirely full interpretation, I think my attempt at interpreting Susan's behaviour, or her part in the relational dynamic, could not be meaningfully engaged with and represented a failure in containment. Her associations appeared to clearly point to an experience of being forced to accept some kind of propaganda that did not feel right to her. I also think that my interpreting 'towards' her at that point was driven by an inability to contain my irritation so as to be able to think about the 'gamey' nature of our interaction.

Although not useful in itself, it did lead to a focus on her perceptions of me, granting her a way of beginning to think about the idea of hostility in the analytic field as represented by my presence at certain points in our interaction.

Patients who have marked difficulties in containing their own mental states find it difficult to tolerate direct exploration of such states and cannot locate or recognize their contribution to various ways of relating. Analyst-centred interpretations appear to help the patient vicariously apprehend uncontained mental states: 'It seems something changes between us when I . . .', 'You seem to find me very annoying when I . . .', 'I sense you are experiencing me as . . .'. In Susan's case she begins thinking about 'hostility' in the analytic field, something usually split off and supplanted by attention-craving strategies. Although it is still not associated with her own internal world, her own motivations, it begins to be contained in the analytic field.

To be clear, analyst-centred interpretations should not be misunderstood as being the same as the therapist's 'confessions'. This is not about impulsively or directly stating what the therapist feels. It is more about alerting the patient to possible ways in which he or she experiences the therapist. Further, if the therapist continuously interprets, in this manner, this kind of interpretation can become problematic and leads to the perception that the therapist is defensively avoiding direct contact with the patient, or is taken to be some form of preoccupation with himself (Steiner, 1994, 2000). When used judiciously, however, analyst-centred interpretations help establish a point of contact, or point of collaboration, where therapist and patient begin to better contain split-off mental states. As Mitrani (2001) clearly demonstrates, interpretations of this nature are essentially interpretations of the transference from the patient's point of view and are dependent on the act of introjective identification on the part of the therapist.

Unsaturated interpretations

Are we ever sure about what we are going to say, or how we say it, when we interpret? Bion (1967, 1989, 2005b), as I understand him, wants us to embrace the fact that we never know exactly how we are going to articulate an interpretation. This does not pose a problem in itself. Rather, at least in part, it reflects the ongoing evolution of experience in the session that represents a potential meeting point of experiencing beyond 'saturated' expectations. Ferro's (2005a) idea that we should, at times, 'speak before we think' rather than 'think before we speak' is important here. He is making the point that our efforts to interpret are often over-thought and saturated. As I utter the first words of an interpretation, I am already changing the analytic field in a way that affects how I further state it, the form it takes, its emotional expression, all, of course, are also dependent on the patient's presence. If the development of meaning is dependent on a dialogical process, what form should interpretations take if they are to help develop hitherto undeveloped meaning in the session? Ferro (2002, 2005c) recommends that we make 'unsaturated' interpretations as a way of engaging the patient in a meaning-making process. It seems that these 'weak' or preliminary forms of interpretation invite further participation from the patient and best engage the containment process.

Saturated interpretations, interpretations driven by theory or a dynamic idea that attempts to give the patient understanding, are not as effective in attempting to help the patient begin to 'name' and give meaning to unmetabolized internal experiences. I am not implying that the more 'saturated' types of interpretation are not useful. I would see the analytic process as more of a movement between unsaturated and saturated interventions where the more saturated interpretations have the effect of putting a 'seal' on the container so attention can shift to other areas. In this way I see saturated forms of interpretation as still emerging out of a dialogical meaning-making process and representing an endpoint.

There are, however, some forms of saturated interpretation that do violence to the meaning-making process and shut down the nature of what it means to 'think' with an other (Carnochan, 2006). If adequate shared meaning and mental capacity have not developed before a saturated interpretation is given, it is often experienced as a tear in the relational field where the analyst's mind is felt to obstruct the emergence of meaning. These interpretations implicitly assume that a single mind produces its own thoughts and ignores, or resists, recognizing the co-construction of meaning in the here-and-now. We are perhaps most vulnerable to making saturated interpretations of this kind when filled with conviction that there is no other way of seeing the situation.

Bion thought that interpretations which require too much thinking about, too much concocting, are usually distractions from what he called evolutions in O, or the constantly evolving nature of the analytic encounter. They amount to intellectualizations that diminish the significance of thoughts that evolve out of moment-to-moment interaction. We might understand such interpretations as becoming bastions of resistance against engaging in the experiencing process where the boundaries of self and other are diminished as the therapist begins to personify various aspects of the analytic field. If the 'thinker' dominates the session, the analyst (or patient) adopts a position where he feels his mind has sole access to the generation of particular thoughts: 'These thoughts are mine, they would not exist if I didn't have them.' The conflict here is between being the sole author of one's thoughts and dependence on another mind, a situation often linked to core internal dilemmas related to envy and possessiveness. With this in mind, Bion thought that the measure of a good interpretation or formulation can be gauged by the relative 'absence' of the analyst:

> The more his interpretations can be judged as showing how necessary *his* knowledge is, *his* experience, *his* character are to the thought as formulated, the more reason there is to suppose that the interpretation is psychoanalytically worthless, that is, alien to the domain O.
>
> (1970, p.105)

For these reasons, interpretations should not be made simply because the analyst has a formulation that comes to mind. Bion saw these interpretative attempts as usually defensive on the analyst's part and linked to the idea of 'cure'. Here the analyst attempts to give an explanation to interpret his way out of the unbearable and difficult task of sitting in the 'emotional storm' of the session. Although such interpretations may have a temporary curative effect, they also run the risk of setting up an addictive cycle in the therapy where the therapist is set up as the bearer of all knowledge (Bion, 1987, 2005a).

Given that the excessive use of projective identification is often linked to attempts to split off and escape traumatic psychic experience, full interpretations that try and interpret splitting are often felt to be quite traumatic. The difficulty arises from the fact that unmetabolized states are felt to be 'present' but cannot be comprehended because the patient lacks the preconceptions to understand what has been split off (Cartwright, 1998). While trying to spell out the meaning behind what the patient is doing to generate split-off states, such interpretations often invalidate the patient's experiences or difficulties and fail to put the patient in touch with the *experience* of managing such split-off states.

What is it then about unsaturated interpretations that convey the containing function? I emphasize three qualities:

1   They encourage collaborative engagement.
2   They have a narrative quality that helps build meaning.
3   They do not attempt to address resistance head-on.

I will focus mainly on the second, the narrative qualities of unsaturated interpretations.

Inviting collaborative engagement

'Unsaturated' interpretations allow for considerable influence and movement in the analytic field. They also have the effect of inviting the patient to collaborate by offering educated guesses, intuitions, possibilities that the patient can elaborate further. Interpretations offered as possible hypotheses have the effect of conveying the opaqueness of our minds and the evolving nature of experience that invites inquiry (Britton and Steiner, 1994).

I have been struck by a similar process evident in Bateman and Fonagy's (2006) mentalizing approach to borderline patients where the therapist adopts an enquiring attitude at the point that mentalizing, or the ability to track the mental states of the patient, begins to collapse in his own mind. I have a sense that this has the effect of inviting the patient into the therapist's mind, noticing and helping him develop meaning at the breakdown: 'I sense you are angry for some reason . . . can you help me understand that', 'I've just lost you . . . do you think it is possible . . .?'. Perhaps this is similar to Bion's clinical approach in sometimes being quite open regarding his own guesses or intuitions (Gooch, 2001). They represent the possibilities of a mind attempting to build meaning within the limitations of what can be truly known, but may feel right.

Meaning-making interactions

Ferro's (2002) version of unsaturated interpretation draws on their narrative qualities. He proposes an 'unsaturated relational model' (p.184) based on the idea that patient and analyst work together to arrive at approximate meanings of unelaborated psychic states. The analyst does this by exploring narrative derivatives that suggest a similar emotional undercurrent. Interpretations here aim to open up possible meanings rather than put a seal on a particular authoritative meaning.

Narrative forms of discourse are somewhat removed from 'external' reality and it is this quality that renders them useful vehicles for contemplating underlying mental states. As the analyst listens, he or she notices different narrative themes that seem to organize the patient's associations.

These are raised as possibilities that the patient can consciously and unconsciously build on in getting closer to articulating and 'naming' particular psychic experiences. In Bion's (1962a) terms, it involves 'sitting in uncertainty' until a selected fact emerges that appears to give meaning to previously disparate clinical facts. In this way narrative themes or derivatives revolve around meanings yet-to-be known by patient or analyst. Let us return to Susan. The relational dynamic, referred to earlier, between craving attention and an 'angry, irritable and distant object' played itself out in many different ways between us. With this there appeared to be a deepening of a capacity to experience difficult emotional states that underpinned these transference–countertransference dramas.

Susan (revisited)

On one occasion Susan happened to call me to try and reschedule an appointment. When I answered she said, 'Oh hello it's me'. At the time I did not know who 'me' was, so I asked who was speaking. 'Me!' she said. I probably sounded a little irritated by this point and on realizing who it was I made the appointment change and cut the call short. I was surprised by my reaction and felt somewhat guilty for cutting her short. My guilt seemed to relate to how a part of her saw me as having a very special place for her in my mind, able to immediately recognize her voice on the phone.

She never raised this in her next session. Instead, she started telling me about how much work she had to make up and was falling behind. She also started telling me that her back problems and other physical ailments were playing up again. She then went on to tell me about a movie she had seen about a woman marine who could 'take all the hits' and never got injured. I said I wondered if she felt injured at the moment and was wondering how she could better cope with it. She said she had been feeling 'down' over the weekend but she was fine now.

The phone call was on my mind so I reminded her of it. I said a part of my mind seemed to go back to the call and I was wondering why. I asked her about her experience. 'You were very nice and gave me your time', she replied. I said I was surprised as I thought she would have been upset because I did not know who was on the line. She disagreed immediately, saying I was the one who should be angry because she had phoned. Susan thought it was odd that I was clearly not angry and it was somehow making her uneasy. At this point she verbalized a sense of feeling that the session felt as though 'it would go on forever'. I responded with curiosity about why the length of the session seemed at the front of her mind and suggested that it appeared linked to her feeling uncomfortable. She said she felt like it was going to take 'the whole day' and it reminded her of how long the days felt at school when she was younger. She recalled trying to pass the time by attempting to speak to others at her school aftercare but they were always busy and would get irritated.

Susan sat in silence for a while and then said she was aware of a strange impulse that she wanted to tell me something interesting but nothing was coming to mind. I suggested that perhaps it was becoming important for her to interest me in something as she was feeling awkward, perhaps similar to speaking to others at aftercare. 'I just wanted a little attention, why couldn't they give me that?' Susan started to voice some anger. We seemed to have stumbled upon feelings about what she later called 'angry rejection' that she had found very difficult to think about previously. Part of her anger was now directed at me for being 'just like others'. She was now openly acknowledging being aware of my irritation on the phone. On leaving the session Susan said, 'So this is what it is to be pissed off, this should get some attention'.

On another occasion, just before Susan was to go on a Christmas holiday vacation, she started telling me that she was feeling 'lost and aimless' at work. She imagined being out at sea feeling isolated and afraid. She went on to tell me about a newspaper report of an angry teenager who had run amok in a high school shooting on the last day of term. The young man, she said, had felt abandoned by his mother. Susan went on to talk about some of the movies she had seen recently which contained a great deal of violence, expressing the view that this leads to an escalation of violence and makes things worse. I said that she seemed to be talking about afraid, isolated, violent people and she seemed to be indicating that this was getting worse. 'People easily become victims', she replied. She told me about the man next door who would not stop shouting at his wife. The wife, she said, would never leave him for the sake of her children. She recalled her father's face when he would get angry with her (or her mother and sister). Susan looked uncomfortable in her chair. 'I could take it', she said proudly. 'Do other patients who end up here get shouted at?' she asked. I replied by saying that she seemed to be wondering about how much she could take. I said I thought she felt good about 'taking a lot' but was also wondering if it was this that lands one in the therapist's chair. While I listened I started to recall a moment I became angry with a good-willed assistant who had tried to help me load my car with shopping. While he assisted, the shopping trolley had rolled into my car, denting it. I recalled how I had driven off in a huff. This thought seemed to help me connect with what Susan meant when she said 'I could take it'. I tried to put it into words. 'I have a sense that "taking it" is somehow an act of goodwill, perhaps you're worried that others – my patients, your sister and mother – can't take it, so you take the hits.' She was silent and tearful and said she had never let her father out of her sight. 'I'm in a spin', she said. 'I feel like I can't leave and go on holiday, I feel like you will become angry. What will happen to you when I leave? What will happen to your other patients if you see them when I'm on holiday?'

In the above fragments Susan and I work towards understanding the meaning of 'anger and irritation' as it emerges in the analytic field. My experience here was that something shifted as we arrived at what 'felt right'. Notwithstanding glimpses of my own irritation, there was an emerging sense that she was able to feel understood. I hope to have shown, albeit briefly, how unsaturated interpretations helped work towards what felt most meaningful as our experience together evolved. In effect, 'anger', representing an area of unmetabolized experience, passes between us as we move closer to how this is being experienced in the narrative derivatives of the session. The denial of Susan's own anger is not directly challenged. Instead specific meaning regarding what is being resisted begins to emerge and she is able to experience some anger which is usually split off. Susan begins to entertain it more in her mind as a meaningful object that need not just be accepted so as to remain fixed and meaningless. 'I can take it', referring to the acceptance of being the object of aggression, starts to become something rich with meaning instead of simply being an unthought repetitive behaviour.

Although her experiences of anger are fleeting, prompting feelings of discomfort and guilt, they seem to hint at moving closer to a depressive solution where all aggression need not be so split off from her personality. 'So this is what it is to be pissed off, this should get some attention' seems to represent the beginnings of her experiencing and integrating her 'attention-seeking self' with split-off aggression. With some ability to better contain these ideas, in later sessions we began to understand more the importance of 'attention' to draw her aggressive object away from putting others at risk. It appears that 'attention' had become constantly conjoined with an expression of goodwill towards others.

I chose not to directly interpret the possible implications of the holiday break for Susan and tried to wait for its meaning to evolve. There are a number of narrative derivatives that suggest an interpretation that could be stated as such: 'You seem to be telling me you're angry with me about the break in therapy, because you're worried you will feel isolated and abandoned.' Perhaps one could add: 'You are telling me about how your feelings of anger lead to escalating anger. You are feeling that it could become unbearable if you expressed it here so it is easier to separate it from yourself and see it in others.' Of course it is always difficult to guess what might have happened. My point is that although such interventions appear 'theoretically' accurate (and in keeping with the narrative derivatives expressed), something felt intuitively wrong about them in the context of my relationship with Susan. I think staying away from more saturated interpretations of this kind allowed us to arrive at a very different and meaningful place. What emerges is not about her anger at me, or even simply about her need to locate split-off aggression in her object. As our experience evolves, a much more nuanced meaning emerges about how she cannot withdraw projected aggression because of the imagined implications for others around her. With this, her 'attention-seeking' self takes on new meaning and helps me better to identify with her repeated needs to draw me in.

In using unsaturated interpretations, instead of directly translating narrative derivatives into transference interpretations, the therapist allows the patient to 'play' with characters and scenarios in his or her story while the therapist tries to follow the ephemeral and evolving nature of experience. It is the difference between making transference interpretations and working within the transference. In this way the therapeutic couple is able to slowly approach difficult unarticulated affect that has not yet found containment or meaning. As Ferro (2004) states:

> The patient must feel he is accompanied in his thought processes, and this can be done by illustrating various steps. It is useless to interpret a patient's communication simply by turning it around: 'You are telling me that . . .'.
>
> (p.37)

In my understanding these steps include therapist and patient working together to get back to the key elements that organize narratives, or what Bion called the 'waking dream', without dominating each other's experience. It also involves the therapist's attempts to place his communications in the narrative framework of the patient. Through this kind of verbal and mental following, unassimilated feeling states, beta-elements as well as proto-feelings and proto-thoughts (alpha-elements) begin to acquire a more bearable and meaningful form. This is in keeping with Bion's view that the psychoanalytic object needs to be a mythical extension of the patient's personal meanings or 'myths'. Bezoari *et al.* (1994) have this to say about the collaborative nature of the task:

> The analytic dialogue appeared to us less and less merely as a field for the gathering of data and the verification of those hypotheses mulled over by the analyst, and more and more as a kind of forge, where interpretations acquire *form* and *sense* thanks to *hermeneutic cooperation* in which the patient possesses equal, though not identical, dignity of function and is the psychoanalyst's best *colleague*, in the full meaning of the term.
>
> (p.38)

Bezoari *et al.* are drawing on Bion's idea that the patient is always the analyst's best colleague in the process. They also appear to be emphasizing interpretative activity that best takes place when commensal relations between container–contained can be maintained. There is an emphasis on a collaborative openness to the process that moves towards a more mutual form of containment between analyst and patient (Lafarge, 2000). Accepting this, however, does not mean that the move towards mutuality represents a more harmonious path. The encounter, according to Bion, is always at some level terrifying as uncontained aspects of experience emerge from each new encounter, requiring that psychological work be ongoing in every new experience.

It could be said that unsaturated interpretations best reflect the inherent uncertainty that is always part of the analytic encounter and the struggle patients and therapists have to endure to connect with each other using their own internal experiences. It respects the opaqueness of the other's mind. Minds can only be known through other minds. Unsaturated interpretations also appear to better engage the imperfections, fumblings and inherent 'messiness' of the meaning-making process in attempting to contain mental states at the peripheries of our awareness.

'Shining through' the resistance

As briefly mentioned above, more unsaturated approaches to interpreting enhance the analytic couple's containing function through softening the way resistance is dealt with. Bion (2005b) indicates that the clinician needs to attempt to 'look at the resistance in such a way that what is being resisted shines through it' (p.67). Returning to my work with Susan, we could say that her aggression is being resisted at all fronts, the idea of her being aggressive cannot be meaningfully entertained without some degree of splitting. But instead of interpreting the resistance directly, we begin to co-construct narratives 'around' experiencing me as hostile, creating a scaffold of meaning that allows it to 'shine through'.

In my opinion if interpretations of resistance occur too soon, we are never afforded the opportunity to see what was being resisted in a meaningful experiential way. The interpretation of resistance is relatively useless unless the patient is able to experience some sense of what is being resisted.

Passion and the analyst's subjectivity

Clearly the above process of negotiating meaning is far from a simple cognitive exercise. One of Bion's greatest contributions is a theory of thinking that is founded on emotional processes. By implication, the emotional engagement of the analyst is indispensable in the analytic field. There are particular links here between his or her subjectivity and the emotional engagement of the analyst that impacts how the containing function is conveyed. We have considered previously the mutative nature of minor countertransference enactments in the containing process. They communicate a struggle (via projective identification) that the analyst survives and therefore somewhat contains the patient's projection in his own experience. What is it that we say or interpret about this process? On what aspects of partial enactments and all other forms of communication does the process of containing depend? We have explored the importance of dialogical engagement in the making of emergent new meaning. But what is it that gives the patient some kind of intuitive direction in reading the analyst's interpretative stance when he listens? Bion is clear that the analyst's interpretative efforts should aim to be 'true' as opposed to being correct according to the strictures of theory:

> In analysis we have to forget whether the interpretation is the right interpretation, or the Kleinian interpretation, or the Freudian interpretation – it is all irrelevant. The only relevant thing is whether it is a true interpretation.
>
> (Bion, 2005a, p.43)

Clearly Bion is under no illusion that this amounts to 'the truth' as measured by objective means aspiring to pinpoint accuracy. Truth or 'fact' refers to emotional experience at a particular moment which is taken as 'evidence' on which interpretations are based (Bion, 1976). They are 'felt' truths. A true interpretation is, to Bion, daringly (and deceptively) simple: to say what one means in a way that can be understood at that point in time. It is a creative act as the analyst engages in a process of 'becoming' and entails the ability to formulate, think, while in the throes of difficult emotions. As Bion put it: 'You have to *dare* to think and feel what ever it is that you think or feel' (2005a, p.13). Containing interpretations involve conveying some of this experience in a tempered way. Much of this is conveyed simply through the analyst's subjective presence, how he positions himself in the analytic field, in trying to understand his patient.

In my understanding the analyst's 'passion' is essential in this process. Bion separates passion from more basic emotional links because it represents the ability to mentally engage with L, H and K: 'By passion I mean one of the dimensions which L, H or K must possess if it is to be recognized as an element that is present' (1963, p.13). Passion is the emotion evoked when two minds are linked (Bion, 1963). It constitutes the analyst's ability to maintain a mental connection with the patient from within basic emotional linkages (H, L or K) without splitting them off. It is, according to Bion, experienced with intensity, warmth, but without a sense of 'violence'. Broadly, I would understand Bion's reference to 'violence' to mean an internal state that does not seek to violate or intrude upon other objects via excessive forms of projective identification. Therefore it represents an attempt to meet an other's mind without intrusion. Conceptually then, it is an emotional state that lies beyond projective identification (Bion, 1963; Davison, 2002) and resultant countertransference experiences.

As the analyst listens and tries to connect with the patient he takes the patient 'in' through introjective identification which evokes various psychic states in him. Passion involves the analyst's mental engagement with this process and, by implication, his own emotional participation, his subjective presence. This appears to have some resonance with Gooch's (2001) experience of being one of Bion's patients. He describes how Bion would often draw on his own emotional experience or presence in making interpretations. In comparison with a previous analysis, Gooch notes how much this led to him feeling less isolated in the process. I understand this to be an expression of 'passion' in the way Bion wrote about it.

This does not mean that the therapist should constantly disclose countertransference states. By disclosure I mean either the analyst's disclosure of personal details or directly making statements about how he is feeling or being affected by the process. Such attempts threaten to breach the containment process in that they are usually vehicles for the projection or intellectualization of feeling states. Further, rather than convey something about the patient's experience, they tend to dominate the patient's experiencing process. In short, disclosures of this nature display an incapacity to transform feeling states into something meaningful to the analytic couple.

Rather than using gross forms of countertransference disclosure the analyst relies on relatively implicit communications that convey a sense of mentally following the patient, tracking the patient, but not breaking with the process of experiencing. Minor comments, unsaturated interpretations and the way interpretations are conveyed elicit this kind of engagement. Implicit aspects of the therapist's communications convey to the patient how he is being held in mind and 'carried through' the therapist's experience. If this implicit process could be put into words it would translate into: 'This is what I am experiencing, how I am thinking, this is how I experience you as a separate person, how it transforms me.' Important here is the idea that the analyst's subjectivity is not talked about as such, it is its direct experiencing that forms part of conveying his containing function. As Bion taught us, there is a great deal of difference here between talking about experience and experiencing itself. 'Talking about' experience through interpretation or countertransference disclosure can often prematurely break with the importance of allowing meaning to evolve alongside the emergence of the analyst's passionate link with the patient.

In this way 'passion' is usually conveyed through what Gooch (2001) appropriately calls 'the appropriate song and dance, that addresses the analysand's emotional experience in the moment' (p.2). It is the emotional tone of the delivery that is important here. Through this the analyst demonstrates how he is engaging his own internal experience, conveying the evocative potential of his internal objects in making him think and contemplate. Further, the emotional tone of the interpretation conveys a sense of separateness but also signals that the therapist is receptive to being affected by the patient (Caper, 1999; Kernberg, 2003).

This kind of mental engagement communicates the struggle between experiencing projective identifications, on the one hand, and the ability to survive and have his own thoughts, a mind of his own, on the other. If stated in terms of the ongoing internal dialogue between 'proper object' and 'dream object', passion is the emotional link signalling these two representations of the therapist's experience in dialogue. It is an internal dialogue that takes place, or is conveyed, within an intersubjective process (Billow, 2000). The outcome is a form of relatedness that allows the patient to hold on to their psychic reality while, at the same time, affording them glimpses of the analyst's subjectivity beyond projective and introjective processes. It grants the patient awareness of the therapist's effort to use his imaginable world as well as its limitations in being able to understand the patient's experience (Lafarge, 2000).

The idea of 'surviving' projective identifications and its links to passion and the subjective presence of the analyst deserve a little more consideration here. It could be said that Bion's understanding of the passionate linking of minds, though relatively undeveloped, anticipates current relational theories of psychoanalysis where the importance of the patient's and analyst's subjectivity are emphasized. In particular, Benjamin's (1990, 2005) views on the role of recognition in psychic development appear to complement the link I am making here between passion and the containing elements of interpretation. She argues that intrapsychic theories tend to have an infantocentric focus that emphasize the role of internalizing the mother as object, but do not explain the importance of the infant's experience of the mother as a separate person with her own subjectivity. Benjamin does not diminish the importance of psychic reality and the process of projection and introjection and so forth. Rather, she is concerned about the tendency in more traditional theories of psychoanalysis to collapse the tension between the person as internal object (subjectively conceived objects) and the person as a separate subject. Both represent different levels of experience. It is only through being able to sense the other's subjective experience that recognition can occur, a sense of being able to feel known by the other as a separate subject.

Benjamin uses Winnicott's (1971) observations about the differences between internal objects and external subjects, omnipotence and reality. For Winnicott, the infant comes to know that the object is real and has its own subjective experience through sensing that internal fantasies of destroying it do not destroy the actual object. There are parallels here with the move from experiencing the object in the paranoid-schizoid position to the depressive position where the patient is able to relate to whole objects. But the focus is different. It is not just about the restoration of a whole good object but the experience of discovering the other.

Susan (revisited)

Susan reported a dream: *Her father was sitting in my chair and she was terrified. She tried to distract his attention by talking about his favourite hobby, fishing, something they used to do together. As he spoke she noticed how much he cared about fishing. She noticed how his voice trembled as he spoke. She was somehow relieved by this and woke up with the thought that she had never noticed her father's 'beautiful eyes'.* This was a dream that particularly fascinated Susan, mainly because it seemed to open up a link with a terrifying object (her father) that brought relief. She had a sense (in her associations about 'beautiful eyes') that 'that brute really saw who I was'.

Given the link in the dream between her father and me (he was sitting in my chair), Susan easily drew parallels between a sense of being 'seen' by me in the last session we had had. 'It was something about the way you said things, not really what you said', she said to me, 'that made me feel like we're in this together no matter what.'

In my understanding, Susan had come across a way of experiencing me that allowed her to feel recognized. Her dream suggests that this is made possible through the analyst's passionate engagement. I think Susan expressed the subtleties of this process when, towards the end of her psychotherapy, she said, 'I used to think you were just here to help me, now I know you know me'. This statement appeared to convey the difference between accepting untested assumptions, a way perhaps of holding oneself together, and being able to experience engaging with the therapist and 'becoming known' through his own passionate engagement as a separate subject.

There is one more point to make here regarding the engagement of separate subjectivities. It seems to me that the therapist has to sit and wait for the patient to connect with him as a separate 'surviving' object. This needs to occur before the patient can start to experience and engage with their own ability to contain experience, to feel their own subjectivity as part of the self. Of course the therapist is always alerting the patient to his own experience, but the extent to which this can be 'known' is dependent first on recognizing it in the therapist's passionate engagement.

In sum, interpretations that convey the analyst's containing function constitute 'passionate' commentaries on the evolution of experience that let the patient know that the analyst is being affected but is surviving his projections. Put another way, passion is conveyed through an awareness of the analyst's subjectivity as he or she attempts to understand the patient's subjective experience.

Point of urgency: breakdown between 'proper' and 'dream' object

When, we might ask, as Baranger (1993) does, is the 'point of urgency' (p.17) for making interpretations that aim to enhance the containing capacities in the analytic field? In the Kleinian approach the point of urgency for interpretation would be when the patient alludes to deep underlying anxieties. A more classical approach would aim to interpret unconscious motivations that intend to make what is unconscious more available to the conscious mind. Still further, we might emphasize the confrontation of defences and aim to interpret the transference. Bion's model privileges facilitating the expansion and flexibility of the container–contained over the interpretation of conflict, deep anxieties, and so forth. Here, processing or transforming emotional events (the containing function) and the psychological work this entails gives rise to new thoughts (the contained) that expand awareness and the reflective capacity of the self. My sense is that the point of urgency in attempting to engage the containing function is when meaning-making breaks down. We notice this in certain 'empty' countertransference states, numbing or 'dead' states, or the other extreme, when we become overly confused and caught up in some element of our own fantasy as it emerges in our minds (in states of reverie).

In theoretical terms I understand this to occur when the therapist can no longer maintain a 'balanced outlook' between his role as a 'proper object' and his role as a 'dream object'. When the role of the 'proper object' dominates, the analyst struggles with mounting defensiveness in the analytic field that makes him inaccessible to the patient as he feels compelled to keep his state of mind intact. This amounts to identifying entirely with the 'proper object' as I use the term. On the other hand, the containing function can also be disrupted when the analyst begins to over-value, or is seduced by, his own reverie in a way that can no longer be used as a useful commentary on the patient's internal world. If these two positions represent breakdowns in the containing process, points of interpretation have a particular function. They attempt to reconnect analyst and patient with experiencing in the present moment. Put another way, the therapist attempts to get back the 'felt' meaning that is somewhat shared between them.

The analyst listens and the process feels meaningful and enlivening, but there comes a point, sooner or later, when analyst and patient lose each other due to the impact of projected states that are being communicated.[1] This, in my view, signals the breakdown of tracking the 'felt meaning' of the interaction that is represented in the analyst's internal world by the

---

1 Clearly other factors can affect the ability to attend as well; for instance, the analyst's conflicts, problems within the setting, his state of mind at the time.

breakdown between 'proper' and 'dream' object. At these 'points of urgency' what is needed is re-engagement through the analyst making unsaturated interpretations that invite the patient to help out and re-establish a containing mental connection: 'There seems to be a number of possibilities here . . .', 'I am unsure but I have the sense that . . .', 'Could it be that . . .', 'For some unknown reason, things feel different today . . .'. All these might be seen as attempts to re-engage and expand the analytic couple's ability to contain split-off mental states and affects.

There are times when complete indifference appears to be expressed in the analyst's interpretations. This poses greater difficulty. Enduring indifference of this kind might be thought of to signal the 'death' of an existing state of mind that is receptive to the patient, the work of −L, −H or −K. Even here, however, when meaningful exchange collapses, risking saying something that is 'felt', no matter how right or wrong, at least signals a significant 'subjective' presence in the analytic field. Bion appears to refer to this when he writes: 'Worse than being right or wrong is the failure of an interpretation to be significant, though to be significant is not enough; it merely ensures that it exists' (1970, p.79).

Conclusion

In exploring how the containing function is conveyed through the analyst's interpretative activity I have emphasized the importance of unsaturated communications in the meaning-make process, analyst-focused interventions and his or her passionate presence. All these emphasize the analyst's participation in the process, how he might be experienced by the patient. His ability to impart a sense of passion and curiosity are central to this. The ability to make interpretations that stimulate curiosity are central to Bion's (1963) idea that good interpretations serve to illuminate K as a basic emotional link and do not emerge from the H or L link.

In some ways focusing somewhat on the analyst's experience may appear to miss the point regarding Bion's idea that the analyst take on projections and focus on the patient's experience in order to transform it and make it more bearable. But the analyst's participation in the process has an important role to play. One might say that all the above elements which have been outlined work to create a degree of distance for the patient, allowing him to apprehend new meaning in a less threatening way. In other words, emergent narratives, difficulties in interaction, need not immediately be conveyed as belonging to the patient. The analyst's interventions first attempt to establish 'common sense' (Bion, 1963) between patient and analyst and add to Bion's idea that interpretations require a 'sense' dimension to them.

Before the patient is able to give meaning to their own internal state ('own' their own internal state) and their contribution to the interaction, they first rely on vicariously apprehending such experiences. Insofar as the therapist's interpretive efforts aim to expand the experiential and affective field, it is the patient's experience of the therapist's interpretative 'presence' that is given priority. Clearly, the impact of the analyst's and patient's subjectivity is always present in the therapeutic process. However, there are points in the analytic process where the analyst's subjectivity is more explicitly revealed, particularly during interpretations and enactments.

Chapter 6

Speculations about proto-containing experiences

Bion uses the container model to explain how the infant's pre-symbolic experiences are transformed and rendered meaningful through the mother's containing function. In the previous chapters we have considered how the containing function leads to psychic change and explored the nature of the containing connection between analyst and patient. A number of authors have considered these questions from different perspectives, particularly in terms of technical approaches that engage the analyst in a containing process (Britton, 1992a; Caper, 1999; Ferro, 2005a; Grotstein, 2000; Ogden, 1997; Segal, 1991; Steiner, 1993). In this chapter I consider possible precursors to a containing mind, how the infant or patient initially comes to have conceptions of the container so that it is 'known' and thus can be used. Put another way, how, as a process of psychic transformation, does the psychic container come into existence as a psychic function? What are the elemental containing capacities of mind? As part of Bion's theory of preconception, I want to explore the idea that preconceptions of the container, precursors, can be found in the *sub-symbolic processes* of interaction. I am aware that there are many ideas here that remain undeveloped. For the time being they simply represent speculations for further exploration.

In perusing this argument further, I am led by Bion's ideas about a proto-mental system and some of his more peripheral ideas about the 'containing' abilities of beta-elements. In essence, I want to argue that proto-containing experiences are emergent phenomena. They have their origins not in mother or baby, analyst or patient; they emerge in interaction as an emergent product of action-movement systems. Such experiences are felt to be a disembodied 'between' state, a subpersonal interactional matrix that can only be referred to by using amorphous terms like 'pressure' or 'flow' in the interaction.

Emergent proto-containing experiences differ from containing proper. Whereas the containing mother gives meaning to projected unassimilated experience, proto-containing experiences emerge in the 'otherness' of interaction between self and the world, manipulated by sub-symbolic processes. As I understand it, the former is an important part of interaction using projective identification, but this belongs to a level of mind that possesses greater dimensionality and a different way of articulating experience (Grotstein, 1991, 2000; Ogden, 1992; Tustin, 1990). As considered earlier, this is an area of mind where alpha-function and the containing function develop or transform psychic contents, they are intrapsychic processes. Proto-containing aspects, on the other hand, emerge from interaction itself through the self-organizing capacities of sense impressions. My hypothesis is that these experiences give rise to nascent preconceptions or 'states of expectation' that make possible the conception of a containing mind. In other words, I am suggesting that the proto-container, although very different from the containing function proper, generates fleeting experiences that act as preconceptions to the containing mind. This idea appears similar to Ferro's (2005a) comments about a sense of containment emerging out of experiences of 'micro-being in unison' (p.7). Such states approximate experiences that emerge out of attunement and a sense of unity between mother and infant (Ferro, personal communication).

My argument elaborates Bion's (1992) conjecture about the 'patterning' of beta-elements which I consider to be linked to a state of primary inter-subjectivity (Trevarthen, 1993). With increasing interest in sub-symbolic modes of relating there has been a great deal of work in the recent past exploring how non-symbolic formats act as a connective between subjec-tivities (Bucci, 1997b; Charles, 1999; Grotstein, 2005; Knoblauch, 2000; Ogden, 1992; Stern, 2004; Trevarthen, 1993, 1999; Tustin, 1990). Most of these authors adopt a broad systemic view of mind where elemental modes of generating experience are viewed as existing in parallel (linked synchron-ically and diachronically) with other tracks of psychic organization. In developing some of Bion's ideas about the patterning of beta-elements, I use some of this work to consider the idea that inherent capacities for imitation and the perception of 'difference' produce rhythmic proto-mental phenomena that generate a background sense of 'moving along', a rhythmic moving toward and away from something. It should be made clear that although I consider some of this work and suggest how it may link with Bion's theoretical system, my intention is not to conflate different perspec-tives. Nor is it my aim to 'fill in' beta-elements which Bion meant to remain unknowable and unsaturated.

Implicit in my argument are some ideas drawn from non-linear dynamic systems theory. Particularly, emphasis is placed on the *Self as process* rather than as based on content or static structures. Here, the structure, function, process and content of the psychic system have reciprocal influences on each other, leading to psychic processes that produce emergent structures and functions and vice versa. From this point of view, the Self is best viewed as being a 'process-structure' (Marks-Tarlow, 1999). A related matter is the idea that some aspects of the personality are self-organizing (Quinodoz, 1997) and find a degree of stability in principles of self-similarity where one part of the personality is able to 'mimic' the form or function of an other. I take from this the view that proto-containing capacities have a self-organizing quality that has fractal-like influences on all levels of experience. In other words, I want to suggest that the 'form' and rhythm of interactive sequences that produce proto-containing capacities influence how internal objects are experienced, how introjection and projection occur, the formation of phantasy, and the like.

In attempting to extend Bion's model and his notion of saturated beta-elements I am highlighting a fundamental paradox. Although sub-symbolic interaction involves the formation of proto-containing experiences that creates the sense of 'having a mind', it relies on what cannot be known and exists at the border between the inanimate and animate, deadness and aliveness, and constitutes the 'unthought' background of the meaning-making subject. At this level, we are contained by what is ineffable and what cannot be known or transformed (Grotstein, 2000). We can only respond (without thought) in the immediacy of the situation by moving along sensory contours that rely on the near-physical patterning influences inherent in the proto-mind. Paradoxically then, it is not thought that allows for the creative emergence of proto-containing experiences but the emergent qualities of the 'otherness' or 'thingness' of interaction.

Preconceptions of the container function

As discussed in Chapter 2, the containing function acts on projective identifications in order to 'metabolize' projected contents. For this to occur, the infant or patient mobilizes a process of 'interpersonal nudging' to realize the phantasy of projecting into an object. Elsewhere I have emphasized the idea that, as a model of change, the container has a seductive schematic quality that is appealing: the patient projects into the analyst, the analyst 'contains' and transforms these split-off parts of the self and returns them anew to be taken back by the patient and reintegrated into the personality. Clearly I am being somewhat facetious here and I do not regard this to be Bion's conception of the container. But it does, I believe, convey a kind of seductive reasoning often implicit in references to the model. This version of the container has great intuitive appeal and conveys a sense of certainty and saturation that forecloses further thinking. Although it makes little logical sense, in terms of how transformation really occurs or what is actually transformed, it resonates closely with common unconscious phantasies (inevitably concrete in nature) about the physical transformation of pain and other intolerable affects. As a reified dynamic it has great appeal to our three-dimensional imaginations: something is put into us so we can transform it. Such phantasies help us forget that the container is an abstraction not a 'real' object. In my experience, this kind of 'seductive reasoning' often leads to countertransference states that amount to the analyst idealizing the container (Britton, 1992a; Mitrani, 1992).

The above model also does not fully account for how the infant has a preconception of a container, expectations of the mother's containing mind into which he can project. Can we assume that the 'need' for a container exists prior to this? Bion assumes that we hold primitive preconceptions of the containing breast which await realization. But the idea of the 'preconception' of 'a container' appears to assume a great deal. What can we conjecture about the elemental processes that make the preconception of a container possible? Put another way, what conditions create 'a state of expectation' (Bion, 1963, p.23) that the mother has a containing mind? I want to explore the idea that the emergence of the container (as a transforming maternal function) is better accounted for by considering the impact of sub-symbolic processes on the proto-mind, the pre-reflective experience of 'being in' experience itself.

At this level of mind the idea of projection makes little sense due to the absence of psychic dimensionality necessary for constructing phantasies that make use of internal/external differentiations. Bion appears to hint at this in some of his writings which I shall now consider. Here I take him to be suggesting that the flux of experience itself forms the bedrock of the containing dynamic. It is the 'patterning' of beta-elements that seem to leave in their wake ineffable sensory contours and shapes that contribute to an elemental sense of 'moving along'.

Beta-elements, non-symbolic processes and the proto-mental system

Bion paid a great deal of attention to non-verbal, pre-symbolic aspects of mind traditionally considered to be outside the realm of psychic experience. In *Experiences in Groups*, Bion (1961) proposes the existence of a proto-mental system to account for the continued existence of inoperative basic assumptions. This is an area where mental and physical entities lack distinction and where emotional expression is undifferentiated. Basic assumptions are essentially prototypical organizing principles that are inseparable from each other. I understand him to be describing a gestaltian undifferentiated mass, a near-physical formation in the mind that emerges through resonance with the 'external' world. The idea of a proto-mental system is an attempt, according to Bion (1961), to understand 'the solidity with which all the emotions of one basic assumption seem to be welded together' (1961, pp.104–105).

Bion appears to take up this line of thinking later in peripheral speculations about beta-elements or sense impressions that have yet to be transformed into psychic states. In his paper on *The Grid*, written in 1971, he makes the point that we should consider the 'existence of a β-element row' (Bion, 1989, p.7) that is not linked with defensiveness (action as a substitute for thought) if we are to investigate aspects of the personality that have a sub-symbolic existence. He links this with his ideas about group mentality that are not accounted for by theories of transference and projection. This part of the personality, he contends, possesses functions analogous to the capillary blood system that responds to external conditions by dilating or lying dormant. Such aspects of the personality exist as emotional potentials that are evoked by various sub-symbolic cues that are timeless in the way they influence the mind.[1] He seems to be suggesting here that this is akin to joining a field of experience that is already there. It is not constructed by thought or the precursors of thought (alpha-elements).

The proto-mental system Bion appeared to have in mind is a system of unformulated experiences that emerge through interaction. It remains inconceivable to our rational conscious minds because it is an area of (proto)mind where the individual is as much 'in the group' as the group is 'in the individual'. The formulation defies distinctions between internal/external, subject/object, individual/group and dynamic principles attached to such distinctions (e.g. repressive forces, the manipulation of experience through projection, or products of alpha-function) raising questions about how unformulated experience might be organized.[2]

Bion uses the term 'valency' in an attempt to derive hypothetical organizational principles that might account for the functioning of the proto-mental system. The term refers to the combining potential of proto-mental elements, units of unformulated experience that are, in his words, 'characterized by behaviour in the human being that is more analogous to tropism in plants than to purposive behaviour . . . the instantaneous involuntary combination of one individual with another' (1961, p.153). The above appears to suggest that proto-mental systems of which beta-elements are a part may have self-organizing capacities. Following Bion, Meltzer (1986) describes the proto-mental system as 'habitual, automatic, unintentional' (p.38), the playground of instinct, habitual behaviours and learned social responses,[3] thus distinguishing it from genuine emotional experience and

---

1 See Bion's (1989, p.23) statements about similarities between Hitler and Tactitis on dimensions beyond verbal thought.

2 Earlier I used Matte-Blanco's (1988) theory of bi-logic to understand polar tensions inherent in the container function. The lack of distinction I am referring to here, between 'internal' and 'external', may appear similar to how the unconscious perceives objects due to the principle of symmetry. However, they differ in the sense that, as I understand it, the logic of symmetry refers to psychic objects whereas I am referring to sub-symbolic processes, non-conscious as opposed to unconscious.

3 This appears to have much in common with Bourdieu's (1997) development of the sociological term 'habitus': aspects of culture grounded in the body and in daily practices of individuals and groups that are beyond thought. It is, in his words, 'a generative principle of regulated improvisations' (p.78) that have an 'intentionless invention' (p.79).

the construction of imagination and the internal world. The former makes itself known through measures of excitement, pressure, based on quantity rather than the quality of the experience.

Meltzer regarded the automatic, unintentional, habitual aspects of proto-mentality to exist outside the domain of psychoanalysis because they are beyond thought and imagination. But might there be room here to consider the idea that such sub-symbolic processes have an important functional role crucial to the nascent sense of having a mind? In other words, aside from being pre-symbolic (on the way to becoming verbal thought) do traces of sense impressions, beta-elements, serve a function in themselves? What are the mental consequences of the constant flow of sensa and sub-symbolic experience?

Beta-elements: functional units of the proto-mental system?

Bion introduces the term 'beta-element' as a way of referring to hypothetical non-symbolic units of experience. He gives beta-elements a number of different meanings and sometimes these appear to contradict each other.[4] For the most, however, he refers to them as representing sense impressions, saturated elements of mind, impressions of objects as 'things-in-themselves'. For Bion, the beta-element 'partakes of the quality of inanimate object and psychic object without any form of distinction between the two. Thoughts are things, things are thoughts; and they have a personality' (Bion, 1963, p.22). At this level of experience, although there exists a rudimentary awareness of the object, there is no clear distinction between subject and object, beta-elements exist as undigested facts.

In most of his writing Bion refers to beta-elements as 'accretions of stimuli' that are evacuated from the psyche. They represent manifestations of sense data that cannot be transformed into meaningful experience and thus are evacuated to produce meaningless behaviours and language, hallucinations or psychosomatic disorders. Once projected into 'external' objects they form 'bizarre objects'[5] that constitute the nearest thing to actual realizations, 'real' aspects of mind as opposed to simply being hypothetical constructs (Wisdom, 1983).

4 In retaining Bion's notion of 'beta-element' I am immediately faced with a number of difficulties regarding what Bion *actually* meant by the concept. He is never specific about what he means by 'sense impressions'. In his characteristic way he leaves them open for interpretation. Despite these difficulties, I retain the concept as a means of elaborating Bion's theoretical system.

5 Bizarre objects are essentially breakdown phenomena felt to belong to the personality, containing traces of ego and superego, but at the same time, treated as things-in-themselves.

But beta-elements do not simply represent pathological products of failed alpha-function. Bion also uses the term to sketch out what he considers to be the primary units of experiencing (Bion, 1962b, 1992). From this perspective beta-elements provide the building blocks of experience that render a sense of being-in-the-world and primitive mentation inseparable. In keeping with this, Ogden (2004b) sees beta-elements as constituting 'the sole connection between the mind and one's lived emotional experience in the world of external reality' (p.1356). It seems important here to make a clear distinction between split-off beta-elements and beta-elements that contribute to generative capacities in the psyche. The latter are best conceptualized as approximating sensory contours generated out of the constant flux of sensa. Beta-elements occur in the immediacy of engagement, prior to representation in the mind through image, sound or kinesthetic impression (the work of alpha-function). They exist as non-conscious analogical traces generating affective contours that emerge in the moment-to-moment processes of interaction.

Bion makes a number of relatively peripheral references to the idea that beta-elements configure in ways that may produce proto-containing experiences, non-symbolic experiences that we may consider to support thinking and containing proper. In *Learning From Experience* Bion (1962b) draws a parallel between the real material aspects of taking in milk and 'taking in' beta-elements. As Bion puts it: 'The patient greedily and fearfully takes one beta-element after another apparently unable to conceive of any activity other than introjection of more beta-elements' (p.11). The link here between material comforts, ingesting milk, and beta-elements is not easy to understand given that Bion mostly refers to beta-elements as only being fit for evacuation. To qualify this, Bion makes it clear that he is talking about a disturbed relationship with the breast. Wisdom (1983) wonders if his equating comfort with beta-elements is a typological error. However, there is another possibility that points to a different theory of beta-elements, a theory which suggests that beta-elements may have other functions in the psyche less elaborated by Bion. Later, in *Learning From Experience*, he refers to beta-elements as 'coherent and purposive' (Bion, 1962b), further supporting the notion that beta-elements might have an edifying function apart from their destructive or evacuative properties. The focus here is on beta-elements as primary elements of experience, the 'stem cells' of experience, 'undigested' sense impressions that are not subject to transformation by alpha-function or evacuated from the psyche.

Bion seems to be making reference to a different path or 'use' of sense impressions, associated with the pleasure of receiving milk,[6] not projected

---

6 Bion considers two different kinds of relationship with the breast. The first deals with the absent breast that is felt to be a bad breast that generates thoughts in place of the 'no thing'.

or awaiting transformation, a stream of sensory impressions that have an edifying role in the formation of container–contained relations. If so, then how should we understand the nature of this interactive, 'tropistic', sub-symbolic base that begins to pattern or contain experience? Because beta-elements have not been worked on by alpha-function, they exist as impersonal units that lack subjective representation. If one accepts this, there appears to be reason to start to consider the idea that proto-containing experiences are born in interaction, impersonal, characterized by traces of sense impressions that are crucial to the formation of the self. Put another way, does this constitute a 'sub-personal' field that has containing influences on the mind?

To pursue this further, the question of how these sense impressions cohere and organize themselves needs addressing. We have already considered the possibility that beta-elements are organized around valences and have a topistic nature. Bion considers this further in *Cogitations* where he muses[7] about how the near-physical, 'indigestible' nature of beta-elements results in them assuming the role of a container. In his words, he asks:

> Are 'undigested facts' then used in the process of 'digesting' other facts? Is their 'indigestibility' a quality that renders them useful for this function, as if it were some kind of container for an eroding liquid which must be able itself to resist the erosion by its contents?
>
> (1992, p.52)

Bion sees this as being similar to parts of a dream that always remain undigested. Perhaps it could be thought of as being part of the dream-product that is the dream itself, providing a solid base – albeit always in motion – on to which alpha-elements can be projected.[8] His thoughts here also appear to have affinities with Freud's (1900) 'navel of the dream', the dream's 'point of contact with the unknown' (p.111), not amenable to analysis but important in holding the dream together. But what might this actually mean? Bion makes mention of there needing to be an understanding of what 'digesting' means in this context. To my knowledge, however, he never returns to this question in relation to the primitive digestive

This is an intricate process that we need not go into here (see p.64). The second relationship is with the good breast that is linked with real milk, satisfaction and the absence of the need for 'thought'. Although Bion makes clear that these two relationships have very different psychic qualities, he is far more concerned with the former. The latter relationship is clearly related to the *presence* of the breast and the reality of satisfaction, the material comforts.

7   We are told that these notes were written in 1959.

8   This appears to be similar to Lewin's (1952) idea about part of the dream acting like a 'dream screen' on to which the 'contents' of the rest of the dream are projected.

capacities of the proto-mind.[9] We can surmise, however, given that beta-elements do not constitute psychical entities, that this would be very different from ideas about the 'digesting' that takes place in the containing function proper where the analyst's mind works on psychical elements and phantasies.

By way of further considering Bion's nascent ideas about the proto-containing capacities of beta-elements let us return to the above statement from *Cogitations*. There are at least three assumptions present here. First, Bion suggests that beta-elements are capable of some form of cohesion. Second, he implies that beta-elements have a particular kind of quasi-functional role in the psyche, laying down strata of experience that become a reified foundation of mind. Third, Bion hints at the idea that there exists an analogical relationship between beta-elements and the 'physical' qualities of the object where the strength and endurance of proto-containing experiences are associated with physical characteristics.

Bion can be read here as alluding to the idea that beta-elements mimic or take on the form and characteristics of physical objects. It is not that they exist 'as if' they were physical objects. Rather, the sensory-affective patterning of experience is guided by attributes of physical objects. In this sense it appears that Bion is alluding to the existence of what I would call a 'mimetic function' in operation at this level of mind, a way of apprehending the object to gain something from its form. A lot has been written about primary forms of identification based on mimicry (Bick, 1968; Ferenczi, 1988; Freud, 1923; Gaddini, 1992; Meltzer, 1975a; Stensson, 2006). Ferenczi (1988) suggests that mimicry is a primordial capability in infancy, a primary unconscious means of accommodating to objects that is 'selfless'. He also links primordial forms of mimicry to the establishment of basic trust. Similarly, Stensson (2006) considers mimicry to be 'our deepest and most extensive way of knowing the other as well as yourself, although without cognitive structure' (p.160).

I would suggest there exists a mimetic process at work at an intrapsychic level that similarly works to take the shape and form of other objects. It is a process that might be seen to be based on transient forms of adhesive identification where primitive phantasies of sticking to an object (not projecting into it) are in operation (Bick, 1968). In conceptualizing psychic operations as part of a non-linear system, it seems possible to think about the 'mimetic function' as being the primitive counterpart of alpha-function. They both represent functions, different ways of apprehending the object, the one more primitive than the other.

---

9 The assumptions Bion is making regarding the containing function of beta-elements are very different from his idea of the 'beta screen' where groups of beta-elements are split off and projected to form somatic or psychotic symptoms.

In support of the idea of a mimetic function Bion (1963), in *Elements of Psychoanalysis*, alludes to the way beta-elements are able to mimic psychic functions. He suggests that the organization of beta-elements occurs through their capacity for agglomeration and dispersal, forming constellations that resemble key psychic mechanisms responsible for thinking proper, namely Ps↔D and the container–contained. In Bion's words:

> The dispersed β-elements, in so far as they seek a ♀, may be regarded as an abortive prototype of a container, a container loosely structured like a reticulum. . . . They may equally be regarded as the abortive proto-type of the contained, a loosely structured ♂ before compression to enter ♀.
> This description can be restated in terms of Ps↔D: the cohesion of β-elements to form ♀ is analogous to the integration characteristic of the depressive position; the dispersal of β-elements is analogous to the splitting and fragmentation characteristic of the paranoid-schizoid position.
>
> (p.40)

Bion appears to be suggesting that there exists a complex referential process between sensory impressions and psychic functions. He suggests that beta-elements are able to form 'an abortive prototype' of the container–contained: crude premature psychic formations that mimic the container–contained relationship. The idea of a crude form of psychic mimicry seems important here where sense impressions, undigested facts, pattern our experience in a particular way so that dispersed elements approximate containing experiences. Bearing in mind that mimicry is never about equivalence, we might suppose that beta-elements may assume the 'shape' of the container–contained dynamic but they lack the capacity for true integration.

As 'abortive' traces they are very different from Bion's vision of the container that gives psychic existence and affective meaning to unformu-lated experience (a vision that relies on the internalization of the mother's meaning-giving capacities). The 'abortive container' appears to gain proto-containing capacities through mimicking the movements and physical attributes of mental and physical objects. Such containing capacities are created in the immediacy of the interaction itself. I understand these two different versions of the container to refer to separate tracks or levels of experience. Further, in referring to beta-elements in this way, Bion appears to be making implicit references to core elements of non-linear dynamic systems theory where separate systems (or tracks of experience in this case) organize themselves using emergent principles, each system having refer-ential influences on the other.

In sum, on reviewing Bion's speculations, I am suggesting that his references to the 'agglomeration' of experience at this level, the gestaltian patterning of sense impressions, are best conceptualized as a subpersonal interactional matrix, a proto-container, that makes use of particular operating principles. The tropistic nature of primitive containing capacities and their organization around movement and physical qualities of the object appear to link with similar processes explored from different theoretical perspectives associated with what is called procedural knowledge in mainstream psychology (LeFevre *et al.*, 2006; Rosenblatt, 2004; Stadler, 1989; Willingham *et al.*, 1989).

In the remainder of this chapter I develop the idea that proto-containing experiences emerge through the rhythmic sequencing of sensory impressions. The kind of experiences I am referring to are perhaps best described as subtle, amorphous experiences of 'flow' whilst engaging with an object, only vaguely conscious. Here, the mimetic properties of beta-elements give rise to a primordial sense of 'moving along' that is inseparable from immediate interaction (albeit it ultimately ineffable). If such non-conscious processes could be represented pictorially, one might think of these patterns or 'abortive prototypes' as holographic impressions, contours of affects that fade in and out of one another but provide a nascent sense of substance on which psychological life can be structured.

Action-movement systems and proto-containing

In 1914 Freud wrote:

> The attention of children, as I have often noticed, is attracted far more readily by movements than by forms at rest; and they frequently base associations upon *a similarity of movement* which is overlooked or neglected by adults.
>
> (p.90, my emphasis)

Although Freud is directly relating this statement to the symbolic nature of a dream of one of his patients, it may also be taken to allude to a primitive form of identification based on mimicking the object. It appears to anticipate relatively recent analytic research that explores the importance of implicit action-movement systems in psychic development. Bucci's (1985, 1997b) Multiple Code Theory, informed by psychoanalysis and cognitive science, attempts to understand the influence action-movement systems have on psychic experience. Bucci considers three essential formats through which experience is processed: the sub-symbolic, presymbolic and symbolic. It is the sub-symbolic that interests us here, an area of proto-mental computation involved in positioning oneself in the world in relation to one's surroundings. In Bucci's (1997a) words:

This mode of processing involves fine differentiations on continuous gradients and 'computation' of analogic relationships among spatial, temporal, or other sensory patterns, within specific perceptual and motoric modalities.

(p.158)

Sub-symbolic formats include all those infra-sensory cues, taken-for-granted automaticisms through which we engage our object or approach a task. The implicit procedures involved in opening a door, climbing stairs, walking, require that we are always implicitly accommodating to our surroundings using our senses and proprioception. Importantly, there are many similar routines and repetitions involved in the frame-by-frame movements of interaction and conversation: changes in posture, gesticulations, manner of eye contact, non-verbal aspects of speech such as tone, pitch, and cadence, non-conscious cues that indicate the beginning and end of utterances in conversation, the way sounds and gestures complement or mirror each other. All these aspects affect the conversational field in particular ways, creating procedural formats that regulate how we engage as we accommodate to each other's presence.

Although Bion (1962b, p.8) saw learned skills and procedural formats as the product of alpha-function, it seems that his peripheral thoughts about the patterning of beta-elements – as discussed earlier – better map on to the non-symbolic nature of procedural processing systems.[10] If we accept this, a number of questions arise as to how procedural formats, sub-symbolic non-conscious systems, influence psychic reality. In terms of the proto-container, I am making a link here between Bion's 'abortive prototype' and the impact that procedural systems have on psychic reality. Different to verbal or imagistic mental processes, procedural knowing is acquired during the process of learning skills or action sequences that cannot be remembered, only enacted.[11] It is the point of convergence for instinct and priming processes where behaviour is modelled through perceptual and motoric faculties within a myriad of contextual cues. As it is based primarily on action and movement it constitutes the immediate pre-reflective sense of 'being' through 'doing', an area of mind that words and preverbal representations always fall short of depicting. We could say that Winnicott's (1988) idiom 'being before doing' is reversed in this area of (proto)mind as

---

10 Bion uses the example of a child learning to walk and suggests that, through attending to these initial skills, experience is processed (acted on by alpha-function) and made unconscious. While this is a valuable model for understanding how emotional experiences related to procedural actions can be transformed into unconscious memory traces and self representations, Bion makes no clear distinction between the ways such experiences are encoded when compared to non-symbolic processes.

11 This is similar to what Melanie Klein referred to as 'memories in feeling'.

it is only through 'doing' that a sense of self can come into existence.[12] Importantly, actions-movement systems do not occur in isolation of an interpersonal context so it appears more accurate to refer to a 'doing together' that is generated at a non-conscious level.

From other theoretical perspectives there has been a great deal written on how non-conscious processes, in the context of hard-wired formats for attachment, object seeking and tracking, contribute to understanding inter-subjectivity and a 'theory of mind'. I shall briefly explore some of the findings here. My interest is not so much in these processes per se, but more funda-mentally in how their existence supports the idea of emergent experiences, non-conscious 'actions' that possibly signify emergent proto-containing experiences. My intention is not to conflate these different perspectives but consider them to constitute different vertices referring to similar phenomena.

Developmental and experimental research has exposed the extraordinary capacities infants possess in processing and responding to sensory input using non-symbolic formats or what I am calling action-movement systems. Findings suggest that traces of inchoate psychic life gleaned from sense impressions are organized around points of correspondence or matching that establish intersubjective moments marked by a sense of being mirrored by the other. The cross-modal transposition of sensory information (Stern, 2000), early imitative behaviours (Meltzoff and Decety, 2003; Meltzoff and Moore, 1977), vocal rhythm matching (Beebe *et al.*, 1988; Jaffe *et al.*, 2001) and rhythmic coupling (Trevarthen, 1993, 1999), all emphasize the way in which the other is tracked through a form of matching or imitation in order to establish a 'way of being with' the other (Stern, 2004). One might say that these are all interactive mechanisms that move towards establishing an affective sense of 'sameness', a pre-reflective sense of 'being me with you'.

The idea that action-movement systems are fundamental to our ability to form systems of implicit meaning is possibly supported by the fascinating discovery of mirror neurons. Mirror neurons grant us a neurophysiological explanation as to how we are able to learn and understand others via pre-reflective processes of imitation. It is the place of 'implicit certainties' (Gallese, 2003, p.172) that contribute to a sense of oneness, an area Gallese sees as belonging to a 'subpersonal' level of experience. The idea behind mirror neurons, that of shared action, has since been extended to include implicitly shared emotions (e.g. Clyman, 1991; Gallese, 2003; Horowitz *et al.*, 1990). From this point of view, empathy can be understood as an emergent or generative phenomenon based on the organization of (pre-reflective) sensory experience across the intersubjective field. Recently, Zanocco and colleagues (2006) use the term 'sensory empathy' to denote a

---

12 This line of argument is in keeping with philosophical arguments put forward by Husserl, Merleau-Ponty, Heidegger and Deleuze.

process activated between the analytic couple at the level of bodily sensation as opposed to through the medium of fantasy and thought. Referring
to Gaddini's (1992) important work on imitative identification, they regard
sensory empathy as 'the ability to assimilate, through imitative identification, what another person is feeling' (Zanocco *et al.*, 2006, p.148), allowing
non-conscious to non-conscious communication, an area of mind that lacks
any imagistic representation.

From different vertices then (neurological, developmental, cognitive), all
the above emphasize correspondences, points of mutuality in the intersubjective field that are largely non-conscious. For my purpose they represent
points of congruence, commentaries on non-conscious processes which
suggest that a form of 'matching' (represented differently in each theoretical
system) circumscribes and organizes proto-mental phenomena in an interpersonal field.

The focus on 'matching' in interpersonal systems, however, does not seem
to provide an accurate conception of primitive experience unless placed in the
constant flux of experience, fleeting changes in perception and affect that
correspond to 'differences' that the infant is inherently adept at perceiving
and responding to. Aside from 'mirroring' processes, novelty and difference
also appear to have an important role to play in implicit developmental
processes, although they often remain under-theorized (Beebe *et al.*, 2005;
Green, 2005a). I am using 'difference' here to simply refer to everything other
than points of correspondence. We might say that 'difference' manifests as
fluctuations in the sensory field or inevitable ruptures or breaks in access to
correspondences between self and other. 'Difference' is not only about points
of separation between objects, it has an important role to play in inherent
contingency detection modules in psychic development (Beebe *et al.*, 2005;
Fonagy *et al.*, 2004; Jaffe *et al.*, 2001). Put in simple terms, we do not simply
want to know that we resonate or are implicitly 'understood' at this fundamental level, we also want to feel our impact on others, how it makes a
difference in shifting the field of experience. Establishing contingencies is a
way of non-consciously establishing a predictable impact of the self on the
other and vice versa. This has important consequences for the establishment
of a sense of agency and affect regulation. There is evidence to suggest that
when contingencies between mother and child are measured as being mid-
range, optimal regulation of affect occurs (Beebe *et al.*, 1988, 2005; Jaffe *et
al.*, 2001). For the purpose of my argument, I view these as points of
divergence, or counterpoints, in the experiential field at a sub-symbolic level.

Entraining sameness and difference and the emergence of the proto-container

The above findings offer compelling evidence about inherent neurobiological
and behavioural systems. What bearing might these different perspectives

have on Bion's hypothetical ideas about beta-elements? My speculations draw on them to suggest the emergence of implicit organizing principles around experiences of 'sameness' and 'difference'. I start with the assumption that mother and infant exist in a bi-directional field in which sensory experience, sound, gesture and consequent proprioceptive occurrences, from both parties, cohere around fields of 'sameness' and 'difference'. The following fragment from an infant observation briefly illustrates this point:

Samantha

Samantha (seven months) looks into her mother's eyes, tenses her upper body and makes the sound 'mmmma'. Her mother smiles, maintains eye contact and straightens her shoulders. She moves closer and replies adding raised intonation at the end so as to exaggerate the 'a': 'mmmmma...a..a'. Samantha responds: 'maaa mmmmma'. They repeat this three or four times with building speed and excitement. Then the mother tries again but this time Samantha turns away and repeats a similar sound. Arousal appears to diminish at this point. Her mother repeats the sound once more but this time the intonation is such that the pitch is downturned at the end imparting a soothing effect.

I use the above fragment to illustrate the way in which the mother and baby implicitly move to negotiate 'sameness' and 'difference' in their interaction. The utterances mirror each other but there is always something different assimilated into the rhythm of the interaction. Samantha, at one point, appears to find the interaction overwhelming and regulates the exchange by turning away. The mother appears to implicitly acknowledge this in repeating a similar utterance ('sameness') but with a downturned tone ('difference').

I move now to develop the hypothesis that these organizations have an analogical influence on psychic reality that produces proto-containing capacities principally through entraining 'sameness' and 'difference'. Returning to Bion, I would suggest that the 'abortive prototypes' of the container, referred to earlier, emerge due to the entrainment of to-and-fro movements between moments of resonance and difference in the interpersonal field. I further speculate that through these emergent rhythmic sequences based on traces of sense impressions, a stabilizing 'heuristic' forms that constantly evolves in its efforts to accommodate changes in the field.

At a phenomenological level we can only conceive of this process as an ineffable feeling of 'flow', a sense of moving away or towards something. It constitutes the non-symbolic background on which Bion's use of the term 'becoming' is conceived in a more primitive form. Although by definition this cannot be 'thought' or clearly conceptualized, proto-containing experiences make themselves known in the form of vague affective states, 'movements' that produce affective contours experienced in the background of all inter-actions. The resultant experience is a sense that the self feels drawn into – or 'falls into' – a process that is 'outside' the ambit of the self leading to a recursive sense of moving towards and away from the self. From this perspective pro-containing experiences are best conceptualized as belonging to a sub-personal field. To be clear, according to Bion's model, in order to have the idea or feeling of a sense of 'flow' the above non-symbolic 'move-ments' have to pass though alpha-functions to become psychic objects. In other words I make the assumption that these non-conscious 'movements' exist in their own right and give form and shape to interactional processes. However, such processes can be experienced at other levels of the psyche albeit in relatively undefined, ineffable ways. Importantly, I would consider attempts to make such proto-containing experiences conscious in our search for discrete objects of meaning have the effect of interrupting this non-symbolic level of generating experience.

How is it that these sub-symbolic processes generate a sense of 'moving along' or 'flow'? My view is that proto-containing qualities emerge because the concept of negation does not exist at this level of experience. At this level of mind the non-conscious perception of 'sameness' and 'difference' does not undergo a categorical analysis. One object cannot be separated from the other, rather they are experienced as different points in a field of sensory intensities. In other words, even absence of the object is experienced as 'present' in its contribution to the affective intensity of the field. In this way I imagine sequences of sensory impressions exist in gestalt formations 'rather like a musical theme that can be played and replayed with variations in tempo, instrument and key, and yet be recognizable in form' (Charles, 1999, p.371). The links between fluctuations in intensity, emergent rhythmic patterns, move us beyond mere sensory impressions as discrete entities to the creation of basic affective relationships between objects. To return to music as an analogy, we cannot see or hear the relationship between a series of musical notes, but we intrinsically group them together to pattern our experience, creating units of meaning. In a similar way, is it possible to think of saturated sense impressions (beta-elements) and their impact on the mind, meaningless by themselves, as forming a meaningful interactive system?

The philosopher Langer (1951) draws an important distinction between discursive and presentational symbols that illustrates how unformulated experience gains a sense of form dependent on the immediacy of experience. Whereas discursive symbols rely on linear linguistic progressions that are subject to laws of negation and a syntactical scheme of expression, presenta-tional symbols rely on the idea that sense-impressions themselves formulate experience. Presentational symbols are based on our ability to perceive forms in sense data. For Langer, sense-organs have a '"reifying" function that underlies ordinary recognition of objects' (p.86). Thus, the flux of experience takes on different forms and patterns where discrete units hold little meaning. Furthermore, due to the absence of negation there exists no 'fixed meaning apart from its context' (p.88). They are presentational because their function as a 'symbol' relies on 'a simultaneous, integral presentation' of elements that display apparent coherence. Could we say that this reifying function impacts the way beta-elements are organized?

Another well-known philosopher, Deleuze (1968/1994), is useful in trying to get us to think about what essentially cannot be thought, what he calls 'sub-representative' occurrences. In essence, he considers the idea that we are agents for the expression of ephemeral intensities. It is the continuous sensual variations of things that give actual objects a lived meaning and significance. This is the basis for his distinction between actual objects and virtual intensities unique to individual experience. Whereas an actual object, a person, may be thought of in terms of discrete identities like being male, tall, fat and kind, the virtual object is made up of relations between the flux of intensities best expressed as a series of 'becomings'. Here male does not mean not female, kind does not mean not unkind, they are experienced as a series of 'becomings'. The person is becoming male, becoming kind, and so forth. Intensities do not inhere within or between objects; rather there is something of all males, tallness, fatness, kindness that exists within a field capable of infinite combinations of these intensities.[13] There are no caesuras, no discrete entities, at this level of experience.

How does this relate to the sense of 'moving along' to which I am referring? What I want to emphasize is that due to the lack of negation entrainment between 'sameness' and 'difference' in the sensory field leads to the emergence of proto-containing capacities in real-time interaction. Further, true to Bion's beta-elements, although rudimentary proto-mental impressions lack any real capacity for integration, their near-physical nature, associations with action and movement rather than thought, lead to particular proto-containing capacities that have more in common with musical expression than the logic of conscious or unconscious thought (Bion, 1956).

Proto-containing capacities

There appear to be a number of factors that have key influences on proto-containing capacities. I focus my thoughts on the 'rhythmic sequencing' of sensory impressions and the role of repetition.

---

13 Deleuze's ideas are very close to Bion's notion of 'obscuring memory and desire' in that he expresses the idea that meaningful experience emerges through a process of 'forgetting' our (mental) attachment to things in order to be moved by the pure ever-changing intensities of the external world.

Rhythmic sequencing and emergent affect

It has often been noted that our communicative efforts have an inherent musical quality (e.g. Blacking, 1976; Kohut, 1950; Malloch, 1999; Mithen, 2005; Trevarthen, 1999). Through gesture, proprioceptive influence and the 'the physicality of words' (Rose, 2004) a responsiveness is generated that remains non-conscious but has a musical quality to it. From birth infants are sensitive to the time contours and rhythms set out in music because our bodies and our movements are by nature polyrhythmic and inherently responsive to pulse and cadence. The 'musical' nature of speech, variations in tone, timbre, prosody, phonation, pitch and harmony constantly influence the intersubjective field. For this reason music provides a rich analogy for mental processes evident in non-verbal and infraverbal[14] aspects of the transference relationship (e.g. Knoblauch, 2000; Mancia, 2003). Much of the time this is the medium through which transference–countertransference 'pressure' is conveyed. Unlike the use of symbolic language, music conveys a relatively loose referential system of meaning: A particular note or rhythm does not itself have particular meaning and is better described as mainly manipulative in character[15] (Mithen, 2005; Sloboda, 1985). In line with this, authors like Modell (1980) and Grotstein (2005) believe that priming, the ability to read each other's gestures, is made possible through 'manipulative' communications of this kind, a way of influencing the sensory field in near-physical ways.

Music, movement and affect share a number of qualities. Rose (2004) draws our attention to a well-known assumption that a sense of motion unites musical expression and affect. It is not sound but motion that goes to the heart of music's ability to 'move'. Movement is created through the rhythmic creation of dissonance and resolution imparting a feeling of motion perhaps best represented by a sense of expansion and contraction, a moving towards and moving away from. Rose associates this with affective cycles of tension and release and draws on research that links rhythmic patterns of tension and release to motoric and kinesthetic aspects of affect. We also know that aspects of neurological functioning related to

---

14 Aspects of the voice that act as signifiers to convey affect through the articulation of sound (Mancia, 2006).

15 It is interesting to note that Freud makes reference to similar musical qualities in pointing out that, as an art form, it is unable to satisfy his analytical sensibilities: 'Nevertheless, works of art do have a powerful effect on me, especially those of literature and sculpture, less often of painting. This has occasioned me when I have been contemplating such things, to spend a long time before them trying to apprehend them in my own way . . . Wherever I cannot do this, as for instance with music, I am almost incapable of obtaining any pleasure. Some rationalistic, or perhaps analytic, turn of mind in me rebels against being moved by a thing without knowing why I am thus affected and what it is that affects me' (Freud, 1914, p.211).

movement are activated when listening to music (Mithen, 2005; Rose, 2004). In Rose's words:

> The implicit motion of the mind, itself, generates states of being and activates affect-motor pathways that somehow transmute the mind's own motion into virtual motion of non-verbal art.
>
> (2004, p.152)

Such rhythmic forms are best represented in the abstract visual arts by Jackson Pollock's *Blue Poles*, Mondrian's *Opposition of Lines*, or art forms that are inspired by fractal geometry.

With these links to music in mind, could it be the case that mental 'impressions' created by sensory experience are organized in valences of 'sameness' and 'difference', granting a rhythmic sense to interaction? Could we say that rhythm establishes a common 'pulse' which has a resonating influence on the mind and makes possible what Blacking (1976) calls 'constructive time sharing'. I would speculate that the rhythmic patterning which occurs as a consequence of this has a number of influences on our minds. At its core the patterning effects of sense impressions possibly grant us a sense of reified form in an action sequence (it is not yet a mental image such as would be represented by a shape), a sense of 'moving along' perhaps similar to the oceanic experiences that Freud wrote about.[16] In this way sensory impressions create experiential contours that give rise to affective experiences characterized by kinaesthetic qualities which have the effect of opening up and closing down the intersubjective field.

Particular affective states emerge as a consequence of the rhythmic sequencing of sense impressions. They are experienced as barely describable 'pressures' very different from feelings proper or what are often called categorical affects. Such affects appear very similar to what Stern (2000) calls the 'vitality affects'. Vitality affects are contours of experience that express the feeling-flow of intentionality that occurs in real time, creating a sense of reaching or stretching of the mind towards something (Stern, 2004). Stern sees the formation of 'feeling contours' and 'time shapes' as emerging out of the analogical shifts that occur in the intensity, rhythm and form of sensations experienced. As he puts it:

> We are immersed in a 'music' of the world at a local level – a complex polyphonic, polyrhythmic surround where different temporal contours are moving back and forth between the psychological background and foreground.
>
> (Stern, 2004, p.64)

---

16 These background experiences also appear similar to Winnicott's (1965) concept of 'going-on-being' and Tustin's (1986) 'rhythm of safety'.

These temporal and feeling contours can be translated into subjectively (using alpha-function) perceived shifts of 'movement' such as fading away, moving forward, exploding, bursting, leaning backwards, flooding. Such affects accompany interaction in a way that creates 'a lived story' and give coherence to the present moment. In Stern's terms 'vitality affects act like a temporal backbone on which the plot is hung' (p.70).

The phenomenology of 'moving along' with the interaction is often accompanied by a sense of feeling 'lost in conversation'. It is the experience of deep attunement where the to-and-fro rhythmic movement of sensuous experience leads to a feeling of 'flow'. It also leads to the sense that something else, something ineffable, is 'carrying' the analytic process. A patient of mine once described this in the following way: 'I feel I am being carried along by the safety of something that I can't know; it is like the flow of conversation is thinking me'. This represents an attempt to think about this phenomenon engaging alpha-function. My point is that its actual source is found in non-conscious processes.

Repetition, 'otherness' and articulating the immediate present

Thus far I have speculated that sense impressions, grouped together around valences of 'sameness' and 'difference', create a form of non-conscious rhythmic sequencing. Repetition, as an element of rhythm, appears to be a particularly important factor in influencing the nature of proto-containing capacities. It has been understood to have a number of different functions in psychoanalysis, I focus here on the role that repetition might play in sub-symbolic activity and then go on to consider other emergent properties that I am conceptualizing as 'proto-containing'.

At the sub-symbolic level of experience repetition might be understood to be a primitive means of conceptualizing or apprehending the object. Inter-active occurrences cannot be thought, instead repetition, as a near-mental action, is used to signify the presence of the object, a way of articulating its immediate presence. It is akin to repeatedly needing to touch an object in order to sense it is there. I find Matte-Blanco's (1988) understanding of psychic dimensionality a useful way of understanding repetition. Using mathematical principles he puts forward the idea that psychic reality exists in multiple dimensions that represent different vertices of experience. In this system an object of greater dimensionality can only be represented at lower dimensions through the repetition of the dimensions that remain out of range or unconscious. To use his example, a triangle represented by the points ABC can be drawn on a two-dimensional plane giving us the image of a three-pointed shape. However, when represented in one-dimensional space it can only be represented as points CABC on a straight line. The point C is repeated in a lower dimension to complete the representation in a one-dimensional plane. Matte-Blanco uses this example to demonstrate how, from a mathematical perspective, we are unconscious of a number of dimensions in psychic space. In terms of the example, we cannot perceive the shape of a triangle when we view it as represented in one-dimensional space. My emphasis is on how point C needs to be repeated and represented as two different points on the one-dimensional plane. I am using repetition here to suggest that a sense of rhythm and movement is generated when an object is apprehended by a system of inferior dimensionality.

How does this apply to proto-containing experiences? Although sensory impressions or beta-elements can be transformed into psychic elements that acquire higher levels of psychic dimensionality, I have argued that some of these elements maintain a functional role in an untransformed state. In this state they lack any real mental dimensionality and therefore cannot represent three-dimensional objects as three-dimensional forms. Instead, they register the presence of the object through repetition. Therefore we might say that repetition signifies the presence of dimensions that cannot be represented.

Translated into the clinical context, let us say that a psychic object is represented by various dimensions: its history, appearance, perceived intentions, emotional attachments, and so forth. However, our ability to apprehend this kind of dimensionality is limited in areas of mind that process sub-symbolic activity. Here all these elements would simply be represented by points repeated around the same object signifying its presence. To return to musical analogies, at primitive levels of mind repetitions are analogous to how musical notes repeat themselves, varying in intensity, tone or rhythm, to signify the presence of a theme or emotion.

The above could be stated slightly differently: repetition is the primary means of apprehending or 'knowing' the object within the constraints of a psychic system that lacks complex dimensionality. It represents a crude manifestation of the K, our best effort at 'thinking', a primitive counterpart of representational thought. It provides an elemental means of resonating with the present moment. It is, as it were, a way of 'holding on' to the fleeting ineffable nature of external reality that is always beyond representation, complex identification or thought and yet is always present. It constitutes, as Blanchot (1969) puts it, 'the ungraspable that one cannot let go of' (p.45).

We are faced with a fundamental difficulty in the immediacy of interaction. It constitutes the essence of what it is to be human and 'real' to the other and yet the connection in the present moment is ultimately impossible to grasp. Perhaps for these reasons, to quote Blanchot again, we are drawn into dialogues where we can only set about 'naming the possible [and] *responding* to the impossible' (p.48, my emphasis). I am suggesting here that repetition may constitute an inherent way of responding to the impossible, a pre-reflective way of resonating with what cannot be known. In this way acts of repetition grant us a way of staying with the present moment, thereby containing it.

It is possible that the repetition and rhythmic patterning which occurs here generates further referential activity or emergent phenomena in the psyche that yields a primitive source of self-regulation. Notably, it appears to contribute to the 'physicality' of the object as well as the sense of 'otherness' characterizing proto-containing experience from a phenomeno-logical standpoint. In terms of the former, I am referring to the idea that repetition serves to impress on the mind near-physical boundaries or contours that contribute further to a sense of 'moving along'. This relates to Bion's understanding of beta-elements as having more things in common with physical objects than they do with mental objects. Their 'indigest-ibility' and tendency towards agglomeration, their closeness to the senses and the body, and their ability to mimic the form of psychical and physical objects evoke a sense of 'physicality'. It seems to me that repetition, as it exists in interaction, further induces an emergent property approximating a near-physical sense of boundary or contour that creates a sense of being 'carried by the interaction'. I am referring here to the repetition of tone, gesture and cadence that occurs between self and other through non-conscious imitation. Certain words that undergo constant repetition in interaction, words that appear to hold little meaning but act like 'tics' in the conversation, may also be viewed as having a similar edifying role.

As well as creating near-physical objects the above also illustrates how the action of repetition has a numbing effect on the mind. Repetitions of voice and gesture act like mantras in the interaction, producing a mental stillness or perhaps a means of regulating affect. I return to my observa-tions of Samantha simply as an illustration.

Samantha (revisited)

After being breastfed Samantha looks satiated and calm, she stares at the breast and utters, 'Uuuuhhhrr'. Her mother responds by turning her slightly to face her and says, 'You fully now?' She repeats this a number of times to which Samantha responds by repeatedly lifting her left arm and touching her face. At one point Samantha's father enters the room. Neither Samantha nor her mother make eye contact with him. Instead the pace of the mother's verbalizations increases and are slightly louder, 'Fully, fully, fully.' Samantha responds by producing a broader stroking motion of her face. Her mother continues to repeat similar phrases but with quieter tones whilst Samantha persists in her arm movements, gradually slowing until she falls off to sleep.

I have in mind here the idea that repetition produces 'mind-numbing' states in the individual that 'nudge' interlocutors into experiencing different intersubjective states because this serves the purpose of regulating affect in the present moment. These aspects deserve greater consideration than I can grant them here. There appear to be thresholds to this kind of implicit repetitive activity. Too little repetition diminishes real contact with the other, but too much repetition creates 'concrete' obstacles associated with autistic modes of generating experience (Ogden, 1992; Tustin, 1990). We shall return to this in briefly considering breakdown phenomena in the proto-container.

I turn now to consider the sense of 'otherness' typical of proto-containing experiences. It seems that the repetition evident in moving towards and away from the object, the rhythmic sequencing I referred to earlier, also yields background experiences that are not felt to be products of the individual's subjectivity. One might say that the emergent rhythm creates an impersonal sense of 'otherness' that patterns and contains the interacting pair. It is not the object itself that is related to or thought about here and in this way the proto-container might be conceptualized as an impersonal emergent 'other'. Whereas at other levels of relating mother and baby are consumed by devotion, love, hate, or care for each other, the proto-container emerges from the 'impersonal in-between', not from mother or baby, but from the non-conscious interactive intelligence that contains them both.

There is a corollary to this situation. If mother or baby become too prominent in their capacities as discrete 'thinking objects', proto-containing experiences run the risk of being interrupted. The unconscious link here is not about seeking a containing object to represent psychic experience in more modified forms (the role of the containing function proper). Rather, motivation is centred around resonating with, and accommodating to, an object's presence so as to build a reified link between the interacting pair. Any attempt at objectifying or analyzing this process has the effect of disrupting the existing rhythm of engagement. The emergent 'otherness' that occurs through repetition is breached, diminishing the non-conscious sense of being contained by the interaction itself. A similar process seems to be illustrated by some artists' refusal to subject their craft to analysis. This is usually motivated by the sense that analysis would disrupt the non-conscious 'flow' of how they engage their object. Here analysis and thought are felt to disrupt 'the thingness' of their creation. Pianist Keith Jarrett aptly describes such a process in saying: 'I have to find a way for my hands to start the concert without me' (Carr, 1991). He describes a creative process that amounts to the wilful suspension of alpha-function so as to connect with and be 'moved by' the build-up of sense impressions that provide the contours of experience. Jazz musicians often refer to these aspects of musical experience as the 'feel' or 'groove' of the music, a sense of being carried by the rhythmic, repetitive movement of the music, a sense that is quickly lost if thought about too much.

Breakdown phenomena and beta-mentality

I have argued that the entrainment of 'sameness' and 'difference', along with all the factors that contribute to proto-containing capacities, give rise to experiences of expansion and constriction of the intersubjective field. I have conceptualized that proto-containing capacities are real-time phenomena which are emergent from action-movement systems. Beta-elements performing a proto-containing function cannot be acted on or transformed (by alpha-function) as objects, nor can they be conceived of as being 'inside' psychic reality or in the external world. From this position I understand breakdown phenomena to occur when beta-elements cease to function as suspended traces of experience that defy distinctions between intrapsychic and interpersonal, subject and object. The pathological states emanating from such occurrences amount to what I call beta-mentality. I use the term because it is the qualities of beta-elements that dominate the patient's best efforts at holding on to mental experience (and a sense of self) when the container function fails.

In Bion's theory of beta-elements, realizations of beta-elements are closest in their breakdown products when they emerge as 'bizarre objects' found in hallucinations and delusions (Bion, 1962b). Similarly, I regard proto-containing capacities most 'observable' when factors that support this psychic function fail. I divide these into three categories:

- hypergeneration of proto-containing factors
- hypogeneration of proto-containing factors
- the appropriation or interruption of proto-containing capacities by other modes of generating experience.

I restrict myself to simply outlining some brief examples to illustrate applications of the theory of the proto-container and return to some of these observations in later sections of this book.

It appears that the persistent repetition of sensory experience can turn contours of experience into objects or obstacles and produce autistic-like defences in the psyche. Ogden's (1992) understanding of the breakdown of the autistic-contiguous mode of generating experience highlights a similar position. Here, behaviour or sensation is auto-generated (Tustin, 1986) to create surfaces around which a fragmented sense of self can cohere. At this level of experience obsessive symptoms can be understood as repetitive attempts to delineate boundaries between self and other.

The hypergeneration of proto-containing factors can also occur as a feature of the interaction. For example, the unconscious provocation of violence, especially in the borderline patient, can be understood as the need to evoke high levels of hyper-arousal and sensation in a desperate attempt to produce something near-physical when the presence of an internal world (the generation of representations of the self) seems terrifyingly absent (see Chapter 12). Grotstein (1991) refers to a similar process where desperate attempts are made to reconstruct the 'sensory floor' of experience.

What happens when sensory impressions lack elements of repetition? Based on the model of the proto-container it appears that the hypo-generation of proto-containing capacities destroys the rhythmic approach to generating an implicit sense that the self is always 'becoming', always evolving anew depending on the context. Often this leads to terrifying feelings of confusion or 'absence' in conversation. Such patients complain of a sense of falling or evaporating. Without automatically configured sub-symbolic ways 'of being with' the other, such patients are exposed to sensory experience that exists free of any contingent relationship with the self and is thus experienced as alien. Here, thoughts are objects and objects are thoughts and the awareness of having a mind separate from others is always traumatic.

The final area where breakdown phenomena occur in this model involves 'interruptions' from more mature ways of generating experience. Proto-containing experience, as I have argued, emerges out of untransformed sensory traces. What happens if attempts are made to transform these elements? In my view other modes of generating experience (including defensive strategies) can act to retard proto-containing capacities. This would involve over-vigilant attempts to think about and understand all aspects of behaviour. It would also involve being overly attentive to aspects of behaviour that have become relatively habitual and unproblematic. Perhaps the clearest example of this can be found in the constant use of intellectualization to assess what analyst or patient is doing in the session. When this occurs the 'rhythm' of the interaction and functional aspects of the proto-container are constantly interrupted, leaving little sense of being 'carried' by the process.

All the above examples have in common a reliance on the mimetic quality of beta-elements where repetitive elements generate background 'physical' qualities to interaction. As I understand it, and in keeping with a dynamic systems view of mental phenomena, this process reverberates though the psyche imbuing mental objects with physical qualities, a kind of beta-mentality. Here emergent properties of the proto-container have referential effects on other ways of generating experience. For example, if there exist deficits in symbolic thinking the rhythmic properties of the proto-container may be misappropriated as the mechanism for producing pseudo-thoughts. Here, thoughts have little meaning in themselves but are used to create some sense of continuity in the self.

Finally, the way in which sensory impressions are entrained in interaction creates particular kinds of sensory contours that influence how internal objects are experienced. For instance, it could be said that constricted rigid forms of interaction contribute to a sense of internal objects feeling brittle or hard. On the other hand, interactions that allow for the expansion of subjectivity through recursive movements between 'sameness' and 'difference' contribute to a sense of internal objects being more permeable and open to integration.

Conclusion

Using some of Bion's ideas about a proto-mental system and the implied patterning of beta-elements, I have put forward the idea that emergent features of interaction give rise to proto-containing capacities. I have conceptualized it as an emergent connection that organizes itself around points of 'difference' and 'sameness' in the interaction and through mimicking 'physical' features of interaction.

This has a patterning effect on proto-mental experience yielding a sense of containment in the immediacy of interaction. At this level of mind it is not so much the object or pre-object that matters, or even the sense impression itself, it is the qualities they impart to a field of experience that can only 'read' discrete entities as contributions to variations in a rhythmic field. There is an implicit acceptance of the saturated quality of experience and therefore no fetching for reason or knowledge. An age-old antinomy is touched on here: in order to truly be oneself, to be known, to think, to give rise to something novel, one has to lose one's self in the interaction. Put another way, the quality of internal object relations depends on proto-containing experiences.

In exploring the emergence of the proto-container I am also suggesting that sub-symbolic experiences set up 'states of expectation', ways of 'knowing' containing experience that anticipate and make possible the use of the mother's containing function (her ability to use reverie and her own alpha-function to make the unbearable more bearable).

A number of technical issues are raised in considering proto-containing capacities. In generating proto-containing experiences the emphasis is more on what the analyst and patient do (and how they do it), as opposed to what is said (clearly these cannot be separated in reality). This does not diminish the importance of interpretation and insight, but underlines the importance of interpretations being made in a way that imparts a sense of 'moving on' in the interaction. I see this as consistent with Bion's (2005b) view that 'true' interpretations (rather than accurate ones) are always conveyed within the context of 'becoming' something else, embracing the moment-to-moment evolution of the analytic couple. Second, partial enactments take on a slightly different meaning in the context of the proto-container. Not only are they our best attempts at engaging with the 'unknowable', but it is possible that they also represent non-conscious attempts at mirroring non-symbolic activity. This is an important part of the analytic process whereby the analyst and patient work together to entrain 'sameness' and 'difference' in a way that creates a deep sense of evolution in the analytic space. Importantly, because this is born out of sub-symbolic non-conscious ways of 'finding each other', this is very different from contrived attempts at empathizing or mirroring the patient's emotional presence. Finally, as a sub-symbolic process proto-containing capacities require pre-reflective responsiveness. This invites an analytic approach that works on tolerating the 'otherness' of interaction and holding off overzealous attempts to analyze the unanalyzable.

Chapter 7

Modes of interaction

Bion's approach privileges relationships over individual minds or objects. From this perspective, thoughts, intentions, experiences become sterile 'certainties' (contrived and manufactured) unless they are related to context and the particular object relationship at hand. Put simply, we need other minds to achieve mental growth. Our attempts to overly assert ourselves as discrete individuals who are able to think in isolation thwart such developments. Returning to Bion's words quoted earlier:

> The breast and the mouth are only important in so far as they serve to define the bridge between the two. When the 'anchors' usurp the importance which belongs to the qualities which they should be imparting to the bridge growth is impaired.
>
> (Bion, 1989, p.26)

Bion's point has a number of implications for the therapeutic relationship. We could apply this directly to any container–contained configuration: The container is only important insofar as it outlines a particular way of connecting with the contained. The moment the container (breast, mother, group, analyst's mind) and the contained (mouth, baby, individual, projections) are privileged as objects over relationship qualities, growth is impaired. But is it possible to privilege relationship over the two (or more) minds that are contributing to the interaction? Part of the answer appears to lie in our innate interest in knowing and tracking the other's mind, defining a link through which we change, and are changed, in relationship.

Melanie Klein (1932) proposed that the infant possesses an innate curiosity about the mother's body and mind. Loving and destructive phantasies about entering the mother's body, as well as using it as a receptacle for projections, greatly influenced Klein's views on development. Following Klein, Bion (1962b) used K (Knowing) to represent an emotional link between objects that draws on an innate curiosity. But he shifts the object of curiosity somewhat. It is no longer just about 'knowing' the object;

curiosity is directed at the link between objects and how transformation occurs within a container–contained dynamic.

It could be said that Bion's realization of the existence of container–contained configurations between objects brings with it suggestions about the nature of asymmetrical relationships between objects that set up particular dynamical challenges related to dependency, negotiating separateness and transformation. How two minds are linked signifies particular ways of managing the asymmetrical nature of the container–contained configuration. Bion discussed three basic relational configurations between container–contained: symbiotic, parasitic and commensal. To these I add the autistic mode and the pseudo-containing mode. These configurations are best understood as ways in which the therapeutic couple are drawn into relating depending on the dominant organizing phantasies in existence between them. In this chapter I consider the clinical significance of these configurations and understand these 'modes of relating' as being different approaches to negotiating the asymmetrical nature of the container–contained and the emotional turbulence that this inevitably brings. Before considering these I want to briefly explore the nature of the asymmetrical relationship between container–contained.

'Forced asymmetry'

> For mental content to be experienced there must be space between it and its container (object) and a perimeter around it.
>
> (Grotstein, 2000, p.89)

Bion thought the infant had acute perceptual abilities at birth and perhaps even before birth. He made the assumption that the infant possesses a rudimentary form of awareness where all perceptions were treated with equal value because they lacked any particular psychic meaning.[1] This is a level of mind where symmetry holds more emotional resonance. But the infant depends on the mother to make these experiences meaningful. In order to make this possible the infant communicates through projective identification, a phantasy that depends as much on seeing the object as an extension of the self (symmetry) as it does on seeing the object as separate and different (Matte-Blanco, 1988). Projective identification diminishes anxiety because the projection can be conceived of as residing in a separate object. I have explored the bi-logical nature of projective identification

---

1 This form of awareness differs from consciousness proper which Bion takes from Freud (1911) to mean the awareness and perception of the psychic qualities.

elsewhere (pp.54–62). Here I want to raise the possibility that the asymmetry inherent in the primordial need for a containing mind is the relational counterpart of the bi-logical nature of mind. Reformulated in this way, the container represents an interruption of the dominant symmetrical logic of the unconscious and introduces a sense of 'otherness' at preconscious levels of mind.

In the previous chapter I put forward the idea that beta-elements, sense impressions, can be organized in a way that provide proto-containing experiences for relating similar to what Ferro (2005) calls 'micro-being in unison'. At this primitive level of mind there are no psychic means of comprehending 'difference'. Instead, exposure to differences in the experiential field generates gradations of experience, 'a sense of flow' in the relationship but no need for another mind to process it or make sense of it. However, this only accounts for how the mind manages or apprehends sense impressions at a most rudimentary level. With the accumulation of unformulated experience, the sense of 'moving together in unison' in the interaction is disrupted by emotional turbulence which signifies that proto-containing experiences are insufficient. In addition to proto-containing capacities, the mind of an other is needed to give meaning to unformulated sensory impressions or proto-thoughts that have managed to pass through alpha-function. With this comes the realization (at varying levels of consciousness) of differences between objects, asymmetries, and the establishment of a dynamic that recognizes one aspect of mind has to assume the containing role, while the other assumes the contained.

Depending on constitutional factors and the emotional climate of core relationships this 'forced asymmetry' between container and contained sets up complex dynamics. Assuming the role of the container or contained, tolerating entering and leaving the mind of an other, tolerating a degree of difference and the tacit acknowledgement of needing another mind, inevitably sets up a degree of emotional turbulence. In addition, container–contained exchanges depend on reciprocal or recursive exchanges between minds. Although, given the primitive nature of undeveloped mental states, the mother or analyst is called upon to perform containing aspects of this dynamic, this is far from a static process. The relational configuration is constantly changing and if it is working well will comprise reciprocal exchanges between mother and infant, therapist and patient. Bion is clear about this when he says that 'the clue lies in the observation of the fluctuations which make the analyst at one moment "the container" and the analysand "the contained", and at the next reverse the roles' (1970, p.108). It could be said then that inherent in every object or mind is the potentiality to be both the container and the contained. Below we briefly see how a mother and baby interact through reciprocal container–contained interchanges while they take turns in letting each other know what is on their mind:

Kayla

Kayla, an 18-month-old baby, cries and looks distressed. Her mother looks concerned and starts to imagine what might be wrong. She responds to the baby, 'Ah, ahhh, should I change your nappy? You want some food? Milk?' The baby looks attentively at the mother's gestures as she speaks. She cries again. The mother replies, 'Okay, okay, you're a little hungry hungry sweet aren't you?' Her mother gets her bottle, still reminding the baby what is on her mind, 'Hungry hungry, Kayla'. A while after taking the bottle the baby looks satisfied and she raises the bottle and gestures towards the mother, 'Hoooo...hoo'. The mother replies, 'Yes you were a hungry little softy weren't you?'

The reciprocal interchange allows the mother to take in the baby's cries, projections of something unnamed, and translates them into thoughts and words. In turn, the baby also demonstrates her own receptivity as a container in attending to the mother's gestures in her attempts to 'think' about her mother's communications. In this example, at an intrapsychic level, we can imagine a healthy exchange of realistic projective and introjective identifications which are gradually modified by both parties. The asymmetry of the container–contained configuration and the anxiety of the baby searching for her mother's mind is eased by gestures that she is able to 'take her in' and think about it. Throughout this process there is an implicit acceptance of 'turn-taking' as the communication about food is processed in both minds.

As mentioned elsewhere, the container function is therefore not always synonymous with the mother's or therapist's receptive mind. In fact one might say that it is equally correct to say that the origins of the container lie in the infant's inherent and growing preconceptions about experience. As Bion puts it, the growth of the container proper 'represents a late stage in a series of stages that commences with a few relatively simple undifferentiated preconceptions probably related to feeding, breathing and excretion' (1970, p.93).

The above observations assume a relatively unproblematic situation where mother and infant are able to use the container–contained configuration with increasing flexibility, fostering ongoing psychic growth. In more pathological states the situation is more complex. Here, projective identifications are used to force unbearable psychic states into the mind of an other so as to split it off or use it to destroy the object. In these cases the reciprocal nature of the container–contained cannot be tolerated as it is equated with the return of something intolerable and is experienced as an attack from the other. The following vignette illustrates this point.

David

David talks to me in a hurried manner, maintaining piercing eye contact as he tells me about an altercation at work. He seems to be searching for a response in my every move. I cannot think clearly and indeed he tells me he doesn't want to know what I think; he only wants me to listen. I shift at one point in my chair and take a deep breath. David, in response, leans back, pauses and looks away. After a short but awkward silence he continues at pace. I try to say something but he cuts me off. I feel my mind racing, I have an image of a skater speeding across the ice with a sense of anxiety that if he stopped he would fall through. I start to have an image of David running a race. I feel inspired by these images and want to cut in and tell him. I lean forward signalling my intent. He lets me start but cuts me off again when I pause. He continues as if I have said nothing and starts to get annoyed when I again try, later in the session, to say something.

There is an acute sense of building anxiety here as the patient attempts to 'push' all his worries and anger into me in the hope that they will diminish. Alongside this, any demands on the patient to think or attend (to contain) to what is happening to me (contained) are avoided.

Common difficulties also appear to be related to the asymmetrical qualities of the container–contained. The consequences of what it means to be 'held in mind' by an other, to experience a mental connection in which the self is articulated and interpreted by a separate person, is of particular importance here.

Shaun

Shaun struggles to meet my gaze in our session and I find myself responding by trying to follow his eyes. I have a sense he is aware of me trying to connect with him and I begin to feel more self-conscious about how he may experience this. He tells me he feels more and more anxious as the session goes on and cannot hear what I'm saying. He complains of feeling claustrophobic in my consulting room and asks if he can 'leave the door open so it doesn't feel so intense'. I agree and he seems relieved. A while later he reports a dream where his mother does not recognize him. He is anxious in the dream but escapes through the kitchen back door. We think about this in relation to leaving the door open during our session and he is able to connect with the idea that he doesn't want me to have thoughts about him. When we explore this further, he imagines that it is somehow too painful for me to think about him. On leaving he suggests that his problems lie elsewhere and it would be better if we spoke about his family and his work situation next time.

The fear of not being recognized, perhaps not existing once entering another's mind, appears to be evident in Shaun's evasion of allowing me to think about him. Difficulties in being receptive to a containing mind might also be managed by attempts to destroy the therapist's capacity to think or the link between analyst and patient (Bion, 1959). Generating intolerable levels of affect in the transference, more direct attacks on the therapist's person or their ability to do their work, are other examples of destructive attacks on the analyst's containing mind.

Difficulties with asymmetrical qualities of the container–contained can also occur when the patient struggles to be receptive to the analyst's verbal and non-verbal communications. In these moments the patient's mind cannot tolerate becoming 'the container':

> 'I don't want you to tell me things that I have to think about, your talking makes me have to listen and think. It is ridiculous I know but I want you to "mind read" me so we can have the same thoughts. That way, we would know each other and "get" each other straight away.'

I understood this communication to be about the difficulties of containing my utterances and performing the psychic work necessary to give them meaning. By implication the patient's fantasy points to difficulties in tolerating the asymmetrical aspects of the container–contained. 'Mind reading', within this context, seems to represent an appeal for symmetry, sameness, without giving oneself over to the turmoil inherent in being contained in another's mind.

How should we understand resistance from this perspective? Following Bion, it seems to centre on the fear that the object is believed to be 'real' and we can know its 'ultimate reality'. Bion is making the distinction here between ultimate reality and the fact that we can only 'have' representations of the object. In his words:

> Resistance operates because it is feared that the reality of the object is imminent. . . . The belief that reality is or could be known is mistaken because reality is not something which lends itself to being known. It is impossible to know reality for the same reason that makes it impossible to sing potatoes.

> (1965, pp.147–148)

From the perspective of being 'held in mind' by an other, the container, becomes intolerable if it is felt to be a 'real thing', an immutable truth, immutable reality. On the other hand, in my understanding, resistance also revolves around giving up the omnipotence of this kind of reasoning. It seems that once this level of resistance begins to be confronted and some omnipotence given up, another level of resistance is encountered: resistance to the pain and uncertainly of giving one's self over to someone else's 'perspective', the opaqueness of another's mind. It amounts to a fear of losing the self in the other's mind.

Container–contained configurations in clinical practice

Bion isolated three basic container–contained relational configurations: symbiotic, parasitic and commensal. He differentiated them in the following way:

> By 'commensal' I mean a relationship in which two objects share a third to the advantage of all three. By 'symbiotic' I understand a relationship in which one depends on another to mutual advantage. By 'parasitic' I mean to represent a relationship in which one depends on another to produce a third which is destructive to all three.
>
> (Bion, 1970, p.95)

Bion is often simply paraphrased or quoted directly in referring to these configurations and the difference between symbiotic relatedness and commensal relatedness is often understood differently by various authors. Indeed, Bion's thoughts about the difference are often very difficult to grasp. Further, although these are terms borrowed from the biological sciences, Bion's explanations and usage of the terms mostly differ from how they are usually used to describe biological relationships between organisms. Perhaps this is partly why there appears to have been little exploration of these configurations in terms of their usefulness in understanding clinical interaction.

To recapitulate, container–contained configurations represent abstract relationships between objects based on asymmetry. In applying this to the clinical situation the configuration can represent many different relationships: between thought and emotion, unconscious and conscious, word and language, therapist and patient, and so forth. Here I use it to predominantly represent relational links between therapist and patient, ways in which the therapist and patient are drawn into participating in a particular configuration in order to avoid the pain of 'being held in mind' and its inevitable asymmetry. They represent predominant modes of interaction between therapist and patient organized around core phantasies. Exploring these types of configurations therefore provides basic templates for decoding phantasies that are personified and enacted in the transference–countertransference relationship. All modes represent different 'solutions' to overcome, obscure or destroy the asymmetrical qualities of the container–contained configuration. Put another way, these configurations may be understood as ways of avoiding or tolerating more realistic representations of the therapist as a containing object.

Although I discuss them separately, these configurations seldom operate in pure form and are better understood as operating in parallel where some configurations dominate various forms of interaction. Let us say, for instance, that the dominant configuration is of a therapist who needs to think of his patient as being particularly ill in order to feel that he can work with her. In response, the patient adopts a sick role to maintain the therapist's perceived affections (a symbiotic configuration). This gets more complex when we consider the multidimensional nature of container–contained relations where the contained in one form of interaction may simultaneously act as container to an other. For instance, staying with the above example, the patient's phantasy of being sick may act as a container for conflict between herself and idealized objects. Still further, the container–contained relationship can become the background container to another configuration. The symbiotic configuration, for example, may be seen as acting as a container for threatening malevolent objects. The result is a dynamic nesting process (Billow, 2003), an image of expanding concentric circles of different qualities that set up complex systems between minds. I turn now to exploring these configurations. I also add two other configurations: the autistic and pseudo-containing modes.

The symbiotic mode

> By 'symbiotic' I understand a relationship in which one depends on another to mutual advantage.
>
> (Bion, 1970, p.95)

The symbiotic mode is perhaps best understood as the prototypical mother–infant relationship as discussed by Bion early in his work. The mother makes herself mentally available to 'take in' projective identifications that are beyond the infant's cognitive and emotional capacities so as to detoxify them and render them more manageable and thinkable. Communication of unassimilated experience is essentially preverbal, unknown to the interactive couple. By beginning to pay attention to these aspects of their relationship the mother stimulates K (Knowing) in the infant and a curiosity about the psychical nature of his mother's mind. This is essentially a two-person system; the presence of a third object is obscured and if made too apparent would disrupt the processing system. To reiterate, 'one depends on another to mutual advantage' (Bion, 1970, p.95). Because the container–contained is a reciprocal relationship, dependence works both ways. The mind of an other is needed, but this mind depends on projected contents. The containing mind is dependent on unassimilated experience because this is the main track through which the mother can connect and 'know' (K) the infant thus leading to their own mental growth.

Mental growth, however, is limited by mutual dependence within a two-person system. The mother, for instance, may express an anxious need to care for her child fuelled by a fear that others' thoughts will impinge on her infant in a destructive way. She protects him by communicating an over-concerned attitude. In return, the child maintains a line of non-verbal communication that only his mother can understand and translate. Although this configuration may serve a protective developmental function, curiosity about the other's mind is limited to attention paid to projected contents and their preverbal nature. Other internal objects or thoughts that allow two minds to connect through imaginative exploration and mature verbal communication are not available in the symbiotic mode. This creates 'blind spots' in the analytic field which the symbiotic couple work together to avoid. This is similar to what Baranger *et al.* (1983) call a 'bastion', a blind spot that arises 'out of complicity between the two protagonists to protect an attachment which must not be uncovered' (p.2).

The analyst or therapist in the throes of a symbiotic transference is to some degree submerged in a folie à deux situation where he experiences some pressure to fulfil the 'role' of the symbiotic object. With this, reverie appears restricted or contrived and often the therapist finds it difficult to think. I think of this form of symbiotic relating as being an inevitable part of the analytic process where the analyst partially enacts particular roles that personify aspects of unconscious phantasy that can then become material for future analytic work. Whether this becomes an entrenched and pathological part of interaction depends on the analytic couple's ability to also begin to use a more commensal mode of relating. We shall return to this shortly.

I understand symbiotic links between objects to be dominated by L or H emotional links which keep the development of genuine thought restricted. Although a sense of curiosity and Knowing (K) is often present, it is only present so long as it serves to uphold the 'knowledge' of the symbiotic union. As Grotstein (1983a) puts it, referring to the L-link, 'L can represent love and need but also the desire to remain unborn' (p.376).

Similar points can be made about the H-link. Symbiosis is expressed in the need to hold on to the belief, for instance, that 'my mother hates me' when it is used to avoid knowing about my own hate or aggression towards my mother. In this configuration, hate functions to link objects and is not aimed at destruction of the object. Here, K is only engaged in so far as it reinforces or reconfirms thoughts about my mother hating me. Any other thoughts are experienced as dangerous 'third objects' that threaten the symbiosis. It appears to me that the symbiotic mode becomes entrenched when the desire to Hate or Love becomes so great that thought or development of this connection is felt to threaten the status quo. It is felt to be a pilfering of the L or H link that is kept like a special gift between two which is secretly communicated but not owned. Perhaps it could be said that Bion's use of K often appears to be superordinate to H and L. In this way he challenges our assumptions about emotional growth, particularly the idea that 'Love is enough' and is always beneficial.

The symbiotic container configuration is not restricted to cases where projective identification is the only link between objects. Similar to other configurations, it also has application beyond the intrapsychic level of interaction. An individual, for instance, may exist in a symbiotic relationship with a given 'containing' group or organization. The group depends on the individual to make up the group; individuals depend on the group for a sense of self or identity.

The symbiotic system thrives on mutual dependence and breaks down once the container or contained no longer depend on each other. For example, once a child is able to think about and put words to her distress instead of relying on projecting it into the mother, the symbiotic link can be relinquished. Likewise, if an individual exceeds the confines of a group's identity or purpose, his or her dependence on the group breaks down and is no longer needed to contain him. Due to mutual dependence, a third object is a threat to the symbiotic system. Depending on the level of abstraction, the third object may be represented by a third person, a separate group, a symbol, an interpretation, and so forth. In my understanding the third object can either be used to progress to commensal container–contained relations or it can threaten and collapse the symbiotic container configuration.

Sam

Sam, an 18-year-old woman, was referred to a therapist (a supervisee) to deal with complications following sexual abuse when she had been five years old. Early in the therapy Sam established a relationship with the therapist where she appeared to omnipotently shun him or regress to a point where she would withdraw and make muffled statements about her 'neediness'. This appeared to mirror aspects of her relationship with her mother where she was viewed as being her 'protective blanket'. During these regressive periods Sam would talk about some of the difficulties she was having with her friends, particularly an inability to trust others and an acute sense of 'jealousy'. Sam seldom made use of words that reflected feeling states in her relationships and relied on the therapist's intuitive suggestions about what she might have been feeling. In response to these kinds of intervention Sam expressed a great deal of gratitude. Although the therapist's intuitions appeared accurate, they never appeared to develop or give rise to the emergence of new narratives or thoughts in the session.

As therapy progressed, and in response to experiencing increased stress in her job, Sam expressed a need to come more frequently. Her rationale was an increasing need for the therapist to 'put things into words' for her so she could feel better. The therapist responded by increasing the sessions, but noticed how he felt a pressured sense of looking forward to the sessions and felt highly valued for his work by the patient. He also noted that for some reason, unknown to him at the time, he resisted taking this case to weekly supervision.

A while later the therapist decided to seek supervision because he was worried about the patient 'constantly being on his mind'. In our discussions it seemed clear that although the therapist was able to 'name' feelings related to jealousy and trust issues, these could never be developed. The therapist had felt unable to say anything about this pattern as he felt it would lead to a loss of trust that would damage the patient. Instead, Sam and the therapist appeared to lean back into a style of relating that fuelled a joint phantasy that my supervisee expressed as: 'as long as she talks and I listen, we're safe'. It appears that thinking about his 'protective role' and interpreting their 'symbiotic dance' had felt too threatening to contemplate.

Interestingly, it appears that Sam's relationship with her mother appeared to suffer once the frequency of sessions increased to three times a week. In response, her mother expressed a need to accompany her daughter to the therapy sessions. It seems likely that the increase in sessions was threatening the symbiotic relationship set up between mother and daughter (where the therapist became the 'third object'). We could suppose that this left the mother feeling empty and purposeless seeing as she had grown to depend on the 'protective blanket' role to establish some sense of self-worth. This case also highlights the idea that symbiotic containment can occur as a defensive manoeuvre to stave off threats of imagined intrusion from other objects or perspectives.

The core organizing phantasy behind the symbiotic mode is perhaps best represented by the phrase 'I complete you'. Here, the asymmetry that evokes emotional turmoil in container–contained configurations is partially resolved by seeing the object as an extension of the self. Henry Rey (1979) describes an extreme form of this configuration found in borderline patients with schizoid features where large portions of the individual's identity remain constantly dependent on the state of the object, its actions and intentions. In these cases people become receptacles for the individual's sense of identity. Because they continually 'live outside of themselves', so to speak, they appear on edge, dependent on experiences that do not feel like their own.

The parasitic mode

By 'parasitic' I mean to represent a relationship in which one depends on another to produce a third which is destructive to all three.

(Bion, 1970, p.95)

In the parasitic mode a third object is produced that is destructive to relating. Let us consider some of Bion's examples of the parasitic relational mode between objects. He takes as a model a man trying to communicate his irritation and in so doing is overwhelmed by emotion that renders his speech incoherent. The container here is the form of speech, the contained is the annoyance or emotion. If speech remains too coherent it will overwhelm the contained emotion. On the other hand, the opposite could happen and emotion could overwhelm speech leading to incoherence. In either case, a parasitic relationship between container and contained is expressed: the 'third object', incoherence or overcontrolled speech, leads to the destruction of all three elements. The 'third object' in the parasitic mode is the product of untransformed emotional turmoil that destroys or attacks the link between the container and contained. If, on the other hand, speech could adequately express the feeling state it can be inferred that the emotional state has been used to develop 'well-chosen speech' and the ability to do this, in turn, allows for the elaboration and development of an emotional state. This represents a move to the symbiotic mode. Note there is no 'third object' here. The reciprocal symbiotic cycle has no product beyond the container–contained. In the commensal mode, on the other hand, the 'third object' is the carrier of great creativity and insight.

A patient I was once seeing had great difficulty using the word 'mother'; she experienced saying the word as somehow awkward. To use her words, she experienced herself as 'angrily stumbling over the word'. She was able to articulate this most clearly when she was feeling more stable and gradually we were able to make sense of these feelings as representing an envious attack on what she called, 'feminist, independent attitudes'. More striking, however, was what seemed to happen when she was going through a period of feeling particularly fragmented. It was apparent to me that she no longer avoided the word 'mother', and the meaning established around it no longer seemed to matter. When I would raise this her response was very different, devoid of the usual affect or meaning that previously caused disturbance. It appears that when she was feeling more stable 'mother' had contained difficult but 'alive' emotion. But when she was feeling more unwell it seems that these difficulties led to her attacking the link between the container (the word) and contained (the meaning) and destroying its significance.

In more subtle forms, the 'third object' often functions in insidious ways to deaden or take away emotional links between objects. In this sense I see the parasitic mode as operating within what Bion called –H, –L and –K links that strip the relationship of emotion, making them feel meaningless, indifferent and lifeless.

Thabo

Thabo came to see me after a three-month period in a drug rehabilitation unit. He had a long history of drug dependence and relationship problems. When I took him on for therapy there appeared to be enough motivation, interest and relatedness to believe that he may benefit from psychoanalytic psychotherapy. We appeared to establish some meaningful contact early on in therapy when he started to try and understand his own 'selfish needs' and his withdrawal from his family. I was struck at this point by how easily I would find myself getting lost in his associations because he would seldom refer to people by name. People appeared to be 'nameless' impersonal figures making it difficult to grasp the discrete or refined qualities of his internal world. After a short period (he was coming twice a week), things appeared to change significantly as he began to fall into long periods of silence in sessions. He did not appear distressed and I struggled to understand or find any precipitating events or reasons (conscious or unconscious) for his withdrawal.

We would get into a situation where he would remain silent and passive and I would feel increasingly anxious to say something that would establish a connection with him. When I did talk it felt contrived, 'silly', too obvious or pointless. He would respond by somehow confirming the futility of my attempts, sometimes openly deriding them, but mostly simply dismissed them with a frown or dismissive gesture. He seemed to grow more distant. Rather than my attempts at establishing contact with him creating better rapport, they seemed to destroy the already tenuous contact, eventually 'forcing' a realization in him that I could not help him.

The above enactment represents a parasitic configuration where my attempts at containment and the establishment of meaningful contact serve to destroy existing rapport rather than build it. It seems that I could not release myself from producing a 'third object', interventions that felt contrived and 'silly', that contributed to the contact between us becoming 'nameless', lifeless and unhelpful.

Links of this kind are usually made through pathological projective identifications where parts of the self are split off with greater violence and omnipotence. In these cases the object (container or contained) ceases to have any independence and therefore cannot defend against core organizing phantasies of envy (Rosenfeld, 1964). In the parasitic mode the creative union between container–contained and its asymmetrical qualities cannot be tolerated and the configuration is annexed so that real exchange between objects is compressed or denuded of meaning through destructive attacks against the container or the contained.

It is often the case that the patient is so imprisoned by envy that they cannot tolerate the analyst's ability to think their own thoughts and so attack the analyst's containing mind by attacking the way he goes about his work. Typical countertransference states range from a sense of analytic paralysis and dread due to constant attacks from the patient, to chronic states of boredom where the therapist struggles to gather any meaningful links between aspects of the material or between himself and the patient.

The commensal mode

By 'commensal' I mean a relationship in which two objects share a third to the advantage of all three.

(Bion, 1970, p.95)

The quote above can be applied directly to the analytic setting where therapist and patient give rise to a third object to the benefit of all three. This is the mode of relating through which optimal growth can be achieved. In my understanding, the third object most readily represents the symbolic products of two minds relating. The commensal mode represents a configuration that the analyst strives towards in using his containing function to eventually arrive at interpretations (third objects) that benefit both analyst and patient in expanding the analytic field. At the sub-symbolic level of experience there also appears to be a 'return' to the proto-container, elemental forms of connectivity that are always in the background but interrupted by demands from the object (for projection and introjection). In both cases, the emergence of symbolic meaning and the 'return' of the proto-container, a third object, sets up new 'nesting' containers for the analytic couple. We shall return to this shortly.

Using the same example of the container–contained involving the relationship between speech and emotion, Bion asks us to imagine that such an event took place in a culture where the form of speech and what is expressed benefit from the background influence of culture and context. Here, the containing relationship expands to include a third object that can become a common reference point.

Britton's (1989) and Segal's (1991) understanding of the container can be understood as container–contained relations in the commensal mode. In their view, a good relationship between container and contained gives rise to a third object and leads to realizations of the father in the Oedipal triangle. In their view, this puts a 'seal' or limit on the child's internal world:

The acknowledgement by the child of the parent's relationship with
each other unites his psychic world, limiting it to one world shared with
two parents, in which different object relationships can exist.

(Britton, 1989, p.86)

Through such realizations a 'triangular space' (Britton, 1989, p.86) is
created that allows the mother and infant (a two-person system) exposure
to the creative influences of a third. The 'father' might be understood to be
symbolic of any third object or influence. Indeed, in the commensal mode it
is the formation of symbols themselves that act as a 'third object'.

Although the commensal mode is synonymous with growth, the realization that the containing mind is also connected and influenced by other
minds or objects brings its own set of anxieties similar to the difficulties
Klein (1935) referred to in working though depressive anxieties. Here
relating is organized around fear of losing the love object. Once projective
identifications have been 'withdrawn' and greater verbal ability achieved,
the patient grows more aware and anxious about damage caused or the
fallibility of the containing object.

The commensal mode begins to emerge when 'the fit' between container–
contained is loosened and there is room to acknowledge the space or
absence between objects as meaningful and generative. With the attention
of the container–contained configuration turned towards a third object the
asymmetrical nature of the configuration shifts somewhat from what I call
vertical asymmetry to horizontal asymmetry. In the symbiotic mode the
asymmetrical division is between mother–infant, vertical. However, in the
commensal mode they turn away from each other allowing asymmetrical
relations to shift towards the emergence of a third object. Put another way,
the container or contained is no longer 'lodged' in either the patient or
analyst's mind in reciprocal interaction, but is felt to be shared, giving rise
to new meaning, new ways of experiencing. In this mode, symbols and their
links to cultural understandings, social groups, interpretations, the proto-
container, or internal objects, contain, or are contained, by the analytic
couple as they collaborate in arriving at a dialogical understanding of the
experience being generated. This is similar to Lafarge's (2000) idea of
mutual containment.

Although this leads to the development of a more mutual space, a space
where two minds come together to contain unassimilated experience, I am
not suggesting that the relationship between analyst and patient is symmetrical in this mode. The idea of perfect symmetry that represents the
absolute unity of experience exists only in fantasy and belongs to what I call
the pseudo-containing mode. Pseudo-containing occurs when the reality of
difference, separateness and the opaque nature of an other's mind is
obscured by defensive strategies that attempt to resist entering the container.

There always exist asymmetries between analyst and patient that fit the abstraction of container–contained. This constantly occurs in the way analyst and patient 'interpenetrate' (Schafer, 2000) each other's internal worlds through mutual processes of projective and introjective identifications in order to understand the other. But the creation of a third object sets in motion a nesting process where the analyst and patient can either be contained by the 'third object' or contain it. This leads to the expansion of psychic dimensionality and psychic space. Symbols now become containers of meaning. In the commensal mode asymmetrical relationships are respected but partially resolved by the creation of a third object. This eventually leads to the analyst and patient collaboratively exploring an array of symbolic communications which at one point they contain and at another are being contained by.

Edward

Edward, a 33-year-old lawyer, came to see me because he feared becoming an alcoholic. He grew up in a working-class family with an alcoholic father who admired his son's abilities at school. With the birth of a younger brother, when Edward was 16 months old, his mother left the family home apparently depressed and not able to cope with two babies. Edward and his brother were raised by a loving aunt and he could do no wrong in his father's eyes.

Edward often began his sessions by making reference to the incompetence of others, ending in statements about his anger at 'the stupidity of others'. These observations were delivered to me like definitive statements which I would find it difficult to 'disagree' with. They were also delivered with such emotional force that it was difficult to think, leaving me feeling like a passive bystander.

In a session after a holiday break, Edward began by expressing his anger with me for not being able to help him more. I responded with an open question about what he felt he needed help with. He replied by telling me about a trip to a foreign city where he was aware of feeling angry towards his travelling colleagues because they always depended on his direction and could not find their way around the city or choose a restaurant for themselves. He also went on to tell me about a 'stupid' builder who he had recently had a fight with because he made a careless decision. In response, I interpreted that their 'careless decisions' or stupidity seemed linked to other's vulnerabilities. I said that I thought he experienced me as 'lost', vulnerable and unable to make up my own mind, perhaps even stupid in the way he sometimes experienced others. My interpretation left him feeling angry. I wondered why and said that I thought that perhaps it reflected how he related to his own vulnerability. He looked uncomfortable and began to laugh in a way that left me feeling that I'd said something terribly wrong.

The session moved on after that as if nothing had happened. In the next session Edward reported a short dream: *He was arguing with a waiter who had got his food order wrong. The manager stood to one side and was trying to say something but neither the waiter nor Edward heard him.* The dream elements seemed to be a clear reference to what had happened in our session two days previously where his show of omnipotent destructiveness served to keep any form of vulnerability or 'stupidity' split off and projected into me with no tolerance for a curious 'third' mind. I did not attempt to directly interpret these elements of the dream. Instead I simply expressed curiosity about the scene and the surface content of the dream. I wondered about how the characters felt in the dream. He responded by telling me about how he felt like a tyrant who wanted things done right, he wanted 'perfect unspoiled food'. I said that it seemed as though it was impossible to get help from the manager who seemed unheard because the Edward character in the dream needed to get this directly from the waiter. Edward did not respond directly but mentioned that he noticed how anxious he became when entering restaurants. I expressed interest in this and wondered if this may be linked to a worry about not getting 'perfect unspoilt food'. He told me that he often felt like he wanted to order everyone else's food for them and was never really interested in his own. It irritated him that they never knew what to choose, he also always wanted to know what others were choosing. I said I could understand how he may feel that his evening would be spoilt if others were not happy with their food, especially if he had suggested it. I continued, saying that I was interested in the way we had been talking about food and I felt as though he experienced me as not serving perfect food and this frustrated and worried him about what I was saying to him and what it would do to him. He agreed and told me about how his mother was a perfect cook but was never around to cook for him. He also felt that his girlfriend was not a good cook, but he noticed that he felt more able to have her visit his house for dinner.

In the above example Edward and I relate in the symbiotic mode where very little can be put into words or metabolized if it challenges the need to split off and project 'stupid' parts of himself into me. My attempts at interpreting this directly led to an intensification of this dynamic but his dream begins to introduce a 'third object' into the analytic space. Instead of interpreting the many possible meanings (its transference references, destructiveness, envy, themes related to Oedipal rivalry) that it may represent, we begin to express a 'dialogical curiosity' about how feeling and thought are expressed around the symbol of food. Through this process we arrive at 'approximate meanings' that work as ways of thinking about vulnerability and omnipotence. This appears to make these emotionally taxing issues more digestible and he is eventually able to entertain how their meaning may have more profound relevance to the analytic setting. In this way the container–contained configuration shifts from an interaction where unassimilated material is 'juggled' between analyst and patient, to a situation where the symbols, jointly constructed narratives and interpretations, become containing or contained 'third objects'. Symbolic references to food contain and give meaning to the transference (in a way that could not be done directly), and in turn we are able, through a shift in our interaction, to contain the symbol in our minds.

Although projective and introjective identification continue in the commensal mode, the main containers are symbols that can be shared and whose meaning constantly shifts (Billow, 2003). If the commensal mode is dominant, the analyst feels less immersed in the patient's projective identifications and finds it easier to engage in states of reverie and suspend dogmatic thinking or enactments. For Bion (1962b), the 'medium in a commensal relationship of ♂ and ♀ is tolerated doubt' (p.92). Here, fragments of meaning exist in states similar to the paranoid-schizoid position but they lack a sense of persecution as they await a sense of coherence that is not omnipotently imposed. Although meaning is generated through the use of symbolic communication, mature adaptive forms of communication, commensal relating has its own set of 'breakdown products'. It is common that symbolic objects, communications, metaphors used in therapeutic dialogue appear to lose their meaning when overused. They become saturated and have little emotional impact. It seems possible here to talk about 'dead symbols' in the same way that we speak of dead metaphors that lose their meaning through overuse. In the context of the container I would understand this to occur where the link between proto-containing experience and continuous commerce between container–contained is disrupted. If this occurs, the nuances of symbolic communications, always changing in some way, cease to evolve with the changing emotional context that is founded on proto-containing experiences and emotional links (H, L and K) between therapist and patient.

The commensal mode is usually signified by a degree of freedom in thinking-along-with-the-patient and there is an expansive opening up of creative contact and curiosity. It is a sense of being able to 'fall back' on the interaction in a way that is often described as a feeling of being 'lost in conversation'. Through this process feelings ranging from deep sorrow to joy are discovered in the emergence of meaning between therapist and patient.

The intuitive give and take of the commensal mode depends on the patient's or therapist's ability to relinquish control of their objects and tolerate the difference or separateness of the object. In my view this cannot take place if the analytic couple do not feel contained by the ebb and flow of non-conscious elements of interaction, what I call the proto-container. In other words, the proto-container provides the background feelings that sustain a sense of 'moving along' towards something.

Perhaps this explains why improvisation is a useful model to convey the essence of the commensal mode. I previously discussed some aspects of improvisation to explore the workings of the proto-container. Although always in the background, its elements seem to surface in a more tangible way in the commensal mode. In improvisation the musician relinquishes much of his ordered or logical thinking about what will emerge in his playing. In its place he attempts to allow himself to be influenced by the music at an intuitive level. We could say the musician loosens his hold on what he 'knows' about his instrument, his playing or others who play with him, and allows himself to be led and contained by the musical interaction itself. In psychotherapy, this is the mode where analyst and patient occupy a space in which they feel freer to see their shared experience as containing previously 'unthought' creative potential. I understand this to be the moments in analysis where Ferro's (2005a) notion of 'speaking before you think', instead of 'thinking before you speak', makes for a creative and productive analytic encounter.

The dominant emotional link in the commensal mode is Knowing (K) where a full range of emotions are subject to curiosity. Perhaps the symbols KH, KL best depict this where the emotional links that connect objects can also be seen as probes, or as ways of getting to know the object through hate and love. Inherent in this process is the capacity to tolerate the inevitable limits of 'knowing'. Bion is clear that ultimate truth is unknowable and this poses a core problem for the analytic couple who are dominated by omnipotent and omniscience phantasies that claim to know the ultimate reality of the object. Working through such phantasies goes hand in hand with the emergence of the depressive position and acknowledgement of the 'loss' of the capacity to possess and 'know' the object. Caper believes this is central to the therapeutic success of psychoanalytic therapies:

> The therapeutic effect of psychoanalysis is partly based on the observation that if omnipotent or concrete phantasies can be converted into ordinary (i.e., non-concrete and non-omnipotent) wishes or phantasies, their impact in the mind becomes far less important. This conversion is no easy task; the phantasies in question satisfy some exciting, instinct-laden wish, or relieve some important anxiety, which means that the support that reality fails to provide for them is compensated for by the charge of excitement they engender, or by the relief from anxiety that they can provide.
>
> (Caper, 1999, p.97)

If this is achieved, analyst and patient work together in the commensal mode to approach O (ultimate unknowable reality) in order to transform this experience into something knowable and beneficial to psychic growth. In my view this relies as much on finding a way to 'face reality' as it does on the analytic couple's creative abilities. Creativity, for Grotstein (2000), is about being able to secure part of one's self in realistically orientated thought while allowing another part to explore unarticulated experiences.

The autistic mode

No idea can penetrate that authority, no idea can penetrate that shell formed around the personality, the group or community. Nothing short of a revolution, nothing short of violence, will crack the shell and release the people within it. That is why I sometimes say that an institute is dead . . . the shell can be so thick that they cannot develop inside it.

(Bion, 2005b, p.11)

The autistic mode occurs when commerce between container–contained is resisted or cannot occur because the psyche, or some area of mind, lacks the capacity. This mode of relating may operate at different levels of psychic maturity but the underlying unconscious phantasies are similar: internal space or conceptions of the inside of the object, its three-dimensional qualities, are shut down, deadened or evaded. In its place objects are used as psychic surfaces to hold the self together. Because the interior of the object is evaded, phantasies that fuel projective identifications as a means of communication or evacuation are not triggered. Communicative projective identification relies on projection into internal space. In the autistic mode ideas or conceptions of internal space exacerbate anxiety and cause further fragmentation. A patient of mine once described this experience as feeling like 'a sense of emptying myself into nowhere'.

Rather than use phantasies related to projective identification, autistic modes adopt an anti-relational stance in so far as sensations, thoughts and emotions are used as surfaces to block relating. Container–contained interaction is obscured or restricted by a narrow-mindedness that focuses on the surface of the object as a means of obtaining some form of cohesiveness. The result has a deadening effect on psychic experience as objects are treated like inanimate surfaces to wall off experiencing.

If we return to Bion's example of container–contained relations between speech or words and emotion (p. 143), it is a case of there being no words to contain the emotion and no emotion to contain the words. The relationship between word and emotion is severed and, in its place, are meaningless objects that block experience. We can generate experiences that momentarily approximate the autistic mode by continuously repeating a word until there is a sense that it loses its meaning and simply becomes 'a thing', a meaningless object.

Bion (1962b) is clear that the fabric which animates container–contained relations is emotion. Whether Love (L), Hate (H) or Knowing (K), as long as there are linking emotions, commerce between container–contained can be established. In Bion's words: 'When disjoined or denuded of emotion they [container and contained objects] diminish in vitality, that is, approximate to inanimate objects' (1962b, p.90). This describes the status of the container–contained configuration in the autistic mode. It appears that this is a particular version of –K, –H, and –L where proto-experiences cease to be developed and are transformed into two-dimensional objects which lack their own discrete qualities.

Bick (1968, 1986), followed by a number of significant contributions (Anzieu, 1993; Meltzer, 1975a; Mitrani, 1992, 1998; Ogden, 1992; Tustin, 1986, 1990), has considerably advanced our understanding of this primitive form of generating experience. She thought that the inability to introject a good containing object retards the development of a multidimensional internal space. Instead, the infant relates to objects as two-dimensional forms, as surfaces to hold the self together, what she called 'second skin' formations. In the autistic mode omnipotent phantasies that focus on the 'edge' of the object dominate. Put another way, there is no container–contained commerce, only elements that cling together to form a primitive and precarious form of containment surface. This is made possible by a primitive form of identification called adhesive identification. Bick (1986) and Meltzer (1975a) thought that this form of relating was driven by phantasies of sticking to an object to gain coherence rather than relying on projecting into its interior. I find Tustin's (1986, 1990) work in this area useful in understanding how this mode of relating (there is still relating to a part-object) can be engaged through the auto-generation of sensual experience to generate boundaries and a sense of coherence. For instance, the sound of the voice, as opposed to the meaning found in words, is clung to as a defining boundary in autistic relating.

These attempts at 'self-containing' can be represented at different levels of psychic experience. All have in common reliance on the 'sensory surface' of the object and the need to block entry into a containing 'thinking' object, whether psychical or external. In Chapter 11 I consider how the autistic mode contributes to the generation of agoraphobic experience by turning dream-thoughts and internal experience into entrapping inanimate objects. In other neurotic states, autistic states can be summoned as ways of blocking experiencing. For instance, as mentioned earlier, obsessive patients often use routine and ritual to create boundaries to their experience as a means of blocking encounters with their own internal world (Tustin, 1986). In more extreme forms we find these states in psychogenic autism where the entire personality is dominated by inanimate relating (Meltzer, 1974; Tustin, 1972).

In the autistic mode phantasies revolve around confirmations that the self, albeit in a very rudimentary form, actually exists. In the same way that the rudiments of internal objects (alpha-elements) are used as surfaces to define the self, proto-containing capacities are also reduced to a similar function. Here, ephemeral, rhythmic to-and-fro interchanges are experienced as threatening tugs away from a more static but secure boundary. Unable to allow proto-containing capacities to have a life of their own between objects, patients using the autistic mode tend to nullify these background containing experiences by adopting repetitive and perseverative strategies that reduce interaction to a near-sensory surface. This is most readily observed in the 'stiffness' and awkwardness of interactive exchanges with autistic and Asperger's patients. In milder forms, proto-containing capacities are reduced to near-physical objects through the constant use of repetition (statements, words and gestures) so they begin to approximate the existence of a dead but defining presence. The process at work here appears to be a particular version of what Green (2000) calls the 'objectalizing function'[2] where the psyche generates its own objects by turning psychic functions, processes, activities into objects in their own right. In the case of what I have called proto-containing capacities, it is non-conscious processes of interaction themselves that are transformed into dead but useful objects.

Often the autistic mode makes its presence known to us in transitory and adaptive forms in therapeutic interaction. These moments occur when there is a need to regulate the self by withdrawing from relating and seeking more primitive ways of holding the self together. I notice with one patient of mine, for instance, how he enters these states when he cuts off eye contact with me for a while and fixes his gaze on the lamp to his left until he is ready to resume contact. Foot and finger tapping, the repetitive rubbing of surfaces, or experiences of hearing one's own verbal communications or interpretations as disembodied noise, are all examples of the autistic mode. Another patient of mine closes her eyes for long periods of time when she can no longer bear the shame that she fears I may see when she talks about herself. It appears that once she breaks off contact a sensory boundary is generated between us through her constant repetitive eye movements while her eyes are closed. Through this process she down-regulates the intensity of contact in a way that allows her to carry on thinking with me. Preoccupation with the 'routine' of the session, the frame and its boundaries, can also be used as an autistic surface to prevent the emergence of new

---

2 Green uses the term 'de-objectizing function' to represent forces in the psyche that work to deconstruct internal objects. It could be argued that the autistic mode functions in this way. However, I emphasize the 'creative' function here, in the sense that elemental experience is used to build 'objects' to protect the self.

experience. These apparently neurotic anxieties (being on time, obsessive interest in the beginnings and ends of sessions, preoccupation with payment, ritualized ways of starting sessions, and so forth) often have an autistic edge to them that block the processing of experience that is jointly constructed as the session unfolds.

There are important observations about the use of interpretation here. In my experience interpretations aimed at drawing the patient's attention to these moments of withdrawal from mental contact in the here-and-now disrupt the patient's ability to regulate his or her emotional life. The experience is one of being robbed of one's own capacity to contain and unbalances the natural rhythm of contact between patient and therapist. This is not to say that encouraging reflection on the autistic mode is not useful after the fact, or when a more robust mental connection has been re-established. When it is interpreted it is best done so in a way that emphasizes the 'positive' inchoate relational aspects of this mode: that it represents the 'best possible way of maintaining contact' with the therapist. This creates an open permissiveness to this level of contact that is easily shut down if the therapist adopts an interpretive attitude that attempts to 'remove' its defensive qualities or ascribe too much meaning to it. In my view, noting its importance in maintaining a basic connection to the object establishes a 'common sense' (Bion, 1963) understanding that has the effect of promoting a benevolent interest in this form of relating that can later accrue symbolic meaning (in the commensal mode). For instance, the patient I mentioned earlier, who shuts her eyes to self-regulate, began to talk about her 'dead connection' with me that kept me 'out, but at arm's length'. Through this our way of being together could be symbolized, helping her better contain moments of shame as they occurred and allowing her to risk greater eye contact with me during these states.

Pseudo-containing modes

Unlike autistic modes of relating where a lack of dimensionality prevents commerce between the container and the contained, pseudo-containing modes circumvent the emotional turmoil inherent in container–contained relations. They do so by mimicking the configuration's existence and perverting its role. In this mode uncontained, unmetabolized experience that has not been integrated into the self appears with an assured and righteous sense of clarity.

Although uncontained mental states are usually thought to be attached to violent or chaotic emotion (the image of emotional overload), overly reasoned calculated forms of thought are also linked to 'uncontained' experience in the sense that such aspects of the self resist containment and emotional growth. While the analyst's containing function works towards an atmosphere of curiosity about experiencing the unknown in the commensal mode, the rigid and apparently well-reasoned patient subtly resists entering a containing relationship and cannot feel the benefits of being held in mind by an other. Bion thought that because we cannot 'know' ultimate reality, all thinking to some degree is a 'lie' because it can only *represent* reality. The degree to which thought approximates a sense of 'truth', however, depends on how much we allow ourselves to be transformed by raw experience. In the pseudo-containing mode 'the contained' is not derived from raw experience that seeks transformation, but is generated by mimicking the unconsciously perceived intentions, needs or functions of the other object. The result is a preponderance of 'premature intellection and story making' (Meltzer, 1992, p.58) that ceases to allow alpha-elements, genuine components of thought, to emerge so that the contained can enter the container.

Zama

Zama is a 33-year-old manager of a personal relations company. She was referred to me because she had 'burnt out' and could no longer bring herself to go to work. She had managed the company very successfully for three years and she quickly gave me a sense that she had invested a great deal in her job. She kept many friends but said little about them aside from being perceived by them as always being 'bright-eyed and on top of things'. Zama had had one six-month relationship with a man two years previously. She had no sense of why the relationship might have ended aside from surmising that he probably no longer found her attractive.

Zama had grown up in a small country town with both her parents. She painted a picture of an ideal childhood in the country spending a great deal of time with her parents. However, in time, a different idea of the family began to emerge. Her mother had been very busy during her childhood years managing the neighbour's farm and Zama started to recall spending long periods of time with her nanny at the age of eight. Her mother had once told her that she had essentially been raised by her nanny, a statement that could not be pursued by Zama and there was a sense that this could not be believed. Her father spent long periods away from home due to work and Zama felt this had led to a great deal of tension between her parents.

For the better part of the first eight months of once-a-week psycho-therapy, Zama talked non-stop. It was often difficult to follow much of what she was trying to convey. At the end of each session she would thank me profusely for helping her. One general theme to her associations that did emerge appeared to be about solving problems at work. It appeared that she went about this in a particular way: she would take young trainees 'under her wing' (she often called them her 'babies') and become obsessed with their performance. When mistakes were made, she would 'smooth things over' by taking on the work herself to ensure that her trainees did not get distressed. Although she was always very animated and somewhat hurried during her sessions, I was struck by how difficult it was for me to grasp a sense of what she might be feeling. Attempts at enquiry only yielded responses like 'much, much better thank you', or 'simply fine'. If I tried to ask for clarification in the hope that she would engage more with what she was feeling she would look upset with me, intimate that I was questioning her integrity, and then attempt to name feelings that she did not appear to feel. We seemed to relate to each other as if we were trying to draw the right feeling out of a box and she would constantly search for signs in my response that led her to believe she had hit the jackpot. Attempts to discuss this transference dynamic led to a great deal of confusion between us. I could not make myself clear and Zama could not connect with what I was saying about the difference between 'thinking about feelings' and being able to feel. I recall having the sense that it was almost as if we were communicating in different languages. Zama responded to this confusion by showing excessive concern for how I was feeling. When I think about it now, it seemed to occur in response to her feeling that I had lost my way and her expressions of concern appeared to be attempts at helping me find my way back.

While I listened I tried to think about some of the dynamic themes among her verbiage: her identification with an ideal maternal object, rescue phantasies, fears of disapproving parental objects, denial of aggression or affect avoidance, the presentation in the transference as being omnipotently resourceful and my countertransference of feeling that her utterances felt like made-up stories. I found it difficult to listen to her and I was aware of a sense of isolation while I tried to make some sense of what she was saying. This seemed to lead to a tendency towards over-thinking things and fretting about diagnosing the underlying organizing theme. I persisted in trying to interpret some of these dynamic themes and underlying feelings. For instance, I put it to her that I thought she felt like she had to rush through things in a motherly way so she could take care of any loose ends in the session because she feared that I would disapprove of any 'failings'. She responded to such interpretations with quick agreement but could not engage with their substance. With these interventions seeming not to advance deeper engagement, I tried to engage her by making simple observations, unsaturated interpretations, about some of the things she was saying, expressing curiosity about the phrases she used. For example, I interpreted how important it was for her to make sure that she responded to me in an approving way and wondered what she made of that. In response to these invitations for discussion and elaboration she would look confused and affronted and would take my comments as commands that she would immediately try and accommodate. In the above example she responded, 'You mean I shouldn't be approving. Yes, I can do that', and then went on to intellectualize about possibilities for changing her behaviour. My experience here was of Zama constantly finding strategies to take over the analytic session so that she became both patient and therapist.

Entrenched pseudo-containing strategies often form part of False Self pathology (Winnicott, 1965). Here, the patient abandons her own needs and desires (her True Self) and takes on the maternal object's needs as her own so as to accommodate to them and preserve a 'good' attachment. Zama seems to do this at all costs and cannot engage with me as a real thinking or containing object. Because the True Self cannot be developed, such patients often battle with a chronic sense of boredom and emptiness. Interpretations are quickly accepted and a way is found of mimicking the perceived intention of the interpretation. Because the pseudo-containing mode short-circuits the process of feeling held in an other's mind, this configuration often leaves patients with no sense of the processes inherent in dealing with unassimilated thoughts and feelings. With Zama, for instance, there was little indication in the initial part of her treatment that she could engage with the idea that her thoughts, or mine, could be explored or developed. Rather, she set about accumulating what she perceived to be the 'right' answers.

The annexing of the container is a common feature of pseudo-containing where patients may often display excessive concern for their objects. Irma Brenman Pick (1995) has proposed that in such situations there is a manic or pretentious 'takeover' of the breast function to overcompensate and triumph over experiences of deprivation and consequent hate. This I take to be consistent with a manic 'takeover' of the container. The dynamic is such that the 'infant "becomes" the breast and shows behaviour which is in part a fake of a very concerned mother' (p.257). In the transference this can often be observed in the patient's non-verbal behaviour where he or she begins to mimic the therapist's gestures, posture, tone of voice and his manner of thinking in a way that is not congruent with processes involved in internalizing and identifying with the therapist as a benevolent supportive object.

Pseudo-containing modes often occur in a transient form in the early phases of the therapeutic process. The patient anxiously monitors the receptivity of the therapist to his projections and reacts to ruptures in analytic contact by apparently working through feelings and thoughts that are still in transit. Extreme forms of this may be found in situations where there is a flight to health. In my experience adolescents typically make use of pseudo-containing modes which make them particularly inaccessible at times. The difficult transition from childhood to adulthood leads to an intensification of omnipotent phantasy and omniscience that involves an attempt to triumph over dependency conflicts. They do so by precociously appropriating the 'adult' container function so as to exclude all other perspectives and meanings. The idea of being 'right' and the adherence to rigid ideas of causality (as seen in the way Zama interacts) is most consistent with –K (Meltzer, 1986). Here any potential meaning garnered from other minds is truncated by narcissistic phantasies. The phrase 'I am you, so I don't need you' appears to approximate these kinds of phantasies.

A similar outcome occurs when the therapist is drawn into adopting the pseudo-containing mode. Here, the container function is nullified and the therapist fails to respond to the patient's need to omnipotently identify with the therapist's role. This serves to obscure the moment-to-moment inter-action between analyst and patient where there are constant reminders of separateness and difference between the container and the contained. Segal (1991) suggests that awareness of difference is usually obliterated by the patient's voracious envy which precludes being dependent on a containing object. The consequent effect, however, excludes the patient from more realistic experiences of being contained or held in the mind of an other. Without there being any tolerance for difference between the container and contained, the ability to make use of a real containing object disappears in the mind of such patients (Segal, 1991). This could possibly explain why such patients may appear to be going along reasonably well in their analysis, appearing to 'heal themselves' with little intervention from the analyst or therapist. But this profile is interrupted by sudden deteriorations that appear to come from nowhere. It is a case of holding the self together but this becomes untenable after a period. Because difference between the container–contained cannot be tolerated, the patient feels trapped in a world where a separate containing mind cannot be used.

The confabulated commerce between container–contained referred to here is similar to what Bateman and Fonagy (2004) call pseudo-mentalizing where the relationship between physical reality and psychical reality is tenuous. In its place 'thinking' mimics creative and imaginative thought. Thoughts and feelings are often extended beyond a particular context and the apparent complexity of thought appears to be based on little evidence in terms of the patient's own behaviours and relationships. As they point out, directly challenging pseudo-mentalization can lead to extreme reactions because it gives rise to a terrifying sense that underlying their attempts to think is a sense of nothingness.

After some time it was clear that Zama's pseudo-containing strategies were beginning to break down. She would go through periods of immense emotional turmoil linked to a terrifying sense that, in her words, 'nothing is linked and everything feels meaningless'. After these intense but brief periods where she would not go to work and took to isolating herself, she appeared to resume where she left off, making little reference to these bouts of internal trauma. Although basic interpretative strategies still were not experienced as helpful, I began to find it useful to simply try and tell her what was on my mind while she spoke. In a way I seemed to be communicating at a distance, letting her know what was on my mind with no reference to hers. It seems that she found these kind of interventions less critical and more about a 'possible story' that she could or could not use. On reflection, I think this stance had the effect of acknowledging the immense underlying persecutory experience Zama was struggling with. Through focusing on my mind, rather than hers, I was able to create a line of communication that imparted some meaning about her own destructiveness in manufacturing a 'make-believe world' that excluded the real needs of her objects.

My interventions in the above case appear to be consistent with what Brenman Pick (1995) terms a 'two-handed' approach that connects with the patient's vulnerability while working with the destructive ways they attempt to deprive their objects. In essence, I seemed to happen upon a way of working with Zama that served to regulate emotional contact between us by inviting her into my thinking first, without linking it to her dynamics. This seemed to generate a sense of curiosity for her and perhaps modelled for her the process of making mental connections between thoughts and feelings. There has to be a caveat here regarding the analyst being drawn into his own narcissistic ramblings that do not serve the process in any way. I would say that the difference lies in the analyst's ability to focus on the ways in which he feels transformed or changed by the object. The curiosity generated by such interventions appears linked to a sense that the patient begins to observe their impact on 'real' objects in a way that is tempered and meaningful. Previously we explored some aspects of these interventions in terms of the analyst's passion (Chapter 5).

Countertransference states linked to pseudo-containing are usually associated with thoughts and feelings that the patient is playing out a role that has little of the intended emotional impact. At times the therapist is struck by feelings of simply 'going through the motions'. Alternatively the analyst or therapist has a sense of occupying the role of critic in an audience while a tightly scripted performance unfolds. A sense of reality is denied due to the lack of connectedness between elements of apparently meaningful content. When the therapist does experience affect it is often linked to a sense of deep sadness about not being able to reach the patient. At times the therapist may also experience emotions contrary or inappropriate to the content of the patient's thoughts and associations. Apparently sad or distressing content evokes a sense of joy, and apparent happiness can evoke immense sadness in the therapist. This tends to occur when the therapist feels immersed in the dramatic nature of the patient's presentation. It seems that these states mirror the perverse nature of this configuration where real emotional content does not undergo transformation but is replaced by a pseudo-containing relationship that generates its own affects to defend against real psychic experience. The contrived way in which the patient presents affect in the pseudo-containing mode often appears to mock the difficulties and struggles that have to be undertaken if emotion is to be made meaningful.

As mentioned earlier, the therapist is easily drawn into pseudo-containing modes when the ability to think as a separate object is given up and more realistic conceptions of the container function disappear. In its place the therapist struggles to engage the patient and continues to reinforce the sense that external objects are unhelpful to the patient. Alternatively, the therapist may adopt the opposite approach and react to the manic 'takeover' of the container by attempting to 'rescue' the patient. Here, the therapist stamps his authority on knowing what is 'right' for the patient and subtly attacks the patient's overly assured attempts to look after herself. In short, the therapist engages in a struggle to win the container back.

In Chapter 9 I explore *The Matrix* movies as an illustration of the pseudo-containing mode where objects devoid of humanity ('Machines' in *The Matrix*) mimic the human qualities of being able to hold things in mind. It is a situation where genuine engagement with experience is circumvented by elevating proto-containing capacities and sensory experiences to the realm of thoughts or mental activity, a process that amounts to mimicking psychic processes. Here, what appears to be reasoned and resolved mature thinking is actually beta-mentality: thoughts that convey very little understanding or meaning and have more in common with the qualities of physical objects then those of mutable thoughts.

Chapter 8

Idealizing the container

Containing, as Sorensen (1995) emphasizes, is an active process that requires an integration of the processes of observation, clarification and emotional resonance. It enables the therapist to dwell in the particular and 'maintain a relationship to the object in the face of the pain of the unknown' (p.7). As proposed in Chapter 3, this involves the therapist adopting a particular mental state that attempts to 'name' unassimilated experience and maintain a fragile mental connection with the patient. Aside from negotiating tensions between seeing himself as a 'proper object' and a 'dream object', this also depends on the therapist's ability to assimilate and integrate projected states using more mature defences (Ogden, 1986). To this end, as mentioned earlier, a fair amount has been written about the use of countertransference in this area, particularly the inevitable nature of partial enactments as a means of beginning to give meaning to previously uncontained mental states (e.g. Carpy, 1989; Feldman, 1992; Ginot, 2007; Mitrani, 2001; Searles, 1979; Steiner, 1993).

Previously I have made reference to how the idea of the container in clinical practice lends itself to misunderstanding. I have often observed how in general clinical discussions Bion's idea of the container function is taken as tantamount to the amelioration of anxiety or as an active effort to make the patient feel more secure. This is closer to Winnicott's (1965) idea of 'holding' as reviewed previously. The clinical focus here is on 'what the analyst must do' to add to his or her technique in order to assist the patient in 'containing' his or her emotions. A related problem appears to occur where, in therapist and patient, the container is invested with idealized promise that is always assumed and never explained (Caper, 1999). The container–contained, perhaps despite Bion's best efforts, often seems to take on a particular 'saturated' meaning that leads to further complications in the development or resolution of transference–countertranference dynamics. It often, in my opinion, leads to enactments that amount to transference cures, deceptive resolution of the patient's conflicts, or therapies that appear to be overly protracted. Based on my observations as a supervisor this often emerges due to misunderstanding the role of the container or it occurs as a strategic defence that works to avoid the emotional turmoil which is an inevitable part of psychic change. This tends to lock the therapeutic couple into a mode of engagement that is bent on assuaging, soothing, or alleviating symptoms. If we are led by Bion's notion that psychoanalysis aims to increase the capacity for suffering, and that all change is unavoidably catastrophic, then this view of the container limits its value.

In this chapter I want to explore possible reasons why we may be vulnerable to 'idealizing the container', particularly in our countertransference reactions to some patients. I present a case to demonstrate some of these points and illustrate the phenomenology of the enactment process. It may be that our own inclinations to help others can ironically contribute to this countertransference state. Mitrani's (2001) words in this regard are worth quoting:

> I wish to express my belief that many of us are drawn to the work of analysis, at least in part, by the desire to do some good. However, paradoxically, this may be the greatest obstacle to actually doing 'good analytic work' and therefore the greatest barrier to truly helping the patient. If unbridled, it may prove to be the most obstructive 'desire' – in Bion's sense of the word – since our patients actually need to transform us, in the safety of the transference relationship, into the 'bad' object that does harm.
>
> (p.1102)

In addition to the above, it seems there is a network of factors at work that can quite easily induce a state in the therapist that I am calling 'idealizing the container'. My sense is that an overly schematic view of the container, an over-emphasis on maternal ideals and defences against 'mourning the container' greatly contribute to this countertransference state. I want to illustrate how the therapist's unconscious identifications with the idealized container engender a quixotic sense of 'being held eternally' and can easily generate in the patient's mind a luring and seductive promise of something that cannot be fulfilled. This mode of apparent benevolence is best understood as an enactment in the symbiotic mode.

Fatima

Fatima, a 27-year-old woman, was referred to me after a brief psychotic episode that appeared to be precipitated by a move away from her parents' home. During the first few months of twice-weekly therapy she was highly anxious and tearful and was often difficult to follow. During this time she would mostly reflect on her sense of falling apart or 'falling off a cliff'. She also complained of feeling withdrawn and unable to connect with anyone. She had wanted to leave home and was angry that she needed to return to her depressed mother and difficult father.

When Fatima was able to be clearer about how she felt she described herself using an image of herself split in two: she stood on top of a cliff whilst a part of her hung off the cliff clutching at her ankles. She seemed to become increasingly distressed when encouraged to explore what this image might mean to her. She thought that the solution, in her words, was 'to amputate it', referring to the 'clutching' part of herself in the image. I began to think about this being an expression of needing to cut me off from interacting with her. My mind seemed to seize on to this image of 'cutting off' or amputating. I began to experience disturbing violent images that mostly involved decapitations or severed limbs, images I had never encountered before. I found myself thinking about the pain this might express related to what Fatima was going through. I was also aware of how often my thoughts would move to thinking about a previous patient who had once cut his arm seriously before attending his session. On reflection, I was clearly disturbed by these images as I listened to her.

In attempting to work with these images, I seemed to deliberately concentrate my interpretations on how damaged and needy the 'clutching' part of her was and how she had disowned it (projected it into me), secretly wanting others, or myself, to notice and care for it. My thoughts shifted to a clear sense that I was acting as a repository for this needy part of her. In a somewhat defensive manner, Fatima spent some time trying to understand my interpretations. She related the emergence of the 'needy' part of her self to her parents' neglect but seemed unable to use this insight in any meaningful way. I seemed to persist along these lines, often aware of thoughts of wanting to sooth her distress and 'carry' her through obvious difficulties she had in connecting with me. It was clear to me that Fatima displayed very little real interest in what I had to say but rather needed me to make reassuring, calming comments. Gradually our way of relating moved in this direction. I found myself reassuring her about her 'difficult parents' and assuring her that it would get better if she was able to talk more about it to me. Importantly, I chose not to raise an emerging tension between us as a point of discussion and exploration. Although my comments appeared contrived and my analytic attitude compromised, the tension between us dissipated and we seemed to be able to move forward. After approximately a year of psychotherapy there appeared to be considerable improvement in her behaviour. She was no longer constantly anxious or tearful and seemed to be able to engage in the analytic work.

Around this time my attention was drawn to observing how unusually soft-spoken I was with her. I uncharacteristically would catch myself talking in a near whisper, motivated it seemed by attempts to calm her. I was also aware of how difficult it had become to end each session. She would appear uncomfortable, sometimes reluctant to leave, which I responded to by feeling that our time together was inadequate and something else needed to be provided. I started to think about inviting her to more sessions as a way of addressing this concern; we had agreed on twice-a-week meetings. I also noticed that I had little access to my own thoughts or reverie when I sat with Fatima. Although, going through some of my notes, I seemed to have started to think about how I had been assuming a 'surrogate mother' role in the transference, my attention no longer appeared to be free-floating and her conversation or my comments never seemed to stimulate further thoughts or images.

Shortly after this Fatima began to complain about a sense of feeling stuck and unable to reach me. She said she felt much better but needed something more from therapy. She couldn't say much about this in relation to me, but spoke about her fantasy of needing a relationship where someone would always be continuously present for her. Her frustrations regarding therapy gradually escalated until eventually she was able to express this fantasy in the transference. Most of the time this took the form of her wondering if I would hold her. The meanings of these fantasies were explored in terms of her need for me to take over and hold the damaged 'cliff hanging' side of her so she did not have to bear its pain. But Fatima could not tolerate thinking about this with me and indicated many times that she was not interested in understanding this further. Instead, she began to put greater pressure on me to hold her, trying to convince me that holding would allow her to 'grow strong'. She began to voice a sense that coming to therapy felt like 'a tease'. I thought this accurately described the way I was feeling about the nature of our interaction at the time: a sense that she was being offered something that she couldn't have. Around this time she began arriving late for sessions, cancelled a number of appointments and related this directly to her believing that coming to psychotherapy felt like a 'tease'. She seemed to become more aimless, unmotivated and somewhat disorientated. In response, and out of concern, I found myself allowing her sessions to run over time. For many months this pattern repeated itself and I was unable to shift it.

Discussion

We could understand much of Fatima's behaviour as revolving around a repetition of her need to split off and project a damaged part of herself into me which was accompanied by an unconscious wish for an 'ideal container' (Britton, 1992a; Feldman, 1992). I understood Fatima's ongoing reference to a need for a merged relationship and her need to be held by me as being part of her search for this ideal. The change in the therapeutic frame, when tension escalated in therapy, also appeared to be a partial enactment along similar lines where she attempted to convince me of her incoherence and the need for me to contain parts of her outside the parameters of therapy. It seems that it was her persistent use of intractable projective identifications that left her feeling impoverished and passive.

My difficulties in working with Fatima appeared to greatly influence the emerging dynamics of this case. On reflection, I relate this to my not dealing with conscious and unconscious identifications with an idealized conception of my role as a container. The point I want to make is that my own rigid conceptions of literally being a container or receptacle for a needy part of her self unduly prolonged the therapeutic process and served to avoid confronting aggressive conflicts that initially appeared in my reverie (concerning violent images of amputation and so forth). In the initial stages of therapy my sense of introjecting 'needy' parts of her appeared to influence how I spoke and seemed to increase my desire to help her, contributing to various transgressions of the therapeutic frame as outlined. In essence, we could understand my motivations as moving towards actualizing her fantasy of ideal containment. In doing so, I was colluding with her need to disown a part of herself. I think Fatima accurately sensed that I was implicitly promising her something that could not actually be given. This was experienced by her as 'a tease', which added to the intensification of her need to be held by me. In this way we were both working to avoid real anxieties that needed to be subjected to analytic work.

My work in this case raises important considerations about what makes therapists particularly vulnerable to such forms of engagement. Clearly, partial enactments are an inevitable part of analytic engagement and I concur with those who see them as a crucial part of the therapeutic process whereby unassimilated unconscious material can be worked on in the present moment. I am referring here to typical transference–countertransference pressures that induce partial enactments that would include the contribution that the analyst's own conflicts may have on idealizing 'the container'. There are, however, more specific factors related to conceptualizations of the container that influence the way it is applied in the analytic setting. In my view these represent potential obstacles to using analytic containing. They include: reified conceptions of the container, overuse of maternal associations, and resistance to processes of mourning as an inherent part of analytic containment.

Reified conceptualizations of the container

This first concern has already been covered in previous chapters. It relates to the overly schematic use of Bion's model of projective identification where the object takes on a reified form somehow actually 'containing' what is being projected. As stated earlier, how 'containing' occurs remains relatively obscure in Bion's work, particularly in his earlier work. This has left his model of the container open to rather concrete assumptions that have more in common with physical phenomena and make less sense in understanding psychical occurrences. As a result it seems that clinical applications of the container model are often translated into rather concrete images that involve the thoughts of an ever-present vessel geared towards taking on what is projected into it. As Grotstein (1983a) has pointed out, the container image lends itself to the idea that the 'container-mind' acts like a rubber band, ever flexible, taking on more projections and expanding as a result.

Perhaps the idea of containing feelings or parts of the self 'inside something' appeals to the limitations of our 'three-dimensional' imaginations (see Matte-Blanco, 1988). The outcome is a seductive one: to be able to take into oneself unbearable feelings and 'digest' them for the patient. It may also be the case that part of this problem arises from Bion's idiosyncratic use of language whereby the term 'container' ordinarily conjures up images of a stabilizing, sturdy, protective vessel (Ogden, 2004b). There are moments in my work with Fatima where representations of these images seemed to clearly play a role.

Fatima (revisited)

In the first session after a two-week holiday break Fatima returned looking distressed and preoccupied about her studies and having to live at home. She looked tired and dishevelled and said that she had not been able to sleep for the last week. She also mentioned some suicidal thoughts. I noticed my anxiety levels rise in the session and was aware that I appeared to be asking a lot of questions about her situation. She started telling me about how difficult her father had been during the holidays. While listening I recall thinking about the holiday break, almost blaming the break for her mental state. As the session progressed, Fatima appeared to feel reassured by my trying to understand her distress. At some point to my surprise I started thinking about what I had been cooking the previous evening! The outcome had been delicious but I was thinking particularly about how I had had to separate egg yolks from their whites during the process. I thought about how my cooking had been influenced by my mother and how I often admired her ability to 'hold it together' during difficult times in our family. Although my dream-thoughts were fleeting and unintrusive, I was aware of feeling a degree of guilt about thinking about such pleasures in the face of Fatima's distress. Although I was unaware of their meaning at the time, the thought of 'holding things together' appeared to make superficial sense to me in expressing how, in part, I felt I needed to just hold things together till the end of the session.

When Fatima was talking to me about how desperate she was feeling, my reverie could be understood to express a kind of compromise between how much distress I could bear to listen to and a wish that I could literally contain her distress by 'holding things together'. Her expressing this difficulty was 'received' as a fantasized psychical form for me to hold on to. My reverie about cooking could be understood to represent the physical separation of objects that were linked to a pleasurable and admirable outcome. Implicit here is the sense that if containing is reduced to images in three-dimensional space, the projection of distress can literally be removed from the patient, colluding with unconscious phantasies that, in part, motivate projective identification.

The above example illustrates how reified conceptions of the container might be used as a transient defence elicited by intense anxiety states. This can occur, however, at a more fundamental level when these ideas are routinely employed due to misunderstanding what constitutes the therapist's containing function. A supervisee of mine once sought help with a borderline patient of hers primarily because the patient had begun to cut himself during sessions. She was worried about the patient but I was interested in her comments about apparently feeling or showing no distress during the sessions. In starting to understand what might be going on, the therapist described her situation in these terms: 'When he cuts or scratches himself, I'm not sure what I feel. I try and damp down my feelings and keep them inside me. I try to get him to express as much about what he is feeling so he can unburden himself and project onto me so I can hold on to it for him.' The image here is one of a therapist who feels she needs to clear a space inside herself in order to 'contain' her patient's distress. She does so by equating her reified image of a container with passivity while taking in as much as she can of the patient's distress and suppressing her own. In this case it seemed clear that the therapist's conception of the container was adding to the patient's need to act out and regress in an effort to communicate his distress through physical means. Once the therapist was able to communicate some of her own distress in a moderated fashion as a way of starting to give thought and meaning to the interaction, the cutting during the sessions began to subside. To return to my conception of maintaining a 'balanced outlook', it appears that the therapist's ability to express some of her feelings about the cutting had the effect of demonstrating how she was being affected (approximately the 'dream object') but surviving (the 'proper object') such projections.

Maternal ideals

A second possible influence that leads to 'idealizing the container' appears to come from static and contrived conceptions of how maternal factors present themselves in the therapeutic process. It could be argued that the valorization of the mother's role in development, particularly in object relations theory, appears often to be directly transposed on to therapeutic technique leading to an overly effusive need to take responsibility for the patient's psychic experience. Making a similar observation, Green (2005a) notes that aspects of child–mother relations most valorized concern those that ignore erotic and destructive dimensions inherent in all relationships. Such aspects include emphasis on the mother's physical presence (as opposed to mental presence) and the need for security and attachment. All these emphasize, in some way, the role of the mother as a receptacle for the infant's needs and focus less on the mother as an object of desire and hate. Lacan (1977, 1994) often criticized object relations theorists for their emphasis on maternal ideals in psychic development. One of his criticisms related to the lack of emphasis on the generative influences that 'absence' has on psychic development in generating symbolic meaning. He took issue with psychoanalytic schools that reduced psychoanalysis to the 'imaginary order', a dual relation which he thought of as being illusory and seductive because it is a form of relating granting the appearance of 'wholeness' based on identification with the image of the self in the other. We could understand this as referring to an over-emphasis on the physical presence of the mother rather than the inevitable 'absences' or gaps that occur between the meeting of two minds. Here the tension between attending to the baby's needs and the mother having a mind of her own is most apparent (so she can interpret and give meaning to preverbal experience). Although I think there have been attempts to approach the generative nature of the mother's moderated 'absence' through Winnicott's and Bion's work,[1] Lacan's point often seems still to hold true in clinical practice when the image of the physical presence of an 'idealized mother' is used as a metaphor to direct the therapist's conscious and unconscious intentions. There is a further implication here. Not only does this tend to obscure inevitable failures in the mother's ability, but it also ignores the infant's presence as an active agent in the maternal exchange (Beebe et al., 2005). In Bion's terms, it obscures the reciprocal nature of container–contained relations.

---

1 Winnicott's (1958) comments on the importance of 'the capacity to be alone in the presence of the mother' and 'the good enough mother' are certainly attempts to think about this problem. Bion's theory of 'no thing' and the importance of maternal reverie and negative capability also mark attempts to theorize the generative influence of maternal 'absence'.

It is possible that similar conceptions influence our view of the container as we imagine it to function in therapeutic dialogue. Luzuriaga's (2000) use of the phrase 'passive good object' (p.150) to depict the therapist as container is a good example of this line of thinking. Similarly, Britton (1992a) sees the container as imparting a sense of being in a safe place, what he calls sanctuary, expressing 'the idea of being inside something good' (p.103). Britton is clear, however, that the container–contained relationship also involves a struggle to find meaning that inevitably involves persecutory anxiety that might be understood to signal the presence of a gap between mother and baby, known and unknown. In my view, understanding the containing relationship as being, in part, about being 'inside' something good is only useful if the tension between these two elements, sanctuary and the struggle to make meaning, is emphasized in the sense that sanctuary creates a situation where new ideas and meaning begin to emerge. If this tension is not considered, the idea of 'sanctuary' quickly resembles an 'ideal retreat', a sense of not just feeling contained in one's mind, but a sense of feeling held forever.

Perhaps even the idea of *maternal* reverie overly colours the therapist's use of his own mind. In line with Gooch's (2001) recommendation, it might be more useful to think of *parental* reverie to move away from idealizing 'passive' perceptions of the maternal object. The above issues emerge in my work with Fatima contributing to a symbiotic stasis between container–contained. I think my attempts to overly accommodate her needs, the tone and whisper in my voice that seemed to creep into our relationship, were attempts to identify with an ideal maternal image.

In terms of the container–contained configuration, ideal containment might be understood to occur when there are expectations of an ideal fit between container and contained (Britton, 1992a). Lamanno-Adamo (2006) describes a similar situation in which the therapist adopts a conception of a *compliant container* where he constantly works towards an ideal or exaggerated accommodation of the patient's needs. This serves the purpose of nullifying contradiction, difficulties, and leads to the disappearance of difference between patient and therapist. In other words, the container is viewed as containing only what is pleasant and is signified in the therapeutic encounter by a stilted sense of mildness or gentleness. Here almost everything is deemed 'reasonable' and there is an 'unrealistic harmony of connection' (p.371) between the container and contained. It amounts to constantly ignoring the real existence of the object, leading to a 'permanent "adulterating" of the object's containing function' (p.380).

Holding and mourning the ideal container

As discussed earlier, 'holding' has an important function in managing narcissistic object relations and the patient's need to hold on to omnipotent mental states in order to form a secure relationship with the analyst. However, it can also act as an obstacle to accessing the analyst's containing function and its associations with introducing inevitable insecurity into the relationship.

When 'holding' is used in a defensive way the analytic relationship often takes on a seductive edge that is not taken up in discussion or attended to by the analyst. For this reason little new meaning is generated but analysis continues. The periods in which I would attempt to shield Fatima from further exploration of her aggressive dynamics might be understood in this light. I suspect that this is a central reason why some analyses continue for many more years than necessary. The therapeutic dialogue becomes entrenched in a 'holding' dynamic where the patient's distress is appeased by the presence of the analyst but little meaning accrues. From this position there is little psychological motivation for internalizing the containing function or 'withdrawing' projections as the therapist's ability to be 'ideal' truncates this development.

We could formulate this as being the result of an entrenched confusion or merger between the 'ideal good breast' and the analyst as a separate 'true' object (Caper, 1999). Following Caper, the narcissistic nature of this object relationship creates an 'understanding couple' accompanied by a sense of relief that is essentially anti-analytical and creates a smug sense of 'like-mindedness' (p.115). Missing from this form of relating is some manifestation of anxiety, guilt, or resistance to interpretation. It is often the case that this dynamic can take on moralistic tones where the therapeutic couple is accepted as 'all-good' and acts against all that is bad in the external world.

In my experience the therapist is more at risk of accommodating to the perceived needs of the patient when powerful negative affects and destructive impulses remain split off and unattended to. As a result, analytic contact remains rather superficial as the therapist colludes with the patient's unconscious wish to split off their hostility. Brenman (1985) proposes that some patients, in particular those who have undergone considerable deprivation, tend to defend against hostility and a superior attitude toward their object by showing a precocious form of concern. This kind of reaction formation makes the therapist particularly vulnerable to enacting aspects of this dynamic by adopting excessive concern for the patient or idealizing their position as a good object. In her words:

> The analyst hi-jacks 'goodness' and sees the patient as a preposterous infant, or alternatively believes that one should provide the so-called total concern of which the patient feels so deprived!
>
> (pp.268–269)

In both of these alternatives the analyst avoids thinking about and confronting the underlying hostilities linked to depriving internal objects. As such, the idealized containing stance maintains paranoid-schizoid links to the object and separation between self and object is held at bay. In the transference–countertransference this translates into a situation where the therapist cannot be related to as a more separate, realistic containing object and idealized phantasies about the therapist's 'concern' or 'capacity to heal' cannot be worked through.

Along with acknowledging the analyst as a separate containing object inevitably comes the need to mourn the phantasy of an ideal container. Previously I put forward the idea that the phantasy of the ideal container is often linked to unconscious motivations related to the therapist taking care of unwanted parts of the self. The need to mourn lies at the threshold of paranoid-schizoid and depressive relating, prompting a great deal of insecurity and resistance to the analytic couple relinquishing the phantasy that the therapist can extinguish psychic pain in the same way that an anaesthetic might take away physical pain.

The importance of containment is often guided by the theoretical understanding that it is the introjection of the therapist's containing function that enables psychic change to occur (Bion, 1962b; Charles, 2004; Grotstein, 2000; Hamilton, 1990; Langs, 1982). In my experience this cannot take place without working through phantasies of idealized containment. To return to the case of Fatima, although the phantasy of the ideal container generated between us fostered some therapeutic change (she was much less anxious and tearful and appeared to engage at a deeper level with me), it was always dependent on my continual presence. John Steiner points out that the therapist is continually needed because no separateness has been achieved between the containing object and parts of the self. Real change and the reversal of projective identifications, he explains, can only occur once the containing object that is omnipotently controlled is given up and mourned (Steiner, personal communication). Only alongside the 'painful recognition of what belongs to the object and what belongs to the self' (Steiner, 1993, p.60) can projections be 'withdrawn'. In a similar way, I think a process of gradually mourning the phantasy of ideal containment needs to be given attention and carefully worked through so that the object/ therapist is less distorted by projections and available for more realistic forms of relating.

Fatima (revisited)

After going through the implications of her needing me to hold her, Fatima decided again that she was going to ask me directly to be held. I said that we had once again come back to a very difficult point between us because if I did not hold her she would feel rejected by me and withdraw. If I complied with her demands, I continued, we would only be avoiding difficult feelings that we needed to try and work with together. I said I would not hold her ('proper object') but I knew this was going to be difficult for her. I told her that it returned me to an image that she introduced a while back (her hanging over the cliff) and I imagined it felt something like she was falling off the cliff ('dream object'). She sat in silence for a while then told me that she had had thoughts of clawing her way into me. She said she felt anxious and angry with me. Towards the end of the session Fatima appeared subdued and felt, in her words, 'like something was missing or had died inside her'.

The following session Fatima arrived on time for the first time in five months. She began by inquiring about my own state of mind and was more curious about what I was thinking. I was surprised by this shift. She then apologised for her behaviour in the last session saying that she thought she had been manipulative and testing and had felt bad for doing this. For much of this session she began thinking about her difficulties with commitment in relationships because she felt weak and inadequate. She also felt it was difficult because 'people had their own lives'. I said that I thought she was, in part, referring to me as being a different and separate person and she was trying to work out how to relate to me and what it meant to be committed to coming to therapy if it was not to be about the wish to be held. Towards the end of the session it was clear that our 50 minutes together had been very painful for her. She ended by saying she hated therapy and felt like she had a needle in her side that had not been removed and now she had to walk out of the session still in pain. This was a difficult image to be left with but I did not respond.

I noted at the end of the session the beginnings of a clear shift between us. In subsequent sessions Fatima was much more able to hold in mind painful thoughts about the end of sessions and the experience of me being a separate, but available, person to her.

Although Fatima's initial response was one of trying to force her internal contents into me followed by a sense that the container/her therapist was rejecting her, she was able to think about this instead of simply projecting it into me. I understood this to be the beginnings of her having to mourn the phantasy of an ideal container and the narcissistic object relations that accompanied this. This was illustrated by more realistic recognition and concern for her external objects, less need to manipulate the boundaries of the session and, more importantly, her ability to more readily use language symbolically in the transference (her descriptions of relationships and the needle inside her). As Segal's (1991) work on symbol formation demonstrates, symbols function as internal representations of loss and absence; they do not substitute for or deny loss but help overcome it. In Fatima's case, she was more able to acknowledge the loss of the 'ideal container' linked to inevitable inadequacies in my own containing ability, and through the use of symbolic language was better able to tolerate separateness. I think this illustrates how symbols themselves serve as internal containers prescribing new meaning to what could not previously be held in mind. Referring back to Chapter 7, the relationship shifted from a symbiotic stasis to a commensal one where shared language and images benefited the relationship between Fatima and myself.

In the latter part of my work with Fatima, the analytic work was more about the restoration of her own containing function through the toleration of loss and separateness rather than the simple introjection of my containing function. This reiterates the idea that the therapist's containment function is not only about containing and modifying projective identifications but also involves tolerating the loss of the 'ideal container' and the emergence of separateness.

Conclusion

There are two main indications that signal that the therapist is entrenched in a transference–countertransference state that represents 'idealizing the container'. First, the therapist's spontaneous free-floating attention, their reverie, appears absent and is replaced by accommodating to the patient's needs in an apparent benevolent fashion. Second, inevitable insecurity and moderate levels of persecutory anxiety appear absent in the process.

Bion (1970) teaches us that all change is in some way catastrophic and for this reason therapist and patient often avoid the real work in psychotherapy. I have tried to illustrate how the therapist may do this through the enactment of a phantasy of ideal containment. More importantly, I have argued that this countertransference state is often influenced by misunderstandings of how change occurs when the analyst's containing function is engaged. Here the seemingly innocuous, but exaggerated, 'growth-promoting maternal attitude' of the therapist hampers the 'withdrawal' or 'reversal' of projections through tempting the patient with an ideal.

Emphasis on the physical presence of the containing object easily translates into an idealized containing vessel, a rigid reified object in the therapist's mind, rather than the ineffable process that it is. Ironically, as explored previously, the containing function proper works against saturated conceptions such as this. It is a transitory and 'in between' concept best expressed primarily in movements between the therapist's use of reverie and his or her role as a 'proper object'.

I see the containing function as being engaged through the adoption of what Green (2005a) calls 'benevolent neutrality'. It is an analytic attitude of 'understanding receptivity (without this turning towards complacency) without giving way to discouragement or irritation' (p.35). Importantly, he distinguishes this from a more 'conventional pseudo-tolerant discourse which will be experienced by the patient as artificial and governed by technical manuals' (p.35). As with many proposals regarding therapeutic technique, they run the risk of becoming disembodied rules, therapeutic compulsions that lack any connection with what might best contribute to a generative and meaningful dialogue. Although analysts today readily throw out Freud's 'surgical' or 'blank screen' analogies, their replacements, the warm, understanding and empathic analyst, often become equally a caricature that can obstruct the generative capacities of the analytic process just as much.

Chapter 9

Some aspects of beta-mentality
On mimicry and thinking in a technological age[1]

Is it possible that beta-elements along with the rudiments of thought can be passed off as apparently meaningful thoughts, thoughts that ostensibly have been worked on by the psyche's container function? Using *The Matrix* trilogy as a platform, I want to consider a form of psychic simulation that might be thought to occur when the containing function is perverted and makes use of the pseudo-containing mode to generate experience. This is a form of *beta-mentality*, a form of 'not thinking' that helps illuminate certain kinds of psychopathological constellations and perhaps some broader aspects of contemporary culture.

Bion (1957) proposed the idea that psychic functioning always comprises both non-psychotic and psychotic dimensions. The former engages reality and deals with emerging conflicts using neurotic ways of coping. The latter hates, attacks, and evades links with reality by employing primitive defences like splitting and evacuative forms of projective identification. In this part of the personality primitive sensuous and emotional impressions, fragments of thought, as well as the perceptual apparatus itself, are split off from reality-orientated parts of the psyche and used against it to attack and destroy its existence. To recapitulate, beta-elements are not in themselves pathological. They are, if you like, the stem cells of psychic experience that await transformation into meaningful psychic experience. But at the hands of the psychotic part of the personality beta-elements and the fragments of thought (alpha-elements) are subject to a different psychic organization complicit in motives driven by the destruction of the link between internal and external reality.

I am not referring to typical 'psychotic breaks' here. There are more subtle alternatives. I use the term 'pseudo-containing' to refer to the perverse takeover of the non-psychotic part of the personality and consider the idea

1 An earlier version of this chapter has been published as 'Beta-mentality in the Matrix Trilogy', *International Journal of Psychoanalysis*, 86, 179–190. Copyright © Institute of Psychoanalysis, 2005.

that primitive sensory impressions and proto-thoughts interact using a particular kind of logic in place of genuine thought. Other than being fit for evacuation via projective identification, beta-elements also have the capacity to form complex psychic structures that mimic reality-orientated aspects of the personality. In short, reality is attacked by simulating its very existence. This, in turn, sets up perverse psychological organizations that work off the contaminatory and seductive effects of split-off beta-elements and undeveloped components of thought. I think the mythic reality of *The Matrix* cogently represents the complexity of this kind of psychic organization.

The Matrix trilogy

The Matrix trilogy,[2] written and directed by Larry and Andy Wachowski, fits the general genre of action-orientated science fiction. The trilogy is most popularly known for its well-choreographed action scenes and groundbreaking special effects. In addition, however, the script, clearly influenced by the likes of Orwell's *1984* and Kubrick's *2001: A Space Odyssey*,[3] is an intelligent commentary on age-old debates about the nature of reality and its relation to our origins, the power and seductiveness of 'the machine', and the mind–body problem. Even the enthralling special effects do not escape the film's astute narrative intentions: to seduce the senses. The Wachowski brothers, in effect, jar their audience into asking questions about the nature of experience: How do we know what is real? Are we truly awake, or do we exist in a dream within a dream? Is there life beyond the senses and their seductive hold on reality? Such questions have always been grist for the mill of philosophical and existential debate. They are also, of course, questions about self-discovery (of both inner and outer reality) and the dynamic forces that drive humankind; it is here that the trilogy's symbolism meets with psychoanalytic conceptions. My intention here is to elucidate how the narrative might be understood as representing ongoing dilemmas between psychotic and non-psychotic parts of the personality, especially the perversion of reality that threatens when the psychotic part of the personality dominates. In many ways the trilogy brings to life the mythic reality – in the bionic sense – of a 'beta-world', a beta-mentality that has its own coordinates, rules and reasons for existence.

The narrative and plot of *The Matrix* are complex and some of the details appear to be deliberately obscured or cryptically stated to add to

---

2 *The Matrix*, *The Matrix: Reloaded* and *The Matrix: Revolutions*. I will use *The Matrix* to refer to all three films.
3 Similar to these epic tales, *The Matrix* has generated a massive cult following throughout the world.

the decentring objectives of the script. This leaves the basic storyline open to greater interpretive possibilities and sometimes confusion. For this reason I begin by giving a thumbnail sketch of central aspects of the narrative that are reasonably well established in the trilogy before exploring the films in more detail.

The Matrix is set against the backdrop of a war between 'the machines' and human beings. We are told that, in an earlier era, the humans 'scorched the sky' and shut out the sun, the main source of power for 'the machines'. In order to maintain their existence the machines have developed a way of using humans themselves as a source of fuel. We are shown glimpses of comatose humans imprisoned in pods, 'plugged in' to a centralized system to generate an energy source. Humans have to be kept 'alive' as a fuel source, but in order to prevent them from 'waking up' to this realization and 'unplugging' themselves as sources of energy, they have to be made to believe they are still living in a human world. Thus the matrix is created, a virtual reality, a series of computer programs that simulate human existence at the peak of civilization in order to deceive and seduce them into believing that this is actual reality. The matrix is a 'neural interactive simulation'; a series of programs that mimics human or earthly forms and is dependent on the parasitic use of the human form and its senses. Through manipulation of the neural connections to the senses the machines continually delude human beings that they are living a normal existence. In this way their sensory apparatus is used against them and it is here that Bion's notion of beta-elements and primitive components of thought are given a mythic reality, a world of sensory and affective impressions split off from their original life-serving purpose.

Apart from the humans that are plugged in to the matrix, there are those who have managed to free themselves and exist in the real world. They live underground, in Zion, a population under siege trying to fight off attacks from sentinels sent from the machine world. Although sometimes difficult to grasp, no humans actually exist in the matrix. It is entirely simulated. In keeping with the decentring nature of the script, the directors manipulate their audience into believing that the matrix is real (like the comatose humans in the film), but in truth it is a world where sensory impressions, beta-elements, are taken to be the thing-in-itself, reality itself.

The story of The Matrix begins with Neo, a computer hacker, receiving obscure messages from Morpheus, a disciple of the 'real' world who believes in the prophecy that Neo will be the saviour of humankind: 'Wake up Neo. The matrix has you. Follow the white rabbit.' In a number of cleverly directed scenes, Neo, along with the audience, is forced into an experience where the differences between dream and reality, past and present, good and bad, are impossible to distinguish. Soon these experiences begin to jar Neo's reality as he is introduced to a perverse 'inside-out' world, a world controlled solely by split-off evocations of experience, a virtual reality. 'You were born into a prison cell that you cannot smell', says Morpheus, trying to help Neo understand the dissociation that has occurred between his 'real' self and his senses.

Neo now faces a choice. Morpheus explains, 'You take the blue pill, the story ends; you go back to your bed and you believe what you want to believe. You take the red pill; you stay in wonderland and I'll show you just how deep the rabbit–hole goes.' In this scene two near-identical images of Neo are reflected in Morpheus' glasses, depicting the binocular dimensions of reality he is destined to traverse, their deceptive similarities and crucial differences. Neo takes the red pill and is 'unplugged' and born into awareness. He requires rehabilitation as his muscles have atrophied and his eyes hurt because, in the real world, he has never used his body or his senses. So begins his odyssey to understand and wage war against the virtual world he blindly believed in. Slowly he learns that he has existed in a dream simulated by the machine world, and although virtual it is a reality that dominates humankind and has the power to destroy humanity.

It should not be forgotten that the word 'matrix' has different meanings. As well as being a reference to complicated mathematical networks that produce lattice-like effects, it is the Late Latin word for womb and is used in the film as a constant play on ideas questioning the meaning of our origins. In effect, it draws out tensions between the womb as the seat of creativity and the womb, a more artificial version, that gives birth to imitations, replications, clones, illusions of what it is to be human.

The 'real world' and the machine world are represented in very different ways in *The Matrix* trilogy. The imagery used is striking with the 'machine world' being shot using a green-filtered lens and the 'real world' shot in blue. Different length lenses are also utilized to make the real human figures look more personable. The computer-generated virtual world is pristine, geometric, bloodless and immaculate. It is patrolled by malevolent, omnipotent agents sent to terminate any 'anomalies' (signs of consciousness or awareness of the system) in the matrix code. It is a world governed by spurious laws of causality that make the distinction between past and future, choice and fate, meaningless. Here, sensuous experience and inchoate mental impressions, always under manipulation, are an end in themselves.

The 'real world', Zion, on the other hand, is very much an underworld situated in the bowels of the earth. It is a dark, dank, fecal-like claustrophobic existence with its inhabitants having to travel through narrow portals and sewage channels in order to evade attacks from the 'machine world'. Humans live in cave-like dwellings and appear to have been reduced to the very basics needed for existence. Replete with biblical and religious references, this, ironically, is the world of faith, belief and love. It appears that the directors intend this to be a symbol of sacrifice where humans have destroyed the world as it once was in order to save what is essentially human and meaningful. We could also take this to symbolize the psychic suffering that needs to be tolerated and transformed if experience is to remain unique and meaningful.

The question of faith – and its implied 'blindness' to the senses – is a constant theme in the narrative. Neo, now also known as 'The One', doubtingly puzzles over what he has been sent to do. He and his crew constantly enter the matrix in search of answers that are guided by a belief in the prophecy that they will soon be freed. They 'plug in' by connecting their central nervous systems to the source of the matrix via the back of the head and leave the matrix via cable telephone. Their bodies remain in the 'real world' but their senses enter the matrix. Throughout this, we are asked constantly to question our faith in our beliefs and what the sensory world has to offer, and indeed whether there are differences between the two. In *The Matrix: Revolutions*, for instance, Neo learns that the Oracle, the guide thought to be the key to freeing humanity, the reason for their belief, is herself revealed to be an 'intuitive programme' written to understand the imperfections of the human condition. She represents belief, hope and humanity that is mimicked to act against humanity. Later, we also learn that Zion, a symbol of their faith, is part of a plan created by the machines to best control 'anomalies in the code'. We are told that Zion has in fact been destroyed and revived six times and Neo, like six others before him, is simply a means through which the machines are able to reinsert their code in order to restart the matrix in a better, more modified form.

To counter ideas about belief and faith, the machines lure humans into seductive versions of themselves where everything is known and therefore there is no need for choice or faith. Choice and free will are mere illusions, mocked and mimicked by the machines and seen as simple nodes in the matrix; a series of on/off responses that have already been determined. 'The only truth is causality', one of the virtual machines pompously explains, 'choice is an illusion created between those with power and those without'.

Pseudo-containing in *The Matrix*

With all this considered, *The Matrix* may well be seen as an allegory about the Lacanian illusory and synthetic ego and its seductive hold on a reality made up of self-reflections that are taken to be authentic for the purpose of circumventing the traumatic implications of the order of the Real (represented by the real, decimated planet). The use of reflection, mirror images, twins, and mimicry to represent the human 'machine' in the trilogy certainly supports this conjecture. Alternatively, the two worlds could be understood as representing variations of Winnicott's True and False Selves in a high-technological age. Of course interpretations abound and, as Zizek (2003) points out in his brief commentary on *The Matrix*, films like this function like Rorschach tests, inviting most theoretical perspectives and personal philosophies to recognize themselves in its creations. My understanding uses some of Bion's thoughts about beta-elements that illuminate the nature of primitive mentation in the psychotic part of the personality. Here, the 'machine world' and its manipulation of virtual reality represent ideographic images that, in part, mirror the behaviour of beta-elements and their overall impact on psychic functioning. I am referring to Bion's most common usage of the term 'beta-elements' to refer to proto-mental units comprising sensory impressions on the mind that are connected to rudimentary forms of consciousness (Bion, 1963).

Similar to Bion's ideas about beta-elements, there is no past or present in the matrix. 'You have sight now', the Oracle urges Neo. 'You are looking at a world without time', as he tries to come to terms with the matrix. Nor can things be made unconscious or conscious. Sensations and feelings simply exist as things-in-themselves. They simply come and go unarticulated by mature thought and taken as fact. It is a scenario where alpha-function is bypassed, the function that imbues sensory impression with a sense of subjectivity en route to generating meaningful experience if it can be contained. Rather than transforming primitive forms of experience, the matrix scenario proposes it is possible to bypass meaning-making activity simply by making use of sensory impressions and existing basic psychological elements (pictograms, audiograms, alpha-elements that have already been transformed by alpha-function) to mimic real human activity.

In keeping with this, Neo has to learn that he has been without thought since birth and has been victim of a manipulation of his sensory apparatus by the machine world. Sensual impressions have been separated from their essential functions of orientation, learning, encoding, and modifying the realities of being-in-the-world as a unifying, whole-object experience. In this way, the virtual world is very much a 'beta-world' where contact with reality has been replaced by a beta-screen.

The logic of the matrix, its 'rules' and the behaviour of its virtual inhabitants, offers a striking and imaginative depiction of beta-mentality. Using computer-generated 'reality' (a reality based on code) as an animated pictorial representation of beta-elements draws on a number of other common associations. They are both primarily non-verbal elements. Binary code and beta-elements are basic, primitive elements that make up the base units of 'experience', whether simulated or real. Both, as units of experience, have the ability to distort reality. Finally, parallels between beta-mentality and cyberspace are also well illustrated by the faceless, disembodied fragments of communication that often typify communication over the internet. There are no better examples, it might be said, of beta-elements in action than those that can be found in the chatrooms and online gaming circuits of the internet.

Objects in the matrix, animate and inanimate, exist outside the laws of reality and can be distorted and mutated. The agents, sent to destroy any signs of 'independent' consciousness in the matrix, are able to project themselves into any object to lodge attacks against representatives of the non-psychotic part of the personality. Their projective capacity enables them to be 'everywhere and nowhere at the same time', as Morpheus explains.

More accurately, figures in the matrix resemble 'bizarre objects' in the sense that they contain traces of the 'real individual'. Virtual figures, as Morpheus points out, reflect a 'residual self-image . . . the mental projection of your digital self'. This is very close to Bion's (1962b) 'bizarre object' comprising ego or superego traces, as well as being a vehicle for unassimilated sensory impressions or beta-elements. Further, in *Cogitations* (1992) Bion refers to 'bizarre objects' as essentially *re-animated* objects; authentic internal experiences (alpha-elements) which are killed off or manipulated and brought back to life in a form suited to the denial of reality. This is done, he argues, largely to placate reality-oriented (non-psychotic) parts of the personality and this too is the very reason why the matrix exists. The virtual beta-world pacifies and ostensibly mollifies in order to keep individuals inert and largely unconscious. But this situation is not simply about the absence of alpha-function in parts of the psyche. It is an active hate-filled attempt to render human existence meaningless, a situation typically referred to by Bion as the reversal of alpha-function. This is given a mythical reality in *The Matrix* as we witness how human beings are stripped of a meaningful existence as they lie unconscious in pods and 'plugged in' to the matrix.

There are a number of principles implicit in the machine 'beta-world' that allow it to dominate. Virtual objects operate on logic that is based on principles of agglomeration and replication; they work together to annihilate awareness and mimic 'normality'. Agent Smith, one of the agents designed to destroy signs of awareness in *The Matrix*, is the epitome of a cold, aggressive superego figure that attacks the link between objects to destroy any capacity for thought. Bion (1959) considered that the primitive superego, what he called an ego-destructive superego, was made up of agglomerations of persecutory objects which generated ongoing psychic fragmentation once internalized. Agent Smith appears to embody this destructive psychic function at the service of the machine world. After being 'killed' by Neo he, like Neo, gains awareness of the rules of the matrix and begins to continuously replicate himself, creating hundreds of objects in his own image. Here we witness further the proliferation of an agglomerated mass of replicated agents as he continues his attempt to control and attack any questioning of the existence of the matrix. Through this he maintains a world of beta-elements and the fragments of thought split off from their ordinary human function, although beta-elements are not always themselves problematic as they await transformation into meaningful experience by the containing function. The matrix represents fragments of experience that cannot be developed further as a result of the attack on the link between sense impressions and awareness. Due to this, beta-elements take on a perverse antihuman quality in the sense that once split off they are used to deceive the self into believing that such fragments of experience are synonymous with what it means to be human. Transformation into meaningful thought is no longer possible and fragments of experience take on a logic of their own akin to Agent Smith's motives where impact and success is directly proportionate to the quantity of objects present. Here, replication of himself and the proliferation of part-objects through unceasing attacks on linking is an asset. What would otherwise be viewed as fragmentation by the non-psychotic part of the personality is taken at face value to mean that there is always strength in numbers.

More generally, this logic can be found in all thought that begins with the reasoning that 'more of something is always better'. This kind of reasoning relies on the physical appearance of things to affirm one's security and is antithetical to beliefs orientated towards the existence of an internal world. With this, there is no possibility of integration or the creative assimilation of such external objects. It is the equivalent of a primitive form of mentation that simply agglomerates and exists according to laws outside of conscious awareness or any kind of conscious control; a mindless following of the forces of repulsion and attraction, like particles that coalesce or separate according to the properties of gravity. In addition, because the matrix is based on mimicry and imitation of human attributes and form, objects in the matrix, beta-elements, are deceptive in appearance. They accumulate and mass together to approximate what might be called a *pseudo-container*, a receptacle of apparent stability, meaning, reasoning and precision. In some ways, the parallel between the machine world and beta-mentality is stretched here beyond the conception of beta-elements being meaningless, chaotic and fragmentary. Beta-elements, viewed through the lens of the matrix, bring us closer to an internal logic that imparts a precarious, but stable and cohesive, hold over its subject through mimicking the non-psychotic part of the personality. To a limited extent, Bion (1963) considers this possibility in trying to understand how beta-elements disperse and agglomerate in the psyche to assume 'abortive prototypes' of the container–contained dynamic. Although beta-elements may appear to cohere in the way that a containing object would, these proto-experiences lack the capacity, or 'valency', for true integration. Earlier, we explored how these ephemeral experiences form the foundation of proto-containing experiences. I am suggesting here that pathological derivatives of this process occur when these primitive experiences are severed from their interactive (unconscious) origins and used to portray thinking proper.

Bick's (1968) understanding of 'secondary skin' formations and Meltzer's (1986) notion of adhesive identification draw on the idea that beta-elements are capable of cohesion. As mentioned in previous sections, in both cases primitive sensations constellate or provide points of adhesion on which the personality can define itself. Bick (1968) believed that the skin provided the infant with crucial evidence of the presence of a primary containing object. In this way sensation functioned to passively hold together primitive parts of the personality not yet differentiated from the body. However, if defects occur in the containing process, the infant makes use of sensory expressions like muscular movements and vocalizations in a cohesive manner so as to generate a defensive 'secondary skin' as a form of self-containment. The coordinated manipulation of the senses is able to produce a believable world that generates a sense of fearless control and pseudo-independence. The matrix, as a representation of a cohesive world, an independent system that denies its dependence on human beings, closely resembles this formulation.

The fecal-like nature of the 'real world' and its associations with freedom and whole-object existence seems to make a particular point about the perverse reversal that has occurred in the trilogy. Whilst the machines mimic 'normality' using their beta-mentality, Zion, the seat of humanity, survives through adopting primitive psychotic-like modes of defence. The underworld generates evocative images of Meltzer's (1992) 'claustrum-dwellers' who have sought refuge inside the compartments of the internal mother. He outlines three main maternal compartments of the claustrum: head/breast, genital and rectum compartments. In the case of *The Matrix*, it appears to be clearly about life in the maternal rectum and its concomitant conflicts. As Meltzer puts it: 'Unlike the other two compartments [head/breast and genital] where comfort and erotic pleasure dominate the value system, in the rectum compartment there is only one value: survival' (p.91). It is here, according to Meltzer, where imprisonment and claustrophobia have their most poignant meaning. What we see in Zion, however, appears to vary somewhat from Meltzer's 'rectum claustrum-dweller' who is intrusively identified with sadism, deceptiveness and cynicism. This, in its extreme, is the dynamic bedrock of the schizoid psychopath. These traits are certainly present inside Zion and its portals. We see leaders being cynical about the prophecy of freedom, we see elements of deceptiveness and sadism personified by Cypher, a crew member who sadistically taunts his crew before killing them as he decides to embrace the matrix and leave Zion behind. But these aspects of Zion are countered by hope and faith in the prophecy. The difference seems to be that this is a whole-object world in retreat, waiting for rebirth. It is a refuge, a rectal-womb, away from persecutory splitting and the separation of body and mind. In this way it suggests a different pathological constellation, a healthier one, where non-psychotic aspects of the personality can make use of psychotic mechanisms – splitting and intrusive identification – for the sake of a last-ditch attempt at preservation of the good object. The conflict thus becomes one of trying to preserve goodness in the face of encapsulating sadism, paranoia and cynicism. Retreat into encapsulation is a lesser evil than having to face the threat of annihilation in the external world. It also appears to be suggestive of a pathological constellation that is linked to the genesis of a particular kind of shame which emerges as a consequence of having to intrusively enter the rectum-claustrum. It is a situation where good and bad, although not confused or interchangeable, are felt to be inseparable, leading to the generation of affect equivalent to the shame of having to expose one's fecal mass in public. This is the view from the non-psychotic part of the personality.

Lost in simulation

The relationship between Zion and the matrix might be understood to be an allegory about high-technological advances, its reciprocal influences on culture, and the insidious influence this has on the personality. The high-tech world, it could be said, 'invites' a particular kind of psychic organization. It invites a kind of mentality that employs certain primitive defences, particularly splitting, depersonalization and projective identification. Its chief purpose is the evasion of thought and inevitable frustration in the service of meeting growing demands for urgency and immediacy. Could it be that this is a reality which lies beyond the individual personality and has a pervasive influence on all our thinking? If so, *The Matrix* warns of the ease with which we are seduced by 'the machine', how much easier it is to 'deposit' ourselves in a beta-world that 'works' because it is supported by an external reality so dominated by 'code' and the computer. In short, proto-mental capacities, otherwise incoherent and unintegrated, are given an order and place – the symbol of the matrix – that is, at times, almost indistinguishable from what is creative and authentic. More profoundly, it could be said that this signals an age where the impersonation of 'normality', supported by man's own ingenious creations, forms the basis of an emerging breed of psychopathology which has no need for neurotic or psychotic symptomatology; a kind of 'sane psychosis' which can be contained and supported by a 'mentality' emulated from the cyber world.

Is this, like *The Matrix*, mere science fiction? What evidence is there in observations of contemporary culture, used as a reflecting pool out of which corresponding states of psychopathology emerge, that *The Matrix* reflects a contemporary reality? Certainly, our increasing reliance on 'the machine' to do our thinking and experiencing points in this direction. The more interesting question that *The Matrix* appears to raise is whether our relationship with 'the machine' has progressed well past simple reliance to a position where we have begun to mimic our own creations. The message here is that we have reached the epoch of our ability to create, think and truly experience. In its place we blindly simulate a mentality that mirrors the expedience and order of binary code, a form of rationality which appears to have greater value than the more inherently defective, though more human, muddle of self-reflectivity, dream-work, and the search for true meaning. The insatiable need for 'strategy-oriented' approaches to living a better life seems to reflect

this type of anti-thinking mentality. We see it more and more in our consulting rooms when patients come in requesting logical strategies on how to
love, how to mourn, how to feel, how to think. Such requests are usually
stated with an odd form of conviction that is best backed up by being able to
produce an acronym for the treatment requested. The empty, mechanistic
nature of such requests almost gives off a sense that such thoughts have been
planted by some hidden order waiting to receive the therapist's (equally
ordered, apparently logical and empty) dictations. Disciples of this form of
reasoning have little sense of why they seek such strategies but obsequiously
sense that it is the 'right way to go about it'. Is it too far-fetched to say that
these kinds of apparently reasonable, but impossible, requests reflect a kind
of 'binary-logic mentality', a beta-mentality, a need for a universal code that
can be implanted, mimicked, without any need for real thought and tolerance of the unknown?

In a similar way, the burgeoning reality TV industry is surely the quin-
tessential example of 'canned' experience or the beta-mentality to which I
am referring. It is an industry that thrives on vicariously living through the
other's senses. There is surely a strange kind of 'madness' attached to
watching individuals make thoughtless and contrived (although seemingly
reasoned) decisions about life-changing events. Here, the reality principle is
not confronted or replaced by hallucination, it is made anew, manufactured
to replicate and mimic what cannot be truly lived.

This form of perverse mentality exceeds the capabilities of Freud's 'guilty
man', and does not belong to Kohut's 'tragic man'. It is closer to T.S.
Eliot's 'hollow men' as pointed out by Newirth (2003):

> We are the hollow men
> We are the stuffed men
> Leaning together
> Headpiece filled with straw. Alas!
> Our dried voices, when
> We whisper together
>
> (T.S. Eliot, 'The Hollow Men', 1962, p.79)

Eliot's words depict an empty, deathly, hollow man. We could take this to
refer to the psychological consequences of *The Matrix* scenario. Is it the case
that we have projected ourselves so much into inanimate objects, com-
puters, material things, all pseudo-containers, that we lose a part of what it
means to be human? Certainly, our dependence on such objects seems to
hold the promise that we can somehow bypass the suffering inherent in
struggling to use and transform feelings and thoughts that resonate with a
'lived' reality. With this, following Bion, we give up the essence of what it
means to be human; to tolerate absence, uncertainty, suffering, so as to
transform emotional experience into meaningful unique experiences. *The*

Matrix scenario seductively suggests that we empty ourselves into inanimate objects and witness what happens when we over-identify with them.

The problems with this psychic solution can be found in the relationship between the machine world and humankind in *The Matrix*. The machines are dependent on the parasitic use of human sensory impressions and fragments of thought, but true to their beta-mentality they are never able to confront, acknowledge, or think about this dependency outright. These are the tell-tale signs that pseudo-containing is at work. The inability to tolerate dependency is also the origin of their deep hate for humanity. The machines' obsession with perfection is always thwarted by an inevitable link to 'humanness' and its imperfections. At its core, it is about the denial of object relationships and hate for the realization that, despite capacities for replication, mimicry and omnipotent deeds, the machines cannot exist, or create themselves, in isolation.

The machines would have us believe that sensory experience, as a thing-in-itself, is all we need. Nozick's (1971) now famous 'experience machine experiment' was designed to challenge this assumption. He asked students to imagine neuropsychologists being able to hook them up to machines that simulated all possible experience while they simply lay floating in a tank.[4] Nozick wanted students to think about why they would, or would not, 'plug in', a way of thinking about what matters other than simply 'how our lives feel from the inside' (p.43). Nozick goes on to argue that what matters is that we actually do certain things. We would not plug in, he argued, because we do not want simply to have the experience of doing something, we want to know we are actually doing it. Our own agency, thirst for truth and awareness of actually becoming a person overrides pure sensation. In *Invariances*, almost 30 years after his initial thoughts about the advent of virtual reality, Nozick (2001) argues that, contrary to prevalent claims, virtual reality will profoundly diminish our capacity for knowledge and thinking. He bases his argument on the observation that virtual reality undermines our fundamental need to actively track our interaction with reality. In sum, it is the actuality of being a person and allowing oneself to be transformed by the reality of relationships that is of greatest human worth.

Of course, psychoanalysis is very interested in how we feel or perceive things 'from the inside', but the outcome of this experiment is one well known to psychoanalysis: there is no value in internal experience without linking it to relatedness and the external world. Even beta-elements, as building blocks of experience, are immersed in a web of relatedness. This is not only the case in the sense that they possess some primitive capacity for agglomeration and so forth, but also in terms of beta-elements being the medium through which internal and external worlds are joined.

4 He made it a condition that once plugged in they would have no awareness of it being a simulation and they would believe that they were actually having the experience.

In *The Matrix*, in the place of acknowledging relatedness is a deceptively lucid and seductive dialogue about purpose, choice, causality and understanding. However, in the end the machines' 'reasoning', in effect, eats itself and is fundamentally flawed due to a denied dependency on the human form, particularly their ability to give meaning to experience, their ability to transform unbearable experience using the containing function. In the virtual world purpose, choice and understanding have no real meaning and are simply equated with a meaningless need for survival. As is characteristic of split-off beta-elements, differences between experiences are impossible to discern, giving rise to symmetry between disparate experiences or elements. This is personified by Agent Smith's ability to 'copy himself' into other persons in the matrix. By way of further analogy, experiences in the matrix are reduced to computerized 'code' that seeks to eliminate 'difference' in order to engineer a 'perfect world' in which all must 'think' the same to perpetuate a false reality. But the need for symmetry makes everything verge towards the same point. Symmetry makes everything exchangeable and, by virtue of this, the idea of meaningful causal connections, a notion dependent on asymmetry or difference, cannot be attained. Ultimately, objects in the matrix exist in an endless looping algorithm, a beta-screen that cannot generate meaning. Here, apparently reasoned and rational communications are imitations, ways of mouthing words that turn words into sensual objects used to crudely define the 'virtual self'.

There appears to be an eroticized edge to this reality. It is most evident in the scenes where Neo goes to meet Merovingian. Merovingian is omnipotent and enthralled in the titillating pleasures of the matrix. He induces women to orgasmic states through manipulation of the code and uses words to demonstrate the perverted sensual reality of the matrix: 'Don't you just love the French language?', Merovingian remarks with a great deal of arrogance. 'I have sampled every language, French is my favourite. Fantastic language. Especially to curse with. *Nom de dieu de putain de bordel de merde de saloperie de connard d'enculé de ta mère*. It's like wiping your ass with silk, I love it.' Statements like this appear to mock the sensual nature of the human world while at the same time their very meaning is dependent on what it is to be human (he would not be able to experience any of this if he did not have access to human sense impressions). He finds great sensual pleasure in mouthing the words for the purposes of an erotized joining together of symbols of excrement and symbols of sophistication, refinery and creativity. It is a celebration of perversion where the mixing of good and bad has no consequence other than to stimulate.

There are parts of the script that raise questions about there being a neat division between the machines and human beings in terms of representations of relatedness, emotion and beta-mentality. Many of the machines appear to experience very human emotions. The Oracle, for instance, displays compassion for Neo's quest and an understanding about love. Are these simply mimicked emotions, apparent feelings as suggested earlier? This is one possible explanation as to why there are aspects of 'humanness' in the matrix. In the other direction, we learn in *Reloaded* that Neo can exercise his virtual reality powers in the portals of Zion, the real world. Does this mean that Zion is another layer of virtual reality that is constantly recycled to perpetuate an endless illusion? These are aspects of the plot that keep us endlessly guessing. In line with my argument about beta-mentality, however, the blurring of a neat distinction between machine and human reflects inevitable dilemmas faced by a pathological organization dependent on split-off beta-elements and mimicry. There will always be seepage between representations of psychotic and non-psychotic parts of the personality because they are held together by the same building blocks of experience. From this point of view human emotions in *The Matrix* represent the inevitable consequences of mimicry where simulation produces its own set of fears and difficulties. Most notably it breeds threats of contamination, the fear of becoming the very thing that is hated, as well as a recognition of 'absence' and the emptiness that lies behind the continual presence of a simulated world. Agent Smith, for example, stalks the matrix driven by hate and the fear that he has been 'infected' by humans. In a momentary lapse of beta-logic Smith forgets the rules of his own making – that he is virtual – and fears that he can actually be contaminated. Here, the boundaries between simulation and reality are lost, bringing him close to deceiving himself that the matrix is real.

The other side of the confusion emerging out of the consequences of mimicry is the sense of lack and emptiness that is ironically part of a world that promises everything, the very thing-in-itself. This is best personified by Persephone, wife of Merovingian, through whom Neo and friends seek access to the Keymaker to give them rights of entry to the source of the matrix. In order to be led to the Keymaker, Persephone makes it a condition that Neo kisses her in a way that she can feel love. She craves feelings of love but can only experience it when kissed by someone who is actually in love. Here Persephone appears to represent a yearning for carnal experience, embodied experience, the essence of what it means to be human in the real world. In Greek mythology Persephone is endlessly trapped between Hades, god of the dead, and her mother, Demeter, goddess of grain and fertility. Similarly, in the matrix Persephone represents a goddess in limbo, an inhabitant of a dead virtual world who craves love and what it really means to be alive and human.

'Everything that has a beginning has an ending'

The finale of *The Matrix*, *Revolutions*, is largely a failure due mainly to its mixed and impossible ambitions of meeting the needs of a 'Hollywood ending' while trying to stay true to its underlying philosophy and storyline.

Most of the time the endless escalating battle scenes drown out an intelligent script. It might be said that the film is lured by Hollywood and thus guided by phantasies of a paranoid-schizoid solution where the plot is driven by the threat of all 'bad' (or 'good') being totally annihilated. The ending, however, does not fulfil its 'promise' of annihilation of bad and idealization of good. Instead, it returns to the central problem of a denied relationship between the machine world and the 'real' world. In one of the closing scenes, Neo is blinded and has to rely on his intuitive power to continue his journey to the source of the matrix. This is the final reckoning with the epithet that 'truth and reality lie beyond the senses'. He no longer needs his senses to 'see' the machines, a turn in the narrative that seems to resonate well with Bion's (1970) claim that ultimate truth (O) lies beyond the senses.

The final solution, however, acknowledges that ordinary existence, beyond the messianic abilities to intuit past the senses, is dependent on an embodied sensuous existence. After losing Trinity, his lover and symbol of humanity, Neo is able to broker an uneasy truce with the creator of the machines, the deus ex machina. It is a truce that, in essence, acknowledges their interdependence and future symbiosis while, at the same time, ensures the elimination of destructive rogue elements (principally Agent Smith who has, at this stage, infinitely replicated himself) that threaten the existence of Zion. The truce leaves one with an uneasy sense of irresolution, devoid of immediate satisfaction. In part, it is consistent with a more depressive resolution where ambivalence has to be tolerated, and omnipotence and idealization given up. Loss is felt on both sides of the divide and a closer, more 'realistic' reading of reality is brought to bear on the coexistence of the beta-world and the human world. Finally, there is recognition from both sides that beta-elements and the fragments of thought (alpha-elements) are ultimately embodied experiences that cannot be authentically replicated or divorced from their human origins.

Chapter 10

Beta-mentality in violent men

The ideas I want to put forward in this chapter relate to a kind of mentality often found in violent men. These observations emerge from interview research with homicide offenders as well as my experience in treating violent men. The interview research involved the use of the Psychoanalytic Research Interview to understand core psychodynamic elements of offenders who commit acts of rage-type murder (Cartwright, 2002, 2004b). It appears that 'explosive' offenders display a particular kind of borderline personality organization. Although defences like splitting and projective identification are typical here, the profile that generally emerges consists of a pattern of projective identification with idealized external objects in a way that protects the self from shame-ridden bad objects that remain hidden, unmetabolized, inside the self. This is similar to Fairbairn's (1952) idea about the defensive internalization of bad objects. It seems that the more typical projective evacuation of bad objects is held at bay by the pervasive use of idealization and over-compliance. As a result, such offenders usually appear typically non-aggressive and over-controlling in their general approach. In what is to come I am interested in raising questions about the nature of these unmetabolized aspects of the personality and the implications this has for understanding their emotional life and treatment. It seems that these suspended states of mind have their own internal logic that is managed by projective identification with idealized objects. Once these defences begin to fail, however, even more primitive mental manoeuvres, such as the agglomeration of affective objects and autistic blocking, are used to defend against unbearable feelings of shame.

In Chapter 6 I have put forward the idea that beta-elements, through interaction, form the bedrock on which the containing function proper can operate. In working with violent offenders my impression is that this process is constantly ruptured by the patient's need to block genuine interaction in order to safeguard the self from a build-up of untransformed sensory and affective experience. Due to an enfeebled capacity to distinguish thoughts and sense impressions, both thoughts and sensations are used as 'objects' to block experience or annihilate threat. The threat that seems to prevent these patients from entering into a working containing relationship appears to be most associated with an immense sensitivity to feelings of shame.

The narcissistic exoskeleton

Men vulnerable to impulsive forms of violence appear to make use of particular defensive strategies. My treatment of violent offenders has led me to understand the core of their defensive organization to comprise projective identifications that create links with ideal objects and serve a protective function. I use the term 'narcissistic exoskeleton' for reasons that I quote from a previous publication:

> I use the term 'narcissistic exoskeleton' for two reasons. First, the external objects that form part of the system have a narcissistic quality to them. They are invested, in phantasy, with parts of the offender's self, and the distinction between self and the external object's needs, feelings and motivations are blurred. 'Narcissistic' also refers to a propensity towards the fantastical creation of internal objects as a means of denying pain (Rosenfeld, 1987). Second, the image of an exoskeleton best depicts the nature of this structure as being situated outside, or on the periphery of, the self, enclosing an interior.
>
> An exoskeleton has a dual function which parallels the kind of object relations evident in rage offenders. It both supports and contains an internal structure whilst simultaneously protecting it from outside threats, much like a rigid sheet of armour.
>
> (Cartwright, 2002, p.118)

The 'narcissistic exoskeleton' maintains a rigid split between an idealized exterior that shields internalized 'bad objects' associated with immense shame, a specific kind of borderline personality organization. Such individuals make use of a number of strategies to maintain the split. Notably, they constantly attempt to appease their idealized object in a way that might be misunderstood as healthy accommodation towards others' needs. This strategy maintains the image of an all-good self free of shame and conflict. In other cases this 'veil of goodness is also maintained through a rigidly held self-righteous, and sometimes attacking, attitude towards objects not perceived to reflect the ideal self' (p.119). Both the above strategies appear to contribute to the apparent normality of such offenders. Based on this formulation the eruption of violence occurs when the defensive system is substantially threatened by some outside factor, usually a relationship break-up which seriously threatens the idealized conception of things. Violence, in these cases, appears to represent a last ditch attempt to annihilate the bad, shameful self as it is exposed and projected into a victim.

In essence there appear to be three main factors that create a vulnerability to impulsive violence: unbearable shame, a precipitating stressor, and the employment of a defensive organization described above.

In *Murdering Minds* (Cartwright, 2002) I focused on the 'narcissistic exoskeleton' as a psychic structure and projective identification as an 'action defence' that leads to impulsive violence (see also Hyatt-Williams, 1998; Meloy, 1992). Other aspects of this kind of mentality have received less attention and are worth exploring as they seem relevant in further understanding transference–countertransference states that often emerge in treatment. In particular I want to consider elements of 'beta-mentality' in violent men and their hypersensitivity to feelings of shame. Earlier I defined beta-mentality as being characterized by confusions between beta-elements and alpha-elements. As a result, the components of thought are treated like objects or sense impressions and beta-elements are treated like thoughts. The way affect appears to agglomerate or build in the psyche, and the use of autistic blocking as a defence against the build-up of affect, appears to represent a particular form of beta-mentality in violent men. I begin with a brief account of a case I treated for a three-year period in once-a-week psychotherapy. The case highlights typical problems that emerge in those vulnerable to rage-type offences.

Glen

Glen was a 36-year-old teacher who had been referred after he had attacked his wife with a kitchen knife, stabbing her several times after a heated argument over finances. She had threatened to leave him and this precipitated the attack. They had been married for six years and one similar incident had occurred two years previously. After the second incident his marriage had not continued and he had sought treatment for fear of a similar incident occurring with others. His wife had chosen not to press charges.

In the initial year of therapy I learned little about Glen's family which he often put down to his terrible memory, something he said a number of people often commented on. From the little I could glean, his father, a businessman, seemed somewhat preoccupied throughout his childhood; he simply referred to him as 'the breadwinner' in the family but could say little about his relationship with him beyond his expression that it was a 'normal father–son relationship'. His mother on the other hand, appeared to be significantly over-involved. He recalled with embarrassment how she would often unnecessarily call his primary school to see if he was all right. She had also been a problem in the past when she would intrude on his marriage with apparent concern for their well-being.

As a child he had a number of close friends and these relationships appeared particularly significant, as he seemed to rely heavily on them. He would often remark that only when he was with his friends did he have some sense of who he was. When separated, in his words, 'I felt like I was nothing, kind of non-existent.' He always had a 'perfect' group of friends he would tell me. 'They would listen to me just like you're listening to me, understanding absolutely everything I say', he continued. When I would ask him to talk a little about our 'perfect relationship' he would reply with statements like: 'You make me feel so good about myself', 'I trust you with my life, with my heart, I can see you are a very good man'. On one occasion I attempted to challenge these perceptions after I had made a garbled comment that made little sense. I said that I thought it reflected that I was struggling to understand him and I knew that would feel somewhat awkward for him. In response he said, 'No, no, no what you said is right, we are on the right track'. He appeared very uncomfortable, as did I. In response, his general demeanour seemed to change. He leaned forward, looked down immediately in front of him and appeared speechless and lost. I was aware of becoming increasingly anxious trying to engage him again. The moment appeared to pass without comment or acknowledgement, but I recall being curious about being left with images of him seeming helpless, lost, that I seemed to associate with those of a cowering animal at the hands of a harsh master.

Glen appeared to be successful in his teaching career, often claiming to have been praised by his colleagues for his good work. In general, in his relationships with others, he would adopt an overly compliant, appeasing attitude, especially in the face of conflict. Through this he was able to maintain an idealized conception of his relationships with others which he could then identify with. In his words he said once, 'I only have time for good people in my life, they rub off on you . . . the bad ones I never notice, I have no time for them'.

The above vignette illustrates how potentially violent men make use of idealizing strategies. The last statement also touches on a rigid moralistic stance that firmly separates good from bad objects and is unforgiving of any vulnerability which is usually equated with the bad object in such offenders. It also has the trappings of an apparently reasoned statement about staying away from 'bad influences'. Statements like this are often linked to observations of apparent normality in such offenders. The concreteness of this thinking, however, its rigidity and righteousness, contribute greatly to the eventual eruption of defensive violence. In my experience violence erupts when the narcissistic exoskeleton, supported by these idealizing strategies, is threatened. My attempts at questioning his idealized view of me appears to leave him dumbfounded, lost, and his demeanour leads to associations that appear to connect with immense feelings of shame and affective build-up which we both attempt to uncomfortably avoid and forget.

Violence in these individuals is never unprovoked. Although it appears to suddenly occur, there is usually evidence that the offender's defensive organization gradually weakens over time as he struggles to minimize and deny the emergence of an unbearable sense of shame. Glen described this as follows:

'I would buy her the best jewellery in town, she was my girl. I would show her how well we were doing financially, but it wasn't enough and she turned bad. I tried harder, made sure I did all the right things. I was the same person, doing the same good things. But this didn't seem to be enough and she started trying to make me feel bad, then I snapped.'

Due to the symbiotic nature of their defensive organization, always in search of idealizing influences, these offenders cannot make use of a 'third object' to help make sense of emerging chaotic experience. This is in keeping with proposals that violent offenders have an impoverished ability to represent experience (Cartwright, 2002; Fonagy *et al.*, 1993; Fonagy and Target, 1996). Without a sufficiently developed means of reflecting on the situation, potential offenders cannot make use of the buffering effects of thought and are thus more vulnerable to any form of provocation. I quote again from *Murdering Minds*:

> Given the poor representational capacity of the psyche the final provocation is experienced as a devastating attack on the self. It cannot be subject to thought and consequently overwhelms the offender and his defensive system. The collapse magnifies the intrusive experience to a point to where it becomes life threatening.
>
> (Cartwright, 2002, p.168)

Violent offenders describe a situation where their idealized self, based on symbiotic relatedness with idealized objects, is felt to be completely annihilated by unbearable shame (associated with bad objects). Because 'bad' experience has been split off it is felt to be alien to the self and is experienced as being forced into them by the victim. In Glen's words:

'The night I became someone else, I lost myself . . . I know I am responsible. But she made me into a terrible person and I couldn't live with that anymore. I know it sounds funny but I had to stand up for good.'

In keeping with Meloy's (1992) and Hyatt-Williams' (1998) observations, the bad object is located in the victim via projective identification in a desperate bid to unburden the self. In the final act, the perpetrator attempts to destroy the bad object in the victim in 'a frenzy proportionate to the devastation the offender has felt internally' (Cartwright, 2002, p.171).

Bateman and Fonagy (2004) point out that displays of rigidity or righteousness, often found in these offenders, are indicators of a non-mentalizing stance. Put simply, this refers to deficits in the ability to intuit or track the mental states of self or others. It is also linked to an impoverished representational capacity leaving their experience in particular areas undeveloped and their thinking very concrete. As a result, it is difficult to see things from multiple perspectives, or others' points of view, leading to rigidly held views that resist change. It appears that in rage-type offenders, it is their feelings of unbearable shame, equated with bad internal objects, that remain unmentalized. In Bion's terms it is as if alpha-function and the containing function have a limited scope, able only to transform experience that has not been contaminated by toxic shame. It seems that this kind of rigidity, as part of the defensive organization, contributed greatly to how Glen appeared to use thoughts like physical objects, as if immutable and existing in physical space.

Toxic shame

A great deal has been written on the link between shame and various forms of violence (Cartwright, 2002; Gilligan, 1997; Kohut, 1972; Lansky, 2005a, 2005b, 2007; Lewis, 2008; Shengold, 1989, 1991). Most agree that shame emerges from a systematic undermining of the self often associated with various forms of trauma or more subtle, but undermining, patterns of relating. Narcissistic wounding of this kind can often be found in the history of violent offenders and trauma may well cause problems where alpha-function and the 'containing process' are overwhelmed by sensory stimuli and undeveloped thoughts (the components of thought). But it is not always the case that impulsive violence is linked to a history of obvious trauma. Shengold (1991), for instance, has pointed out that over-stimulation and over-involvement, not typically considered to be trauma, may equally contribute to pervasive feelings of shame. In such situations, the child has no room to learn how to contain his own mental states: there is no need to think in an idealized world. It leads to a situation where the individual feels like he has been promised 'everything' but in the end, once separated from idealized relationships, feels like he has nothing. Offenders often feel a great deal of shame about a defenceless exposure to these parts of the self. In working with Glen, this seems to have been an important dynamic in his relationship with his mother.

'My mother always looks out for me. It changed when I moved out of home and set up with me wife. I can only say it was like a hole in my heart because she [his mother] gave me everything . . . People said my mother spoilt me, I think she loved me with all her heart.'

I want to say a little more about the nature of affect and its regulation in violent offenders. It appears that exposure to shame is experienced as unbearably toxic and this becomes the central reason for the erection of the defensive system referred to earlier. Given the nature of suspended affective states, it would be accurate to say that rage-type offenders are out of touch with these feelings but feel profoundly and deeply. Although difficult feelings are felt to be inaccessible for use, there is a sense of endlessness and timelessness attached to suspended affective states. This is perhaps best described as a background sense of dread. It contributes greatly to a sense of escalation and panic when evoked feeling states come to the fore. When the situation escalates out of control and feels overwhelming and endless, the only defensive recourse is to locate this distress in his victim. It is less simply about pent-up cathartic discharge and more about the desperate need to locate it in a physical form and annihilate such unbearable feeling states in an object external to the self.

Violence is associated with the sudden re-exposure to a split-off, undeveloped part of the self that is unwittingly dislodged by the victim. This is vividly illustrated in *King Oedipus* as symbolized by the scarring on Oedipus's feet. As the story goes, Laius condemns and disowns Oedipus, his son. He leaves him on the mountain and pierces his feet with a nail. When they meet again many years later, Laius orders him off the road 'to make way for his betters'. Whilst passing him, however, one of the wheels catches Oedipus on the foot, provoking the attack that leads to him killing his father. Oedipus does not know this is his father, nor does he know about his shame symbolized by the early scarring of his foot that is once again damaged or shamed. But it is still very much present in an unmetabolized form waiting for provocation.

Shame, it could be argued, is at the core of what inhibits self-reflection and the ability to think for fear that it will bring attention to unwanted parts of the self. Ironically, this only compounds the problem further as these men often feel immense shame about their own inarticulateness or ability to think, which is sometimes confused with poor intelligence. The polar dimensions associated with shame, its intense defensiveness and cowering stupor, are often observed in the therapeutic relationship with violent men. The offender's gaze oscillates between avoidance and penetrating stare. The latter generates a feeling of immense intrusiveness, perhaps giving the therapist a sense of how the patient feels when engaging with others. I am often struck, however, by how unconscious rage offenders are of this dynamic. Although those struggling with unbearable feelings of shame are often conscious of 'scenarios of vengefulness' towards others (Lansky, 2007), rage offenders seem to keep this largely out of awareness. In its place they are able to marshal certain defensive strategies that reinforce the split between good and bad objects. This is 'hidden shame' (Lewis, 2008) at its extreme and there are attempts to reduce everything related to shame or bad objects to concrete, unmetabolized forms. Paradoxically, this appears to make the offender more vulnerable as these states remain uncontained, leaving the offender having to endure a tangible but unidentifiable sense of feeling exposed and intruded upon. I turn now to trying to understand in more detail the nature of what might be called the split-off bad-object system.

Beta-mentality

Glen (revisited)

Glen found it very difficult to think about his own vulnerabilities and would employ particular strategies to deal with this. Over time it became more apparent how lifeless relationships felt to him and how he would constantly try and prop them up by idealizing their capabilities. There was very little space for thinking or reflection in his sessions and he would stay very close to the description of actual events rather than what they might mean. For instance, he would spend a great deal of time telling me about activities he would do with his children. The narratives did not seem as idealized as the other relationships he had discussed but were filled with practical details that seemed to deaden my ability to listen. On one occasion he told me about the difficulties he was having disciplining his adolescent son when he came to visit. It was particularly about his son being 'angry and selfish'. I thought this might have been an opportunity to explore aggression in a way that was not too threatening for Glen. But when I tried to express curiosity about what might be going on in his or his son's mind he would say something like, 'because he is an angry young man' and launch into the detail of what happened that week. He found it very difficult to think about how his son's or his own mental state might contribute to the problem.

Although it was difficult for him to talk about his own psychic states, on one occasion we stumbled upon what Glen called 'flash pictures'. In this particular session he was talking about an aggressive shopkeeper who always seemed so 'moody'. Glen felt like he may do something wrong in his shop and didn't want to face his wrath so he chose to avoid shopping there. I began to inquire about this man's aggressiveness, to which Glen responded with some irritation, 'He is just aggressive. What else is there to say?' In response, I suggested that he sometimes felt uncomfortable with me, especially when I asked him to think about 'bad' or 'aggressive' things. 'There is enough bad in the world', he responded. 'It is enough that I get these "flash pictures".' I thought he was referring to flashbacks of his violent attacks on his wife, but on further enquiry this was not the case. What he described were sudden images of 'eyes with no face' that seemed to be looking at him. I tried to get him to say more about these experiences. 'It feels threatening like, like someone looking down on you like you're nothing', he said. 'This happens sometimes even when they seem like laughing eyes.' Glen said at the time he found no value in discussing these images further as he felt they had nothing to do with his current problems. In time, he started to notice that such experiences occurred when he felt pressured by me to talk when he had nothing to say. The 'eyes' began to take on meaning related to watching or witnessing something going wrong. Still later in his therapy, they became my eyes, 'making fun of him and tripping him up'.

Two central dynamics appeared to oscillate in the transference–countertransference relationship. In the first, I was clearly a highly idealized figure. He would often comment on the so-called skill with which I was able to help him, or he would discuss aspects of my life that he felt were impressive or ideal. I felt drawn in by this experience but found it very difficult to have clarity on what I actually felt about him or the situation. Our interaction was characterized by what I came to call a kind of 'meaningless intensity' that would escalate as the session continued. It was difficult to retain material from the sessions or to differentiate clearly between persons being discussed. The affect in the room never appeared attached to specific subject matter and it was very difficult to have a clear narrative hold on what the therapy was about.

The second mode of relating in the transference–countertransference was characterized by a sudden drop-off in affect and intensity. On these occasions Glen would become more rigid in his posture, appeared to be more intro-spective, but spoke in a rather detached way that made me feel very absent while in the room with him. Later in the therapy he was able to say how very difficult these transference states were for him to tolerate. In his words, 'I don't have a name for the feelings . . . things get impossible because I begin to feel surrounded by everything, I don't know where I am and talk just becomes noise to me. The only way I can stop it is by stopping things around me or by trying to harden up inside . . . People, even you here, don't feel real to me when this happens.'

The above fragments raise two key issues often found in violent offenders. First, typical of a borderline profile, there is a persistent difficulty in processing information and feelings, leading to an escalation of affect. Glen's poor memory, a lack of narrative continuity, poor representational capacity, and the 'meaningless intensity' that would often occur in sessions appear to point to this. The second issue is related to how affective intensity was often followed by a numbing or dropping off of this intensity that appeared linked to particular psychic strategies aimed at managing the build-up of unmetabolized affect.

I would formulate the above dynamics as follows. It appears that the idealizing transference, where we see the narcissistic exoskeleton at work, permits Glen to projectively identify with symbiotic objects allowing him to escape the eternal difficulties of having to generate his own thoughts or experience. The primary difficulty here is not being able to process (through alpha-function and the containing function) unbearable feelings of shame leading to a 'meaningless intensity' between us. Put simply, in this version of the symbiotic mode Glen is able to engage his object in the avoidance of shame linked to bad objects. Apart from leading to an impoverished and static sense of self, these strategies cannot deal with the inevitable build-up of negative affect. I propose that a group of second-order defences are called upon here evident in the way affect builds in the psyche and then suddenly 'drops off'. I understand this to be linked to how uncontained affects begin to take on the 'physical' qualities of beta-elements leading to an internal reality that is experienced as a near-physical entity.

To explore this possibility further I return to Bion's model. Beta-elements are, in essence, untransformed sensory or affective impressions, rudimentary impressions made on the mind that are left suspended in the psyche if not acted on by alpha-function. Apart from being fit for evacuation through projection, beta-elements also form the most primitive units of our experience. They are the 'stem cells' of psychic experience capable of transformation into alpha-elements, the basic psychological elements or components of thought. Alpha-elements remain unconscious and are not yet meaningful thoughts. They exist like disorganized 'snapshots' of experience, pictograms, that still have yet to be organized in some meaningful form (Ferro, 2002, 2005b). The acquisition of meaning and genuine thought depends on the operation of the containing function and Ps↔D.

As mentioned earlier,[1] this is partly made possible by the internalization of the containing function of primary caregivers. Such a process, following Bion, not only makes genuine thinking possible, but also enables mental contents to be assimilated and stored in the psyche, leading to greater

---

1 I have emphasized the idea that internalization also involves a process of mourning the 'ideal container'.

integration. According to this view then, meaning is dependent on the processing of sensory impressions, performed by alpha-function, which otherwise would not be able to take on a psychological form. If this cannot be done, primitive forms of experience are simply left in a suspended state.

Bion's model is fairly novel in that it proposes an emotional processing system that is responsible for the continuous creation of thought deposits – alpha-elements – that form a division between conscious and unconscious; a division that creates a contact barrier between self and external reality. Here the subject, in effect, continuously 'dreams' himself into existence. It is a continuous process of 'becoming' oneself through the perpetuation of this contact barrier.

What goes wrong in rage-type offenders? It seems to me that toxic experiences of shame either cannot be acted on by alpha-function or cannot be rendered meaningful by the container function. Glen's interaction with me appears to illustrate difficulties in converting or translating primitive forms of mentation into meaningful experience that can, in turn, enrich the engagement and build meaning through symbolic communications. This deeply affects one's sense of self and leads to the build-up of beta-elements and components of thought (alpha-elements) that cannot be successfully integrated or transformed. This is how Glen described this experience:

> 'There is a part of me that has a life of its own, I can't control it; it goes up and down as it pleases. People tell me things then they just disappear, like I forget them, but I can still feel these things they are always sort of there. . . . I can't get rid of them.'

On another occasion, talking about his experience of me:

> 'There is always something bad behind what you say, even if you are talking about positive things . . . If I let you talk too long it's like I fill up with something that starts to feel threatening and I start feeling irritable. It's not anger, just irritation. I think about a lot of things, they come and go, but these feelings stick around a bit until I shut off.'

For Bion (1962b) beta-elements are attached to primitive states of consciousness that have no particular meaning. Here, all impressions of self and others are felt to have equal value and can only be experienced in the form of a vague but lurking sense of 'pressure' being exerted on the mind. Although Glen appears to be aware of the presence of affect in the sense that he becomes aware of his own discomfort, much of his experience cannot be developed psychologically and assimilated as part of the self. In essence, experiences of shame associated with anticipated 'bad' objects appear to be always present at primitive levels of mind. It amounts to a peculiar situation where they cannot be remembered or forgotten. This is similar to the case of Amelia to be explored in Chapter 12, where this psychic conundrum is expressed in the sense that things cannot be dead or alive but always exist as both. Glen's description of his own experience appears to depict an aspect of his internal world that exists on the periphery of his experience, an area where feelings and thoughts are ever-present but inaccessible. Put another way, it depicts a sense of being haunted by a presence that is felt but has no history.

It should be made clear, however, that I am not referring to the virtual collapse of alpha-function. Even in the most psychotic cases, alpha-function is still able to process some experience (Bion, 1967). It is the experience of shame that cannot be processed. Even here there are times where we can see alpha-function at work in the 'flashes of awareness' that Glen cannot develop further by using his containing function to develop meaning. The 'flash pictures' appear to carry with them some of the qualities of beta-elements where they cannot be developed into meaningful conscious thought and appear as aberrant experiences not belonging to the self. Although Bion meant alpha-elements to remain an abstract concept, it appears that these momentary experiences give us a glimpse of this level of mind, usually unconscious. As Glen reports, these experiences feel like an assault on the self when they occur. Rather than alpha-elements becoming fruits for creative experience, the breakthrough of authentic experience, the sudden appearance of these pictograms, appear to be a traumatic experience. They suddenly appear and there is obliviousness to how one thought might lead to another or how mental states evolve and develop between minds.

The build-up of unmetabolized experience has further implications as it leads to deficits in the ability to discriminate between the perception of feelings, intentions, physical sensation, motives; all sophisticated mental events. In theory I understand this to occur because inadequate containment of toxic shame leads to confusion between beta-elements and alpha-elements. Although alpha-elements represent inchoate psychological fragments, without containment they remain very concrete experiences and fall prey to various other mental manoeuvres that have more in common with beta-elements. First, in keeping with Bion's idea that primitive sensory experiences lack differentiation and are felt to have 'equal value', there is often a felt symmetry between mental events in terms of meaning. This can be found in my interaction with Glen where my enquiring about aggressive experience, interpreting his difficulties in relationships, maintaining eye contact, showing interest in some of his difficulties, were all experienced as potential attempts to shame him. It is the emotional valence of unprocessed affect, or the impact of interaction as a sensory event, that has the most influence here, not the varied potential meanings of my different intentions, motivations and actions. I would surmise that the unreasoned escalation of events or emotions that could not be contained can be traced to these kinds of confusion. For instance, in the lead up to Glen's aggressive acts towards his wife, his wife's intentions in talking about future financial plans, her need for security, her anxiety regarding the precariousness of her own work environment, were all equated with his own felt inadequacy about his earning capacity.

Because psychic representations remain undeveloped, confusion between the mental and physical realms is also a common feature. This often manifests in a kind of 'what you see is what you are' mentality. For example, size is equated with goodness or quality, quality is equated with quantity, success is equated with financial gain. Although this kind of mentality is often apparent to some degree in most, it dominates the mind of the violent offender. Mental events are dominated by sensory input that simply registers the presence of physical reality but misrepresents psychic reality. Here, the components of thoughts are treated more like sense impressions, beta-elements, and are felt to have a very real physical presence. With a retarded capacity for genuine thought formation or reflection, action, the conventional approach towards the material world, is felt to be the most apparent solution. Bateman and Fonagy (2004) term this the teleological mode in borderline patients where reasoning is based on direct cause–effect relationships in the physical world. This contributes to a particular kind of mentality that appears to mimic the 'laws' of physical form and action. Projective identification, for instance, relies on concrete phantasies that psychic objects can be evacuated and annihilated. I do not want to say anything more about projective identification here. The link between projective identification, as an 'action defence', and violence has been covered at length elsewhere (Cartwright, 2002; Hyatt-Williams, 1998; Meloy, 1992). Other aspects of this kind of mentality have received less attention and are worth mentioning in a little more detail as they seem relevant in further understanding the transference–countertransference states mentioned earlier, including the sudden drop-off of affect encountered with such offenders and their apparent normality.

Apart from making use of projective identification, unmetabolized affect linked to 'bad' objects appears to be managed in two ways: through the agglomeration of affective objects and the generation of 'autistic blocking' to contain the build-up of affect. It seems to me that rage offenders mostly tend to use projective identification for creating a link with an idealized object. The projection of unbearable affect only accompanies the act of violence where it leads to a phantasized destruction of the object in the victim. On the whole, however, when aspects of idealization and splitting are challenged (the narcissistic exoskeleton) a second-order level of defensiveness and psychological organization is exposed. It is characterized by a sense of self or a sense of coherence being managed through oscillations between the build-up of affect and autistic blocking.

I propose that affective build-up, typical in rage offenders, occurs due to agglomeration of sensory impressions and affective objects. Following Bion (1992), agglomeration refers to how undigested beta-elements, instead of being transformed or assimilated, appear simply to mass together or agglomerate. As Bion points out, this often gives the appearance of coherent whole-object relating but the experience is more about a sense that these parts of the self have a life of their own where proto-emotions and the components of thought cohere around events that have a similar emotional valence. Without adequate containment, isolated experiences adhere to a kind of reasoning that draws on imitation of the physical world. This emerges in reasoning often found in violent men that draws on the logic that 'there is always strength in numbers', or where 'quantity is always seen as better than quality'. Glen would often defer to this type of one-dimensional logic when referring to relationships with others. For instance, he would reason that the stronger he could be in therapy, the better he would become at dealing with his feelings. He also felt that the longer he could 'sit out' problems in his marriage, the better his marriage would become.

If this kind of mentality is prominent in the individual, it gives Oedipal anxieties a much more primitive meaning. Feelings of jealousy and inadequacy, for instance, linked to exclusions regarding the parental couple, are felt to be annhilatory, or push the individual towards feelings of disintegration and non-existence. From this perspective, it might be said that the massing together of beta-elements and proto-thoughts is used as a primitive strategy to counter such deleterious conceptions.

In *Cogitations* Bion wondered whether indigestible experience had an important function in holding the self together whilst other experience was assimilated and made meaningful. As quoted earlier: 'Is their "indigestibility" a quality that renders them useful for this function, as if it were some kind of container for an eroding liquid which must be able itself to resist the erosion by its contents?' (1992, p.52). Previously I associated this with the proto-container; here I explore the extent to which agglomeration leads to hypergeneration of proto-containing strategies.

Perhaps this can be applied to understanding the way in which violent offenders use agglomeration as a principal method of holding the self together when idealization begins to fail. Through using affective impressions as a source of building coherence, the patient defends against 'lived' psychic experience. I see this as part of an autistic containing mode where the strength and might of being able to 'hold things together' dominates over thought-filled contemplation and the integration of internal objects and their corresponding affects. Although the build-up of affect is negative, because it is felt to approximate a real physical object it is taken to delineate the boundaries of the self and represents a form of beta-mentality.

There is room here to assume that the build-up of affect initially occurs because splitting and projection, as a means of organizing experience, is not easily deployed in 'bad' parts of the self. As discussed earlier, typically, 'bad' experience is locked deep inside self, shielded by a profoundly idealized world. It could be argued that this hampers ongoing interaction between Ps↔D, disintegration and integration, where experience accumulates (D) but is not subject to disintegration or normal splitting.

As well as agglomeration of affect producing a near-physical sense of cohesion, the boundaries also appears to eventually block affect. To return to Glen's experience, as quoted earlier: 'Talk just becomes noise to me. Eventually I feel myself harden inside, things stop. But people and things, even you here, don't feel real to me when this happens.' This seems to describe a generation of 'autistic blocking' in the transference where potentially meaningful experience is transformed into autistic objects as a further means of defensively shoring up the self. Without the container function in proper operation a more primitive version of holding the self together is sought. As pointed out earlier, we all experience this process in transient ways. For example, a word or sentence if repeated continuously, or subjected to intense scrutiny, quickly loses its meaning and is felt simply to be an object, a sense impression that feels more linked to the physical world. More importantly, the word is then felt to block thinking or meaningful experience. This says a lot about how precarious systems of meaning and the containing function are. But for those prone to violent acting out this process is adopted as a means of defending against extreme vulnerability. Here, repetition and over-exposure to building affect denude objects of meaning and turn them into instruments that block experience.

Implications for treatment

In light of the above problems I see treatment as an attempt to deal with factors related to unmetabolized aspects of the psyche that are linked to shame and the bad-object system. Poor representational capacity makes psychotherapy an arduous process leaving one with a sense of tremendous immobility and inflexibility. Often such patients appear markedly ill at ease with the therapeutic process, particularly the therapist's attempts to think along with the patient and other associated aspects of his or her containing function. Although not verbalized, there is sometimes a sense that the patient feels that the therapist is just 'making things up' in a meaningless way. This appears related to their inability to follow or intuit the mental states of others, particularly when they come close to activating feelings of unbearable shame in the personality.

Given the logic of what I call beta-mentality, a near-physical way of approaching the world, it is not uncommon for such patients to feel as though the therapist wants to literally 'move things around' in their mind. It is a sense that the therapist is able to physically change things in the patient's mind and is accompanied by a great deal of paranoia. As Glen put it once:

> 'Sometimes I think about things here when you say them. I don't know what it is but I know that it is because you have done something to me. It is like you have made me do it. You made me think these thoughts with your thoughts . . . I don't like it, it makes me suspicious.'

In order to try and begin to initiate a productive therapeutic relationship one has to tolerate 'rationalizations of goodness', idealizations, and attempts to emulate the good seen in the therapist that is linked to the narcissistic exoskeleton. This involves having to tolerate and collude with behaviours and thoughts that prompt an idealizing response. It means tolerating rigidly held righteous beliefs, over-obliging submissive strategies and fantasies of a symbiotic union that exists separate from the real world. Some degree of actively 'going along' with the patient is required because the idealized self still needs to defend against underlying unbearable shame if he is to make contact with the therapist. Further, the idealized self 'is believed by the patient to represent the self in its entirety and is the basis on which most achievements have been based. With this in mind the therapist needs to exercise some caution in challenging these beliefs and ideas. That is, until the patient is able to think about himself in different ways and, in so doing, have other internal resources to rely on' (Cartwright, 2002, p.182).

As indicated previously, the level of uncontained anxiety often makes it very difficult to think about the patient or the therapeutic interaction. Sessions are felt to be rushed and quite 'meaningless' but intense at times. The build-up of affect associated with this aspect of the transference often makes it difficult for the patient to continue coming to psychotherapy. Some anticipatory comments regarding how this may cause a premature end to psychotherapy can sometimes be a helpful means of beginning to address this problem (Cartwright, 2004a). In many ways, especially during 'autistic phases' of interaction, it is useful for the therapist to adopt an approach that is more about translating and helping the patient to name affective cues as opposed to attempting to adopt an interpretative approach proper. Simple interventions can help the patient start to link thoughts with feelings so as to encourage psychic growth, flexibility and some degree of self-acceptance while gradually being exposed to aspects of the bad-object system that are perceived to be intolerable. Examples of such interventions might be: 'I wonder what that man might be feeling?', 'Perhaps your experience changes when I . . .?', 'How does that feeling differ from this?', 'Do you think irritation is like anger?', 'Your feelings seem to change when . . .?'.

As I see it, the principal aim of therapy is to find a way of thinking about and containing the unbearable shame that is linked to this process. The first indication of real progress with rage offenders is usually the ability to be conscious of their own vengefulness rather than splitting it off (Lansky, 2007). Through fostering more possibilities where the patient can engage with the therapist's more contemplative stance – the ability to hold the patient in mind – more meaningful contact is gradually built up and the patient becomes more able to relinquish the hold that his defensive organization demands. As is the case with working towards a depressive solution, in the Kleinian sense, this makes possible a process of mourning the consequences and impact of one's behaviour on others.

In Glen's case this entailed him beginning – for the first time it seemed – to think about his own feeling states in relation to his mother. It was a rudimentary, but very difficult move, as it meant having to relate to the shame this aroused in him. Mourning meant having to tolerate and attend to his own vulnerability and its impact on his behaviour; something he had always vehemently denied feeling in his relationship with his wife.

Encouraging the patient gradually to 'name' bad experience broadens their own containing capacities and the work of alpha-function. It requires that the therapist take an active stance in getting such patients to see their world from different perspectives. Often, due to the unmetabolized nature of experience where the agglomeration of affect overwhelms the therapeutic space, the therapist has to work hard at simply slowing down the speed of interaction to make this possible. In essence, the task is to develop a rudimentary sense of a 'third object' being present in the room, another perspective that attempts to 'open up' mental space. Referring back to 'Modes of Interaction' (Chapter 7), this could be understood as the therapist attempting to facilitate a move towards the commensal mode.

One last point: it is often assumed that such patients will be aggressive and, given the presenting problem, management of aggression should be the key focus. In my view, making this assumption, and attempting to work with aggression from an anger management perspective, serves little purpose at this point. Such an approach will simply be taken on compliantly as part of the defensive system and tends to block further exploration of the problems of shame and the processing of concrete objects. The problem here relates to the fact that they can be told that they are aggressive and so forth, but seldom are able to grasp its felt personal meaning in the early stages of psychotherapy as it still exists in a much depersonalized, unmetabolized way.

Conclusion

There is a lot missing from this picture regarding the driving dynamics behind violence; constitutional factors, the role of perversion, attachment difficulties, the Oedipal level of experience, the role of situation factors, etc., are all important. I have attempted here simply to shed some light on some aspects of experience as commonly found in rage offenders. While potential offenders use the narcissistic exoskeleton to defend against shame through projective identification with idealized objects, I have attempted to show that the unmetabolized experience linked to shame is organized around a form of beta-mentality. The agglomeration of beta-elements and the components of thought, its near physical nature, as well as the generation of autistic objects, create a means of holding the self together in a way that approximates a physical representation of the container as opposed to its fully developed psychological counterpart.

Chapter 11

The autistic mode in agoraphobic syndrome[1]

There seems to be common agreement about the general formulation of agoraphobia being a regressive flight away from Oedipal fears to more primitive modes of relating. However, the quality and nature of this regressed state, the primitive dynamics of the agoraphobic experience itself, have been less clearly formulated. Here we are faced with questions related to how agoraphobic experience is generated, why such symptoms should be 'chosen' above other symptomatology, as well as how it may differ from other phobias or forms of psychopathology in general. Above all, further understanding agoraphobic experience will hopefully lead to better help and progress in our technique with such patients.

In this chapter I want to put forward the idea that a very primitive autistic type of relating forms the bedrock of agoraphobic syndrome. Here, agoraphobic fears and related defences represent a regressive compromise that both terrifies and protects, both prevents and allows contact with the external object. There are three essential points I want to make. First, a key dynamic in the generation of agoraphobic symptoms involves a regressive retreat into the maternal object where the fear of disintegration is halted. From this vantage point external objects can be used as autistic shapes where they become substitutes for boundaries of the self, a form of protective encapsulation. This fits a general mode of engaging with internal and external objects that I have called 'the autistic mode' (Chapter 7). In addition to the commensal, symbiotic and parasitic modes of interaction that Bion (1970) suggests, 'the autistic mode' amounts to a further way of understanding how container–contained might interact. I use the word 'autistic' here to refer to states of mind that make use of mental objects and sensory impressions to seal off and block experiencing (Tustin, 1990). Second, it appears that, as a consequence of autistic encapsulation the

1 An earlier version of this chapter has been previously published as 'Autistic defenses in agoraphobic syndrome: "flat" objects and the retardation of projective identification', *Journal of the American Psychoanalytic Association*, *54*, 109-135. Copyright © SAGE Publications, 2006.

defensive use of projective identification is retarded. Projective identification is often used as a means of ridding the self, in fantasy, of bad objects by projecting them into external objects. My observations suggest that this process is retarded due to the agoraphobic's perception of space. This leaves them less able to use projective defences as a transitory means of 'unburdening' the self.

Finally, in keeping with Ogden's (1992) ideas on different modes of generating experience, I want to put forward the idea that agoraphobic experience occurs when the dialectic between the paranoid-schizoid and autistic-contiguous modes of generating experience collapses. Alongside considering changes in the transference dynamic of the case to be discussed, we will briefly consider how the theory of container–contained configurations might apply.

These observations emerged in the treatment of a 33-year-old woman who had become agoraphobic after experiencing a panic attack. I saw her for twice-a-week psychoanalytic psychotherapy over a period of four years. She proved very difficult to treat and it was only after I was able to understand the transference as being generated out of autistic experience that progress was made. To illustrate this I will trace a number of occurrences in the transference–countertransference relationship and the therapeutic process that led me to these conclusions. Towards the end of the chapter I shall briefly explore some of the technical implications this may have for understanding agoraphobia and the therapeutic process.

The psychodynamics of agoraphobia

Agoraphobia remains a rather amorphous diagnostic entity most often precipitated by the onset of panic attacks. It covers a number of fears that include claustrophobia, the fear of enclosed spaces, streets, open places, buildings, buses, and so forth. As such fears usually co-occur in the individual, Compton's (1992) suggestion that agoraphobia is best understood as being a 'syndrome' appears appropriate. The *Diagnostic and Statistical Manual of Mental Disorders IV* (American Psychiatric Association, 1994) isolates two key situations associated with agoraphobic anxiety and fear:

- situations where escape might be perceived as being difficult
- situations where it is perceived that help is not available.

A number of psychodynamic factors have been found to lie behind this clinical picture. Space does not permit a full review of the literature here (see Compton, 1992; Pam *et al.*, 1994). I shall simply highlight the main dynamics that have been implicated in the syndrome before concentrating my efforts on understanding the nature of primitive psychic states and defences that occur in agoraphobia.

There is broad agreement that both Oedipal and pre-Oedipal concerns contribute to the symptomatic profile of agoraphobia. Stripped down to its most rudimentary dynamics, agoraphobia has mainly been understood as having its origins in a regressive flight away from unbearable anxiety states precipitated by Oedipal-related concerns[2] (usually in the form of panic attacks). Such fears and conflict include fears about sexual temptation and promiscuity (Abraham, 1913), castration (Busch et al., 1999; Lewin, 1935), unresolved aggressive conflicts (Deutsch, 1929) and fear associated with new-found independence (Deutsch, 1929; Ruddick, 1961; Weiss, 1935). This formulation finds support in the fact that agoraphobia often occurs after major life transitions, particularly in early adulthood, a time when such conflicts and fears are in ascendance. Following general principles of the formation of phobic symptoms, the specific Oedipal fear is then displaced on to more 'acceptable fears' and projected into external situations where the anxiety can be avoided in a way that cannot be done internally. In this formulation regression is viewed mainly as a means of avoidance and emergent symptoms are viewed as being the result of Oedipal dilemmas.

There is general acknowledgement that the agoraphobic state also arises due to 'fear of fear', a fear of re-experiencing unbearable states of anxiety. However, although such fears may account for some of the conscious reasons why individuals protect themselves from 'unsafe' places, this formulation, on its own, fails to account for unconscious processes and regressive defences that contribute to the phenomenology of agoraphobia. Furthermore, this explanation does not account for why fear of anxiety should occur in particular situations and not in others (Compton, 1992).

Despite the general acknowledgment of the Oedipal problems that the agoraphobic faces, doubts have often been cast about this being a complete formulation. In his seminal paper on the subject, Ruddick (1961) put it as follows:

> Although the hysteria seems to develop around a crisis of the oedipal conflict, frequently the sources stem from far deeper preoedipal and pregenital difficulties, and one can rarely say that the agraphobe is simply a hysteric.
>
> (p.537)

Support for this can be found in those who argue that agoraphobics often show signs of having a personality disorder or deep character deficits

---

2 Deviating from this main formulation, some argue that the initial anxiety associated with agoraphobia is solely physiological and lacks any associated psychological content. Freud (1895) put forward this view in arguing that agoraphobia was precipitated by 'Aktual anxiety'. Alternatively, some are of the view that such anxiety is precipitated by a hysterical reaction to trauma.

(Goldstein and Chamberless, 1982; Pam *et al.*, 1994). Further, approaches that emphasize the importance of separation anxiety, attachment problems, over-dependence and over-protection (Ballenger, 1997; Busch, 1995; Bowlby, 1985; Gabbard, 1992; Goldstein and Chamberless, 1982; Milrod, 1995; Pam *et al.*, 1994; Roth, 1996; Shear, 1996) also suggest that pre-genital conflicts play a significant role in the formation of agoraphobic symptoms.

Returning to Ruddick, he argues that 'failure at the earliest oral level of incorporation and of the formation of a functioning superego' (1961, p.543) contributes greatly to agoraphobic experience. This leads to a situation where, in his words, 'the street and the outside world were structured as an attempt to concretize or localize an ego boundary' (p.543). In an earlier paper Weiss (1935) also found that the retardation of introjective processes were involved. Still further, Lewin (1952) extended his previously 'phallo-centric view' of claustrophobia and agoraphobia by underlining the import-ance of fantasies of engulfing or penetrating the interior of the maternal object that, in turn, begin to represent a bounded claustral space. As well as advancing arguments for the importance of pregenital concerns, common in all these findings is the recognition of a need to link inchoate concep-tualizations of psychic reality, internal space, ego and bodily boundaries, to the development of agoraphobia.

Kleinian analysts, with their primary emphasis on primitive object relations, have perhaps been most influential here. Klein's (e.g. 1932, 1946, 1955) emphasis on early oral incorporation phantasies, projective identi-fication and phantasies about the interior of the mother's body has led to considerable interest in the primitive origins of claustrophobic and agora-phobic states. Segal (1981), for instance, suggests that the use of patho-logical projective identifications best explains agoraphobic-related fears. Pathological or intrusive projective identifications[3] are used to rid the self of part-objects that threaten the fragile ego by projecting them, in fantasy, into external objects. Of course, the defence is only partially successful as the evacuated projections create phobic objects in the individual's external environment. Others, particularly Meltzer, Bick and Tustin, have concerned themselves with even more primitive mental states that give rise to autistic ways of relating to the world.[4]

---

3 As discussed earlier, Bion (1962a) makes a valuable distinction between omnipotent, patho-logical projective identification and normal or 'realistic' forms of projective identification. Whereas the former functions as a means of holding omnipotent and destructive control through annexing it, the latter performs a crucial developmental task in communicating feeling/mental states, in turn, making them available for transformation by the object that receives the projection. Intrusive projective identification (Meltzer, 1992) perhaps best describes the internal situation discussed here.

4 Although such a statement may appear oxymoronic, these authors convincingly show how inchoate forms of relating always exist in autistic psychic states.

As discussed earlier, Bick (1968) identified the use of brittle 'second-skin' formations in the psyche created due to failed containment by an external object. The individual essentially uses the 'skin' as a form of self-containment that shuts off a need for dependency on other objects. As a result, containment is equated with imprisonment or confinement and thus related to claustrophobic phenomena. In *The Claustrum*, Meltzer (1992) develops a theory of claustrophobic states based on the use of intrusive projective identifications with an internal maternal object in order to escape mental pain and individuation. Through projective identification, the patient penetrates the internal object, essentially annexing it for himself. This has all sorts of consequences for identity formation and individuation. Most important here, however, is Meltzer's theory that claustrophobic phenomena – including agoraphobia – have their origins in the penetration of an internal object that, in turn, becomes entrapping and threatening principally because it has been deceptively penetrated and awaits 'recriminations' for this.

Such primitive forms of relating rely on the defining qualities of the 'invaded object' and the patient is able to take on these characteristics for purposes of their own self-definition through the use of adhesive identifications (Bick, 1968; Meltzer, 1974, 1975a). The individual defines himself by adhering or 'sticking' to the form of another object – the object's surface is taken to be one's own. Tustin (1986, 1990) shows that this kind of autistic encapsulation is continuously auto-generated through using objects as sensation-generating, two-dimensional surfaces. The sensate surface forms a protective capsule which, at the same time, gives rise to a sense of continuity with the object that denies separateness. The essential function of the defences here is to create a 'rhythm of safety' (Tustin, 1986) in order to stave off the threat of disintegration. She argues that encapsulated states of this nature are always, to some extent, present in phobic patients. A number of other authors have also found autistic defences to have an important presence in various 'neurotic' presentations (e.g. Anzieu, 1989, 1993; Grotstein, 1983b; Klein, 1980; Mitrani, 1992). In such patients, parts of the personality remain unthinkable and unable to articulate experience. They function like autistic 'cysts' that block various avenues of experience.

In acknowledgement of the idea that autistic defences can be found in various forms of psychopathology, Ogden (1992) has proposed that autistic means of generating experience should be viewed as being in a dialectical relationship with paranoid-schizoid and depressive modes of generating experience. In his view, different forms of psychopathology correspond with the collapse or retardation of the dialectic between these modes of generating experience. We shall return to this argument in exploring its relevance in understanding manifestations of agoraphobic experience in the following case example.

Ms A

Ms A came to see me approximately one year after she had suffered a panic attack whilst travelling alone on holiday. Prior to the panic attack she recalled being worried about not being able to find 'a place to stay' in the city she was visiting. She grew increasingly anxious after the incident and, despite having close friends in the same city who offered their support, returned home immediately. Soon after this Ms A developed severe agoraphobic symptoms which essentially kept her housebound for almost two years. She was highly anxious about leaving home, driving, and being in any enclosed space. By the time our treatment commenced she was able to leave the house for short periods of time, but always had to be accompanied by her mother or a family friend.

A year before the initial panic attack she had graduated from university and was a qualified health-care professional but had not gained the confidence to work. Ms A continued to live at home with her mother and father. She had one older brother who had left home but would return home for extended periods of time when 'things were not working out for him in the outside world'. Ms A and her brother had grown up in a household where their father had been largely absent and their mother was clearly over-concerned and anxious about her children's ability to function away from home. Although her mother often appeared caring and concerned, Ms A would often complain that there was a growing sense of distance between them that worried her a great deal.

A particular dynamic appeared to exist between family members that seemed to be relevant for understanding Ms A's condition. Her father's withdrawn approach seemed partly related to his being a rather introverted and shy man. This had clearly created much anxiety in my patient and led to conscious attempts to try and involve him in social activities. Based on this, they developed a close intimate relationship that placed her in a position of guilt as her father and mother had increasingly grown apart.

Ms A had first experienced a panic attack in adolescence whilst attending a school concert hosted by a male teacher. This initial episode had always puzzled her. She did recall, however, that she was concerned about her parents at the time as they were not getting along. Ms A recalled many instances of separation anxiety in her history and felt that people always appeared to be leaving her. Although separation problems abounded in her history, interpretations related to underlying anxieties in this area were mostly denied and were not available for interpretation for a long period in the therapy.

During the initial six months of therapy Ms A was markedly distressed about her high levels of anxiety. As is the case with most agoraphobic patients, she was constantly preoccupied with her physical symptoms. From the outset she adopted a particular style of communication that seemed typical of what Compton (1998) calls 'anxious thought', a dispersive manner of communicating that tended to fill the entire therapeutic space. She would talk endlessly about her troubles, often second-guessing herself and undoing previous thoughts in a way that was very difficult to follow, although not incoherent or illogical. Thoughts and ideas could only exist momentarily before being reined in, criticized, or questioned in a way that made their original intention relatively meaningless.

Patient: [anxiously, and with some pressure of speech, discussing her concerns about her father's growing isolation] I walked with him yesterday around the garden, no I didn't, we just talked about what he was doing. Lonely, very lonely. . . . Well not really he has my mother. I could take him out but then how would I feel? Maybe it will make him feel better but it could make him feel worse. I could call him, he could call me. But I suppose phoning is not the solution, I should see him. . . . But I don't feel well myself. I'm feeling worse this week, better than the week before though. Well, not really because I feel a little giddy. I was feeling depressed, no not depressed but kind of sad about not being able to go out on my own, well I wasn't sad but needed to be with my mother. I'll ask my father if he wants to walk, but I usually walk by myself. I feel tired, I'm not sure why. I wanted to go out last night, phoned a friend. I was at school with her, she had another friend who spent a lot of time with them. I'm not sure if I'll go overseas again, well maybe. My father could be sick I suppose; shy, but he's fine.

Analyst: You seem to be concerned about your father but also want your own space.

Patient: Perhaps, but not really. Well . . . yes. But I feel he is lonely, well he does work. My mother never talks to him. . . . Only when she wants something done. I feel like I'm safe at home with my mother, but she doesn't do a lot. She never openly cares. . . . She does, but not really with care so I don't think it's that. He's busy with his work. There is nothing wrong with him; I can talk to him but not really. I will be by myself. It's not right, my father is fine; the world is cruel, people are cruel, well not really. I just want to stay safe in my room but I'm really fine . . .

Analyst: You seem . . . [interrupts]

Patient: I am tired, it's been a rough week; my mother has been away, I feel safe in my room. There are so many things to say, my father looks worried sometimes, I know I can't help. Well I can, but what should I do? I did a bit of work today, well not really. My head hurts, my legs hurt, I'm anxious sometimes; I see nothing I can do. There are some friends coming down. I was thinking if I should visit. The one friend is a friend of my brother's; the other is a friend of a friend. We could go for tea. Well I think we could meet at her place; no I'll see.

Analyst: Just earlier, you seemed concerned about your father, but it feels difficult to think about, something is cruel that makes you want to retreat into a safe place.

Patient: Yes. . . . My week has been good, well some things were good. I could do some of my work. It is a safe place my room . . . but there is no safety, I have to keep on moving and doing things, saying things. I feel a little better then . . . I was worried today. No, scared. I think I need to see my GP again, it's my ears, I want to see if that's linked to panic, feeling dizzy sometimes . . . I'm worried about going to work, she is nice but I don't say much then I feel panic, I don't know what to say. She's involved in charities much of the time. She's also working full-time, she has similar interests, her friend's sister is an old colleague, I think. My body feels heavy, tired. I could go home after this, I could go and see a friend. She connects with me like I feel here, less anxious. . . . You are good to me. I must go now.

It is difficult, in the space of a brief vignette, to convey the impact that this manner of speech had on the therapeutic situation, especially the non-verbal implications of her ruminations. But hopefully this gives the reader a sense of the way the patient presented throughout most sessions. Initially, this appeared simply to be in keeping with her state of anxiety, a caricature, in a way, of the anxiously neurotic patient. However, this manner of speaking remained unchanged even when her manifest anxiety appeared to subside towards the end of the first year of treatment. Although some reassurance about her anxiety had appeared to help assuage her distress, none of my interpretive interventions appeared to have had an impact. It was very difficult to follow her and I often felt confused and directionless in my thinking. Her frenetic manner of speech and the sense of feeling 'talked at' made it difficult to know my own feelings when I was with her. With the little I could follow, my understanding of the case at this point was that Ms A's agoraphobic state appeared to have its roots in separation concerns that had remained unresolved due to particular concerns involving Oedipal conflicts, notably Ms A's role as a 'replacement wife' to her father. Her agoraphobia appeared to represent a regressive solution to this unconscious conflict whereby Ms A 'returned to her mother' and projected her guilt and fear of leaving on to the outside world. This in turn kept her from having to face her own fears about separation.

In a similar way to some of the formulations mentioned in the previous section, I understood her 'anxious thought' to be the result of such projections. Although these projections protected her from an internal resolution, locating such conflict in her external environment had made it an unbearable place to inhabit. It was a dynamic that appeared to amount to the workings of an extremely harsh superego that was projected into me in the transference leading to excessive fear in relating to me. At the time this seemed to explain my sense of feeling almost 'robotic' and markedly unemotional towards her.[5] Almost everything I tried to convey to her felt overly harsh or intrusive, even the simplest comments.

At points I tried to draw her attention to how her 'anxious thought' seemed to be related to anticipations of danger and cruelty that she perceived in me or others. I also encouraged her to consider the amount of emotional strife that seemed to revolve around her concern for her father as an attempt to raise her awareness about the possibility that these conflicts were being projected onto phobic situations.

Despite tacit agreement with such comments, my interventions did not seem to deepen Ms A's associations and no progress appeared to be made, especially in terms of her manner of relating to me. Her communicative style began to baffle me. In time though, once I was able to pay closer attention to my countertransference, her manner of relating and speaking and the way she perceived space, I began to understand the core dynamics of the case very differently.

Ms A often alluded to the importance of being 'inside her room' at home where she knew her concerned mother was available. There was a contradictory sense that her mother was essential to her well-being and yet she hardly referred to her and I was aware of knowing relatively little about her. A similar dynamic appeared early on in the transference, although it took me over a year to understand it. Therapy had clearly become a 'safe place' for her. Despite her anxiety, she often commented on how tranquil, calming and safe it was when she was 'inside' the room with me. She would often try and understand why she felt so different with me as compared to the 'harsh outside world' and was curious about the way psychotherapy worked and why she felt 'soothed' by the process. Amidst her anxious musings she tried to understand what was happening between us but was sure that it had little to do with our verbal exchange. In her words, 'It has

5 At the time, I understood my feeling state to be a combination of the incarnation of Ms A's harsh superego as well as my own defences against its destructiveness.

nothing to do with words or what is said in therapy, there is something else
. . . a kind of connection'. Towards the end of each session she would often
thank me for 'truly understanding' her, 'really connecting' with her concerns. 'Connecting' with others was something that took on idealized tones
and her fantasies in this area related to putting herself in positions where
she felt mothered in an idealized, magical way that I came to know as a
kind of swoon-like state.[6] Most relationships with others appeared to
follow this dynamic. When they did not, they were deemed relatively useless
as this essentially meant the 'connection' had been lost. I grew curious
about the disparity in our apparent experiences. Although Ms A was
preoccupied with her notion of connecting with me in a 'meaningful way', I
often still felt remarkably 'wooden', numbed by her vocalizations. I felt out
of reach and unimportant to her and, as mentioned earlier, I seemed to
have very little access to any feeling states whilst sitting with her, leaving me
with a sense of meaninglessness about our interaction.

I began thinking more about the importance of 'connecting' for Ms A and
the disparate feeling states that appeared to surround this dynamic.
Somewhat challenged by these observations I began to relinquish any
attempts to discern clear narratives or meaning from her utterances and
instead began to focus on the impact of her speech patterns on my experience. It was a time where I attempted to re-engage the containing function
through actively suspending knowing about the case so as to better connect
with my dream-thoughts. As discussed earlier, this involves the analyst
relating to himself as 'dream object' (held in tension with his role as 'proper
object') in order to engage the containing process (see Chapter 3). I began to
experience Ms A's utterances as being more like 'noise' set between us, a
form of interference that was trying to create a barrier between us. It seemed
clearer that in direct contradiction to her conscious aims of wanting to reach
me, words were being used to keep me out. But more profoundly they
seemed to be used as 'surfaces' against which she could define herself. It was
as if her words were used to weave a boundary around herself, but the
boundary could only be formed through contact with me, even if it was only
in the form of 'noise'. Her manner of generating experience with me left little
room for experiencing anything other than the point of contact between us.
Everything other, and the spaces they represented, shared little relationship
with this part of herself.

The idea that words were being used as a barrier as well as being a means
of establishing coherence gained momentum when I began to consider other
therapeutic material. She had had a dream in an earlier session that now
seemed more understandable: the dream was simply about two ships in the

---

6 'Swoon-like' appeared apt as it depicted the way she almost 'fainted' into the other/mother
creating a mindless, somnambulistic connection with the object.

middle of the ocean that were in danger unless they touched side by side. In her words, 'touching kept them safe'. It also appeared significant that she described the ships as 'peopleless', lifeless and inanimate. Although she gave few associations to this dream, in retrospect it seemed to confirm elemental aspects of her relating where points of contact between objects were points of self-definition and safety. The way 'touching' was represented in the dream also seemed to shed light on her idea of 'connecting', with the absence of people resonating with the 'wooden' inanimate feelings that appeared in the countertransference.

Representations of boundaries in the psychotherapeutic space also took on a similar meaning. Previously I had been aware of Ms A's need to 'keep time' in the sessions and her acute awareness of the beginning, middle and end of the sessions. All I had been able to say about this related to it being a means of controlling anxiety in the session, a partial interpretation that appeared to have little impact on the therapeutic process. Although I think there was a clear link here between anxiety and control, I had missed the significance of how she related to – and created – such boundaries as a means of auto-generating inchoate self-boundaries. The more I listened, the more it was apparent that she struggled a lot more with the middle of sessions as it represented, in spatial terms, the furtherest point away from a source of self-definition. This was also the point at which her ruminatory, dispersive manner of speaking escalated. Through these observations I came to understand this as a desperate means of auto-generating a sensory boundary in the session that offered an elementary form of self-cohesion. Other representations of 'boundaries' in the session like the 'rules' – her words – of therapy, her implicit ideas about how the therapy should run, were rigidly adhered to. Far from being a real sense of engagement with me (as Ms A had regularly claimed), Ms A seemed to be using the therapeutic space to recreate rudimentary boundaries that doubled as parameters of the self. With this in mind, the 'connecting' she spoke of appeared to be more about an affective experience that emanated from self-soothing sensory investment in contact boundaries – the edge of the object – rather than being about any real investment in the object and its interiority.

After some time I was able to draw her attention to the way she appeared to be relating to me and the therapeutic space. I spoke to her about the way I thought she was using words and that although she was trying desperately to reach me, she mostly spoke to build a safe shield around herself, a way of creating 'a home away from home'. At first she perceived my interpretation as a statement that essentially rejected her way of 'connecting' with me. But in time the essence of what I was trying to convey became more manifest. She began to talk about the protective function of what she called a 'wall of words' and how this appeared to reflect the way she related to space in general. Once she remarked, 'I need something up close to me, so that it becomes me, to push up against it, otherwise it feels terrifying and I just can't stand it'. In time, Ms A also grew acutely aware of how she needed me to 'be' in the sessions. In her words, she needed me to be 'kind of unreal . . . like just something . . . so you're there to me but, at the same time, I tune you out'.

The autistic mode and paradoxical entrapment

Ms A's manner of speech and her preoccupations with contact boundaries as described above suggest the presence of a rudimentary form of object-relating. It involves the auto-generation of surfaces that allow the patient to position herself 'inside' the object so as to feel 'bound' by it in order to stave off pending disintegration.

Ms A's initial sense of feeling soothed and calmed by me appears to represent a sense of being, in phantasy, inside me or the maternal object. Through her constant ruminations and repetitions Ms A appears to use words to surround herself, creating a sensory boundary of protection. From this point of view, words are used as autistic 'flat' objects as opposed to being signifiers of meaning, depth or interiority. Her thinking about time, rules and 'connecting' with me also suggest that she related to her own thinking about particular objects in a similar way. Here, the sensorial and physical qualities of thinking appear to hypertrophy in her mind. Using Bion's model, alpha-elements and narrative derivatives take on some of the qualities of beta-elements. Earlier (Chapter 6), I explored some ideas related to the organization of beta-elements to form 'abortive prototypes' of the container, proto-containing capacities. It appears that in Ms A's thinking, as expressed in her need to 'connect' and its particular qualities, these capacities stand in for the container proper and mimic its function.

Clearly, I am not suggesting that the above represented her entire experience, or that her words did not possess some symbolic qualities and so forth. I am simply trying to convey a particular level of experience where words were used as flat sensual surfaces against which she could define herself. Indeed, Ms A illustrates her capacity for symbolization in her representation of this protective autistic boundary in her dream and its representation as a 'wall of words' later in the analysis.

Ms A's idea of 'connecting' with me, its representation in the dream and consequent awareness of my emotional unresponsiveness, further added to the idea that points of contact were used as surfaces or protective boundaries appropriated for the purpose of self-definition rather than as a means of engaging with the object. I have tried to show that boundaries of the therapeutic relationship also took on a similar meaning. As Ogden (1992) points out, however, although the autistic mode needs to make use of hypertrophied boundaries to shut out the emotional world and suspend the ability to attribute meaning to experience, this mode also represents a rudimentary form of relating through sensation-bound surfaces. In other words, although words block experiencing, they also represent a point of contact with the object. For this reason Ogden terms this mode of generating experience the 'autistic-contiguous position' to depict the key dilemma delineated by this emotional state where isolation and rudimentary contact exist side by side.

The use of autistic defences in the case of Ms A suggests that her agoraphobic fears had their source in an impossible dilemma between disintegration and suffocating encapsulation. Auto-generated surfaces stave off a catastrophic disappearance of the self but, at the same time, isolate and suffocate. Space, both psychical and external, cannot be tolerated because it is equated with disintegration of the self. Here, giving oneself 'room to think' or the idea of psychic containing space is near impossible and is replaced by verbiage and constant ruminations about physical symptoms.

Although taking residence inside the maternal object – through auto-generation – itself delineates some conception of space, it is highly idealized and frozen in time so it becomes wholly predictable and unchangeable. Her idealized clinging to a 'connection' with me seemed to reflect this. Significant relationships also appeared to demonstrate this quality. As long as others close to her complied with her fantasy of idealized 'connecting', their immediate presence brought welcome relief from agoraphobic fears.

Within the context of this formulation the separation anxiety, experienced by Ms A, appears to take on a particular meaning. It seems linked to the fear of having to, in phantasy, 'step *outside* the primary object', outside a self-generated cohesiveness, and has less to do with the fear of the loss of *relating to* the object. Rather, fear and panic appear to have their source in the loss of the *immediacy* of the object's surface as an inchoate means of self-definition. Spaces inside and between objects are felt in a very concrete way to be terrifying voids in which the self cannot be recognized.

I would also venture to say that Ms A's agoraphobic experience was further complicated by the retardation of the use of projective identification as a defence. As alluded to earlier, interpretations related to terrorizing split-off and projected parts of the self had little effect on the therapeutic process. Although this is by no means reason enough to doubt such a formulation, there appear to be other grounds for considering this possibility. I base my observations here on the agoraphobic's terrifying conception of space, as well as retrospective observations in the case of Ms A that suggest that the subsidence of autistic forms of relating gave rise to a greater sense of interiority/exteriority and a new-found use of projective mechanisms to better manage her anxiety.

Ms A (revisited)

After approximately two years a number of events occurred in the course of our therapy that appeared to indicate changes in Ms A's way of relating. She was much more engaged in the therapeutic process but complained of a new-found sense of distance between us. She also grew increasingly curious about my own experiences in the session as well as what might be going on in my personal life:

Patient: I can feel the wall of words when I talk to M [a friend]. But I don't do it so much with her, well not really. We were getting closer, she was getting to know me, well kind of I guess. But we don't connect, I feel it is right, but not safe, I don't have my wall, we don't connect in that soothing way, it's different. I can understand her, her thoughts, she is interested in listening to me, especially about what kind of work I will be able to do . . .

Analyst: You experience her differently . . . even as you speak here it seems that you feel something different.

Patient: Yes, but I'm unsure what you think about this. I come and you help me, but I don't know anything about your life; whether you're married, kids and stuff. In a way I don't find you as empathic as before, something seems to have changed. It feels like something is different and it is worrying.

Analyst: It seems important in a new kind of way for you to know more about me. I imagine that you have begun to have many ideas about my personal life, it interests me that this seems linked with your feeling that I have grown distant from you . . .

Patient: I worry that therapy is taking a negative turn . . . like I'm kind of falling. I'm much better now, kind of, but I hate that our connection has changed.

In stark contrast to the previous transference–countertransference constellation, I felt engaged and real to her in a way that had appeared out of reach before. Although invasive in her enquiry at times, I found myself welcoming her engagement with a quiet sense of relief. It seemed linked to a sense that we had survived the stifling effects of her autistic encapsulation where there was no curiosity or thinking about her objects.

Significantly, Ms A's growing 'awareness' of my presence appeared to lead to increasing irritation in her. She had grown concerned with what she saw as a 'negative turn' in the therapeutic process because she felt that I no longer 'connected with her'. She insisted on wanting to know how I was surreptitiously manipulating the situation in a way that had changed our relationship for the worse. In time, it became clear that Ms A was convinced that I had 'some plan in mind' that I wasn't letting her in on. She grew increasingly anxious about this, often insisting that we 'connect' in the way we had done previously, otherwise she would terminate treatment.

It was difficult to understand Ms A's growing irritation and suspiciousness. I had a sense that it had something to do with the changes in our style of relating and an increasing awareness of separateness, but I could not find a way of saying anything about this to her. We explored her interests in my personal life and came to some understanding that it involved getting to know how others outside herself might 'feel and think'; something new that had led to a number of fears and perceived consequences. Despite this, she persisted in wanting to know about my personal life. Given her escalating anxiety about my 'manipulativeness', I found it important to disclose minimal details about my marital status and whether I had kids so as not to buy into her sense that I was deliberately holding back just for the sake of it. In time her irritation appeared to give way to a new set of narratives about her perceptions of men and fears that she was unable to attract their attention. Her references to men, male behaviours and her sexuality had been markedly conspicuous in their absence throughout our work together. Their emergence appeared to confirm changes in her object relationships that were mirrored in the transference. In a session around this time Ms A had a rather detailed dream that further illuminated these changes (I have included her main associations to the dream in parentheses for the sake of expedience).

> Ms A was in her car (her mother's car, a safe place) outside my practice waiting for the beginning of her session. She had parked almost touching the wall that surrounded my house (safe barrier, a safe house, non-existent in reality). She left the car but then felt stricken by anxiety as to whether she was arriving 'on time or in the middle' of her session (anxious about not 'sticking' to rules, in the middle of something, 'there would be no place for me if it was the middle'). Ms A went back to her car, and after entering the car felt reassured that she had the correct time. She began to feel claustrophobic in the car so decided to make her way 'inside your house'. She walked hurriedly, with a clear sense that inside would be safe if she thought about my house as being her own. Once entering my practice Ms A found me lying in my chair (a flirtatious pose) and the contents of the room had been changed around (not familiar or comfortable, someone had 'been inside' and changed it around). In the dream I was talking to others who sat outside the therapy room in a 'casual way'. She described the others in the house as 'male-biker-types' (rule breakers, deceivers of the law, rude, oversexed, dangerous on the road). Ms A was ambivalent about staying for her therapy session but decided to despite the fact that it felt strange and 'intruded upon'. She stayed because it was her 'time and space for therapy'.

The dream is rich with spatial references and possible Oedipal references that appear to say something new about the transference and the unfolding intrapsychic changes occurring at this point: She had left her mother/car only to find her surrogate-therapist-mother had changed into an oversexed dangerous man/father. The many permutations of this interpretation were gradually explored later in the course of Ms A's therapy as she grew more able to hold these ideas in mind. At another level, however, I was intrigued by the dream's ability to capture Ms A's agoraphobic conundrum as well as the move away from this stasis. It appeared to illustrate an opening up of psychic space and the interiority of the object as a container. The initial part of the dream seemed similar to her first dream about 'the ships'; a representation of being inside the mother/car with boundaries (the sides of the car and her references to time) and 'touching' delineating the contiguous boundaries that secure the space but also stifle her.

But the second part of the dream appeared entirely different as represented by the changed therapy room and movements beyond 'the wall' into another space. The 'space' is populated with dangerous masculine, oversexed, 'deceivers of the law' with which I was also identified. Significantly, at the end of the dream she makes reference to 'time and space' being her own. As well as being references to the deceivers of 'Oedipal law', and clues as to the trigger that may have initiated her regressive retreat in the first place, this part of the dream also appears to signify a new-found use of interiority and a capacity for projective identification. Based on the tranference–countertransference paradigm operating at the time and the dream content, it appears that Ms A was now able to risk entering new objects and psychic spaces (my personal life, 'inside my house') and move away from autistic rigidity and predictability. Her sense that I was somehow deceiving her with my intentions seemed to be associated with the latter part of the dream where I had become someone who was male, dangerous, 'separate' and sexual. As mentioned earlier, I had always been struck by the absence of anything that might be construed as sexual in Ms A. The dream seemed to demonstrate the tenuous links she was beginning to make with her own sexuality (and associated destructiveness) through the use of projective identification, thereby using me as a receptacle with which she was identified ('this is my space and time'). In doing so, Ms A was now able to use her version of my sexuality to vicariously explore the danger of her own libidinal needs.

In many ways elements of the above dream soon became a reality in the therapeutic process. Ms A began to comment on my 'new casual approach' to the session. These perceptions unsettled and sometimes irritated her as she struggled to understand what this might mean. In a remarkable way this was most vividly played out in how she began to experiment with changing the position of herself and other objects in the therapy room. She would move a picture or an ornament and comment on the difference in feeling this evoked in me. On two occasions she tried lying on my couch for similar reasons (an act very far removed from the rigidity of her posture that typified her earlier autistic pose). On these occasions it was her thoughts about my 'sexual feelings' in response to her actions that dominated the inquiry. In my understanding, the therapeutic space had now become a projective surface that could be 'played with' and transgressed in a way that could be experienced once removed through the use of projective identification with an external object. Importantly, this also sets in motion the possibility of these psychic states eventually being transformed through containment. Instead of making use of the autistic mode where relating to objects and thinking take on the qualities of beta-elements, Ms A begins to make use of mental space, the analyst's mind, as a transformational space where projected mental states can be thought about, experienced, and made more tolerable for the patient.

Risking interiority and the rebirth of the projective space

The above account is an attempt to capture some of the key elements that marked Ms A's transition away from autistic encapsulation. This appeared to be ushered in by the transgression of previously rigidly bound surfaces and the use of space as a projective screen. The gradual contemplation of my own imagined internal states appears to revive a capacity for projective identification (and concomitant paranoid experiences). With this, Ms A oscillates between engagement with me through projection and the yearning for a return to 'autistic connecting' where the contiguous defining lines of the self yield the illusion of continuity with the object. However, as previously explored (Chapter 3), although separateness is obscured when projective identification is in use, the idea of internal/external is never completely extinguished otherwise the defensive purposes of the defence would be defeated. I have tried to show that Ms A's employment of projective identification allowed for the modification of experience through a freer, articulated use of psychic space. Here projective identification, through 'sensing' my thoughts, is used like a probe, testing the waters and seeing where such imaginings might lead.

In retrospect it could be said that the use of projective defences, particularly projective identification, appears to have been retarded when Ms A's agoraphobic experience predominated. One inference to be drawn from such an observation is that retardation of projective identification contributes to the symptomatic presentation of agoraphobia. Such a proposition requires some clarification as it runs contrary to the conventional understanding of agoraphobia. Reasons for the retardation of projective identification appear to lie in the nature of autistic defences and consequent psychic reactions.

As mentioned previously, space, in the autistic mode, can only be crudely conceptualized and thus lacks a sense of depth and interiority. With this, the use of the object for projective identification is retarded as it is dependent on conceptions of the 'inside' of the object, either as a containing space or a place of refuge. Space also appears to be equated with disintegration and thus cannot be used, or annexed, for the purpose of projection. We see this represented in Ms A's 'ships' dream and her inability to make use of my own experience or 'subjective' presence when her agoraphobic fears were prominent.

Associated antecedent defences, particularly the use of splitting, also appear to be impaired in the generation of agoraphobic experience. Although Ms A's relating could be described as dispersive and chaotic, her thinking could not be organized around various oppositions as an intermediate means of managing anxiety. It appears that this kind of temporary dissociation – a normal transient form of splitting (Ps) – caused by separating good and bad experience is felt to be too close to the experiences and fears of disintegration for the agoraphobic. It could be said that the psychic act of 'splitting' itself approximates a spatial representation – between two objects – and is therefore abandoned as a means of managing anxiety. Instead, it is replaced by blocked experiencing, the annihilation of space and the autistic stifling of experience.

I used the word 'retarded' with particular intent here as far as the phantasy of projective identification is concerned. Meltzer and Bick (1960) distinguished between four 'life-spaces', or geographical zones, associated with the self that help clarify my formulation. The four life-spaces are:

- the outside world
- the inside world
- the inside of external objects
- the inside of internal objects.

The varied relationships between these life-spaces provide a very useful means of conceptualizing different kinds of psychopathology. In the case of Ms A, and agoraphobic states in general, I am suggesting that although the agoraphobic is able to occupy the internal object through the use of intrusive projective identification, the parallel use of the defence does not take place with external objects due mainly to the use of the external object as a contiguous surface. In other words, retardation of projective identification occurs as far as the external object and its containing space are concerned. It is the terrifying equivalent of finding nothing of oneself reflected in the other's pose or one's surroundings. With the agoraphobic, space is not a place for something to exist, grow, be created; it is simply equated with horror and nothingness. This has implications for the dynamic formulation. The more unbearable anxiety becomes, the more refuge inside the internal/

maternal object is sought. This triggers the increased use of autistic defences and a concomitant increase in claustrophobia because no temporary solution can be found in the unburdening of the self into external objects.

The above ideas run contrary to conventional understanding of the role of projection or projective identification in the symptom formation of phobias. Weiss (1935), however, made similar observations to my own. He concluded that while projection may be the main mechanism involved in other phobias, he found little evidence of projection being used in agoraphobia. Later, he linked this to the idea that anxiety emanates principally from an inner danger associated with an ego-state characterized by an unbearable sense of 'ill-being' (p.48) linked to loss of self or identity and a sense of derealization that was often accompanied by somatic complaints such as dizziness and fainting sensations (Weiss, 1964). In sum, Weiss viewed agoraphobic anxiety as being precipitated by a sense of ego disintegration. In his view, this emerged from a struggle within the ego over the repression of 'ego states' associated with libidinal urges.

This psychic state appears similar to the fear of disintegration that I have described. Others have described this state as a sense of 'falling for ever' (Winnicott, 1965), 'nameless terror' (Bion, 1962a), or the experience of encountering 'black holes' in the psyche (Grotstein, 1990). In my view, the use of projective mechanisms and associated paranoid experience is not necessary to complete the formulation. Although not referring particularly to agoraphobia, others have also suggested that projective mechanisms are stifled in states where autistic experience and adhesive identification predominate (e.g. Grotstein, 1983b; Meltzer, 1986). It is extremely difficult to 'measure' and evaluate whether projection, displacement or other mechanisms are involved here as many of these claims are based on different models of anxiety (Compton, 1992). For this reason it still remains an open question. Further claims, however, would need to be theoretically consistent with broader formulations of agoraphobia and be able to be clinically demonstrated.

By way of summing up, I have found it useful to contextualize the above dynamic in terms of Ogden's (1992) understanding that autistic-contiguous, paranoid-schizoid and depressive modes of generating experience operate in synchrony, each in dialectic partnership with the other. In other words, all three are, to some extent, operative at any one point in time. It is the collapse of the dialectic in the direction of one of these particular positions that corresponds with various psychopathological presentations. There is little space here to elaborate fully on this model and its possible different pathological presentations (see Ogden, 1992). Suffice it to say that each mode generates particular anxieties and corresponding defences. The depressive mode manages anxiety through a mourning process contingent upon the realization of whole-object relating and one's destructiveness towards the object. The outcome is greater integration of previously split-off parts of the self and a growing awareness of the continuity of experience and a sense of history. The paranoid-schizoid mode manages persecutory forms of anxiety through using fantasies of splitting and projective identification. Although these kinds of defences help account for psychotic experiences, they also form an essential part of our developmental make-up whereby, through projective identification, we are able to make use of external objects, containers, as sources of transformation. These ways of managing experience differ greatly from the autistic-contiguous mode, where the key anxiety is much closer to questioning the very existence of the self as an experience. Here, the agglomeration of experience around sensory surfaces is used as a protective shield.

With the above model in mind, I have attempted to show that agoraphobic experience has its roots in autistic entrapment and the collapse of the dialectic between the autistic-contiguous position and the paranoid-schizoid position. As a result, autistic anxieties do not seem to be modified by projective identification due to primitive, terrorizing conceptualizations of space. The dialectic between the 'self-defining' defences of the autistic-contiguous position and projective defences of the paranoid-schizoid position is severed, causing the hypertrophying of autistic blocking. This stifles attempts to engage in the creative, meaning-making qualities of the containing object.

Ogden's model is also useful as it illuminates concurrent manifestations of different modes of generating experience in the clinical setting. Psychosis is never simply generated out of paranoid-schizoid modes of relating, and neurotic manifestations also make use of projective identification and splitting (paranoid-schizoid mechanisms). Similarly, as mentioned earlier, Tustin (1986), Klein (1980) and others have convincingly shown how autistic defences are often present in neurotic presentations where depressive and Oedipal forms of relating are dominant. This is consistent with Britton's (1992b) argument that Oedipal concerns and the depressive position are inextricably linked. A similar presentation has been discussed here where the autistic mode of generating experience is coloured and symbolized (walls and other boundaries, etc.) by the depressive (and Oedipal) mode and vice versa. Understanding agoraphobic experience this way offers a partial explanation as to why such patients are often described as having a clear hold on reality but at the same time are always very close to catastrophic feelings of non-existence.

Some implications for technique

Viewing agoraphobia as being generated out of autistic defensiveness as well as the retardation of projective identification has important implications for the treatment of such cases. As indicated earlier, my use of conventional interpretations related to Oedipal conflict and the use of projective mechanisms did not seem to reach the heart of my patient's problems in relating to her world. The bedrock of Ms A's pathology appeared to be much closer to the location, or re-establishment, of a self through the autistic mode. I have tried to demonstrate how Ms A moved from an autistic mode towards making more adaptive use of projective mechanisms (the symbiotic mode) and the interiority of an external containing object.

Crucial in this transition is the safe-sensing of a cohesive bounded self, the self as a prototypical container that has an inside and an outside. At some stages in the transference she used almost every object she could find (me, her words, boundaries of the session) to define her existence in my presence. Only once I was able to understand her need to use objects as an important means of self-definition was I better equipped to tolerate and hold in mind the apparent stasis that typified the countertransference. Being able to identify and make use of autistic forms of relating in the transference brings with it a considerable amount of emotional strain on the therapist's part. It also requires an acute sensitivity to crude non-verbal ways of generating experience in the therapeutic relationship. Most of all, the process asks that he recognize that his empty 'thoughtless' presence, although apparently meaningless, has enormous importance for the patient in helping to slowly regain rudimentary aspects of self-experience that otherwise could not be tolerated. Here, the therapist's main function involves finding a way of tolerating such experience whilst trying to remain 'alive' to the patient. As Ms A put it, once she had a clear understanding of earlier parts of her therapy, 'I needed you there, even though you were not there to me'.

In such cases a clear understanding of the paradoxical nature of autistic defences is needed. They block or stifle experiencing but also allow for primitive, contiguous ways of relating that generate new tolerable ways in which the patient slowly learns to *be* (or *re-be*) in the safety of the therapeutic relationship. The emphasis on autistic defences translates into an analytic focus that pays attention to the way the patient uses the therapeutic space not only as a means of blocking new experience, but as a means of re-establishing contact with the therapist's mind in the only way that truly feels tolerable. At this level, the patient will make particular use of the boundaries of the session, sensuous experience and alpha-elements to give expression to an emergent self. The sound and tone of the therapist's voice, the feeling of the chair or couch, the rhythm of the conversation or periods of meeting, visual surfaces in the room, or symbols that depict boundaries are all examples of this phenomenon. In time I was better able to tolerate the experience of being used as a 'flat object' and found ways of helping her make sense of her experience by symbolizing its existence.

Due to the more obvious neurotic and phobic presentations of the agoraphobic, one may be quick to assume that associated defences should be addressed in treatment. In other words, it may be easily assumed that repression, projection, displacement, castration complexes are central here. I have tried to show that such an understanding, although accurate, does not adequately address a more basic problem that the agoraphobic faces in relation to fears of disintegration and the disappearance of the self. At this level of experience, relatively complex defences like repression and projective identification assume a certain interiority (of self or object) that cannot be articulated in the autistic mode. One implication of this is that continued use of interventions that assume a complex interiority will only foster more rigid use of autistic barriers as such assumptions about psychic space are too intolerable for these patients.

Summary

Using the case of Ms A, I have attempted to illustrate the presence of primitive autistic defences in the generation of agoraphobic experience. The partial collapse or retardation of projective identification with a containing object as a means of 'better' managing intolerable feeling states also appears to be significant. My observations echo Mitrani's (1992) call for greater discrimination between autistic mental states and other primitive mental states, most notably paranoid-schizoid experience.

Chapter 12

The dead alive self in borderline states

Borderline patients are often seen as difficult and disruptive, prompting negative reactions and loss of empathy in the therapist early in the therapeutic process (Cleary *et al.*, 2002). It is well known that borderline patients make considerable demands on the therapist and the treatment process. But there is now accumulating evidence indicating that treatment can be more successful than we previously believed (Bateman and Fonagy, 2001, 2004, 2006; Clarkin *et al.*, 2001; Clarkin and Levy, 2006; Gabbard, 1998; Gunderson *et al.*, 2006; Linehan, 1993; Linehan *et al.*, 2006). The symptoms of borderline personality disorder (BPD), as specified by *DSM-IV* (APA, 1994) also appear to remit more quickly than previously thought (Cohen *et al.*,, 2005; Skodol *et al.*, 2005; Zanarini *et al.*, 2005).

Currently there are two approaches to the treatment of BPD that have acquired adequate empirical backing through the use of random controlled trials: mentalization-based psychotherapy (Bateman and Fonagy, 2004) and dialectical behaviour therapy (Linehan, 1993). Leaving aside the detail and differences of these approaches, it is clear that both require acute empathic understanding of borderline states as an essential part of the treatment process. It is well known that borderline patients have an enfeebled capacity to process experience. Therefore in most treatment approaches there is increased emphasis on being able to track the moment-to-moment experiencing of patients to help gradually contain and expand their ability to bear thinking about their own experience. This is compounded by the fact that it is often easy to misjudge the emotional and cognitive capacity of borderline patients because they appear to understand complex mental states (Bateman and Fonagy, 2004). In reality, however, borderline patients display a number of deficits in their ability to track mental states and form psychic representations of their own experience. In working with borderline states the therapist often finds himself engulfed by powerful affects and subject to interminable confusions between different feeling states, self–object representations, intentions and thoughts.

My experience of supervising and treating certain borderline states has led me to focus on how certain patients get caught in interminable states of confusion when faced with the possibility of containment. It is well known that splitting and projection of negative affective states are used to excess in borderline states and may bring some relief to the self. Relief is dependent on the awareness, at some level, of a separate object able to 'take on' projections. The problem here, however, is complicated when intense destructive affective states are linked to a sense of 'aliveness' in borderline patients. It leads to a confusing 'push–pull' situation where some relief is gained from unbearable psychic states being understood or 'held in the mind of an other'. But it leads to an equally difficult situation where the terror of recognizing the object as separate from the self is equated with 'taking away' the very means on which the patient is able to survive. Put another way, at some level the borderline patient feels she needs unbearable psychic states to remain psychically 'alive'. Destructiveness is 'taken back', kept unmetabolized because it is felt to keep the self alive and protect the self from even greater internal terrors. The outcome is best understood as belonging to the parasitic mode where interminable confusions between container and contained lead to the proliferation of unmetabolized experience or beta-elements that have, in turn, further destructive effects on psychic functioning.

In this chapter I focus on fragments of a psychotherapy with a patient, Amelia, who spoke eloquently about such experiences as she gradually learned to withstand difficult affective states and put them into words. This, in time, fostered the capacity to better think about her experience, thus enabling her to build up a more stable mental picture of herself in relation to others. I have written the case in a way that attempts to demonstrate how my clinical observations are also informed by various countertransference thoughts and states of reverie as I attempt to engage her in the containing process.

After meeting for twice-a-week psychoanalytic psychotherapy for three years, Amelia, a 23-year-old student, gave me a poem she had written about her sense of feeling 'liquid' or 'evaporating'. She called the poem 'Dead Alive'.

It's dead alive
My body is water and blood, dead and moving
It's dead alive
Fractions of me fail to breathe
But I'm still here,
Seeping through others, suffocating others, drowning in others
Looking for reflection

I understood this poem to be a poignant attempt to represent, to symbolize, a core dilemma that Amelia had constantly struggled with over the past three years. As well as representing protean, dream-like states, otherwise generally termed depersonalization, that characterize the experiential world of borderline patients, Amelia used the poem to depict how she felt numbed by experience, inanimate, only with a background sense of aliveness. Her reflections on the poem touched on two struggles. First, Amelia agonized about the inseparable coupling of feelings of 'deadness' and 'aliveness', hence her sense of being 'dead alive'. 'I need to be dead to be alive and alive to be dead', she said. My own reaction to her statement was one of immense frustration and confusion, perhaps because it defied any apparent logical reasoning. On reflection, it is likely that implicit in Amelia's response are suggestions of what it feels like to be caught up, trapped, in such an interminable state. As we shall explore shortly, to confuse matters further, the sense of aliveness that Amelia refers to here is not linked to positive affect as one might automatically assume. The second aspect of the poem that Amelia seemed to be moved by concerned her reference to the 'itness' of her experience, the sense that she was an object to herself. This seemed to point to a growing awareness of her 'dead alive' self constantly compromising the ability to process and represent experience, making it difficult to connect with herself as a subject, 'me' as opposed to 'it'. It is worth noting that parts of the poem appear to express a degree of 'hopefulness' in her struggle. There is also a suggestion that part of her struggle is of an interpersonal nature, holding out for a 'good' containing object. We shall touch on some of these aspects later.

Before continuing, it should be remembered that this poem was written after three years of psychotherapy during which time Amelia had gradually built up a growing ability to track, represent and think about her own unbearable mental states. In other words, she had become more able to contain and give meaning to her 'dead alive' internal state. This marked a significant point of progress in our work. It included being able to internalize the ability to better track and intuit feeling states and inchoate thoughts, a forerunner to being able to allow contained, meaningful mental states to emerge. Bateman and Fonagy (2004) make this the central focus of psychotherapy with borderline patients and see the restoration of implicit and explicit forms of mentalization to be the key to progress in the treatment of BPD patients. I turn now to describing some fragments of this case that seem to expand somewhat on Amelia's 'dead alive' self and related experiences.

Amelia

I met Amelia after she was referred to me by a psychiatrist who had hospitalized her. She had been cutting her thighs with a razor blade on a regular basis when she found it difficult to tolerate being alone in her flat. From the psychiatrist's assessment the cuts were superficial but he was worried that they would lead to a suicide attempt as she often expressed suicidal ideation.

On meeting her in the hospital for an assessment we talked mainly about her need to cut. She had this to say: 'I call cutting my transformer; it transforms my emptiness and this chaos into something real, I can feel it.' On asking her if she wanted to change this about herself she was ambivalent, claiming, 'I would be a nobody if I stopped cutting, I wouldn't feel myself.'

Her cutting was the reason she had left home four years previously. Her mother had tried to get her to stop cutting herself by 'laying down the law' but it had backfired and her self-destructive behaviour escalated. Eventually it was decided that she should move away from the family home and her mother found her a flat nearby. This was largely motivated by her mother's thoughts that she needed to learn how to be independent. Amelia's mother worked as a local health-care worker in the district and had considerable experience in treating borderline pathology using dialectical behaviour therapy. Amelia had a very ambivalent relationship with her mother that swung rapidly between intense hate and love. At times she felt her mother was the only one who would be able to help her, but this was often followed by intense anger claiming that her mother was motivated by self-interest and just wanted to make her into a 'good little girl'. Amelia was fond of her father and described herself as feeling safe when she was with him, although she also felt him to be 'weak and submissive' in dealing with her mother. Amelia had an older sister, Fiona, but had lost contact with her after an argument two years previously that centred on Fiona no longer tolerating Amelia's constant suicidal claims and 'manipulation'.

On one occasion, trying to establish her motivation for change, I happened to ask her if she had tried to change anything about her life and if she liked anything about herself. I was surprised by her vitriolic response. 'You cognitive behaviourists are all the same, you think thinking can change emotion . . . you just think you can manipulate thinking . . . it is emotion that changes emotion', she shouted, 'Go and read Kohut and Freud!' I could feel myself hardening, freezing up, under attack. I retorted, somewhat arrogantly, 'Oh! I'm curious how you think emotion changes emotion, tell me about your theory'. She responded with even more anger, 'So now you want me to be the psychologist, great. You can't help me if this is the way it is going to be.' She turned around and looked away. I tried to steady myself and said, 'Perhaps you don't want to be here, you don't have to be here you know'. She did not respond. All this occurred before we were able to discuss my role as a therapist and how we might work together.

Although anxious and pretty dumbfounded about what to say at this point, I tried a different approach, trying to better meet her in her own experience. 'I have a sense that something I'm doing has really got you feeling uneasy with

me. I asked you about change or said something about good things about you.'
She was silent and started to pick away at the arm of the couch with her
fingers. I continued, 'I wonder if you might be worried that already, we've just
started, I'm not hearing you and so you feel manipulated or pushed by me?'
'How can I trust you?' she shouted. I responded, 'I thought that that is what
we are trying to find out so we can see if we can work together.' She seemed
a little reassured by what I had said and went on to tell me that she had no
friends she could trust, but that there was a woman at work who seemed to
understand her and would buy her little gifts to make her feel better when
she was down.

After meeting for two sessions we discussed treatment guidelines for
twice-a-week psychodynamic therapy, my responsibilities in the treatment
process and a crisis plan. Amelia's visits were often marked by stark contrasts
in presentation. Some days she looked dishevelled, angry and irritable. These
sessions were often about accusing me of being only financially invested in the
treatment and wanting to abandon any hope of getting better. At other times
she was markedly regressed and mute, talking to me in a needy, infantile
voice. There were also times when she would come to her sessions looking
immaculate, appearing relatively coherent, positive and motivated. As treatment progressed some of these self states appeared to be associated with
various anxieties and happenings either in the session or more broadly.

At one point in treatment, Amelia walked in angry, slumped down in the
chair, looked around the room and appeared to be unable to make eye
contact. She began to shout at me and seemed somewhat disorientated.
'There is nothing here. I can't stand it, there is nothing to hold on to.
Everything is all supposed to be good and I'm supposed to be well.' At one
point she got up and put my clock under a pillow and held her ears saying it
was too loud and was hurting her ears. She then moved the two empty chairs
in my room further apart and said that she needed to do this because
otherwise 'it meant we were lovers'. I could not get past her anger in this
session and it was impossible to engage her whilst in such a dissociated state.
Although attacking me verbally with all her might, I was struck by a sense of
emptiness that appeared to lie behind her rage. It felt to me like a 'personless'
state. I started to feel that these affect storms, although destructive, at least
carried some sense of aliveness in their affective expression. They seemed
to be a desperate attempt to keep herself related to me when she was at
her worst.

Most of the time, Amelia appeared lucid and coherent, what she called
'work mode'. She held a part-time job as an office administrator of a small
business and would talk in great detail about her efficiency and productivity at

work. But these bouts of 'efficiency' were driven by near manic attempts to please others, leaving her feeling depleted at the end of the day. 'I help everyone else,' she would say, 'but they all avoid me, even though I'm the first to do anything . . . so I try to live in the real world but I end up feeling invisible'.

It was noticeable too that at these times Amelia would talk merrily with me. She would talk about feeling intelligent and full of life. She would talk about understanding her 'borderline self' with sophisticated ease. But after these apparently light-hearted sessions, she would go home and cut. It became apparent to me that often her cutting escalated after such sessions and while things appeared to be going 'well' in her sessions, her weeks were littered with confrontations with others.

Discussion: the dead alive self

With the help of hindsight I have become increasingly aware of particular confusions that occur in some borderline states where destructiveness becomes fused with a sense of aliveness. A great deal has been written about the role of destructiveness in borderline patients. It could be understood to represent an attack on the good object or bad object, an appeal for rescue, a failure of mentalizing, an attempt to regulate affect, among others (e.g. Bateman and Fonagy, 2006; Cohen and Jay, 2006; Gunderson and Ridolfi, 2001; Linehan, 1993; Silver, 1985). Here I focus on it being an expression of 'aliveness'.

Amelia's description of cutting as being a 'transformer' to counter fears of losing a part of herself is not an uncommon experience in borderline patients. Although there may be different underlying dynamic reasons why cutting occurs, it is often used as a means of regulating affect when feelings of dissociation escalate. In Amelia's case something unreal, chaotic is made 'real' or physically present. Equally important, it is associated with a representation of her self as being alive. Cutting does not only appear to be precipitated by negative affect. Amelia presents her apparently adaptive 'work self' to me but then goes home and cuts. We might think of this as being her best attempt at relating to others, albeit it in a compliant and ingratiating way. The effect, however, is that she is left feeling empty, needing to cut to feel in order to connect with some sense of self again. She also appears to adopt a similar strategy interpersonally through her unconscious motivation to get into fights with others.

Early on Amelia attacks me and assumes, perhaps similar to her mother, that I want to change her and that I am interested in the 'good' things about her. It seemed uncanny how we immediately appeared to slip into an enactment that she often played out with her mother. I chose not to make this link as there was a clear sense that this would simply inflame the situation further. Although not understanding the situation, being able to reflect on and simply acknowledge that something I was doing was affecting her deeply (an analyst-centred interpretation) seemed to make her feel a little more understood (as associations about a person at work who understood her seemed to suggest).

My growing sense of confusion between what appeared to be real and unreal, destructive and helpful, seemed to reflect an interminable confusion occurring between us. Amelia's references to being 'good', perceiving our relationship to be about her being 'good and well', seemed to put her in touch with an empty, terrifying, dead internal state. It appears that in response to this terrifying situation, cutting, fighting with others, although destructive, at least made her feel real and alive. Here a central confusion, as reflected in the countertransference, occurs between representations of self and corresponding affect. It might be expressed as follows: 'I feel dead when I'm good and alive when I'm bad.' The dilemma appears to exist as an endless perverse riddle between us.

It is well known that borderline patients make extensive use of splitting and projective identification. However, it appears that in particular borderline states where this kind of perverse dynamic dominates, the patient is met with a problem: because destructiveness is coupled with aliveness, any attempts to split off and project destructiveness are felt to threaten the very essence of what keeps them psychically alive. Although Amelia comes to psychotherapy and, in part, wants to attend to and change her destructive behaviours, such efforts threaten to take away what feels real and alive to her. In this situation, the analyst's well-intended attempts to 'take on' and understand destructiveness are ironically felt to immobilize hope.

This internal situation represents a static situation where psychic movements between disintegration and integration of psychic objects, Ps$\leftrightarrow$D, can no longer operate successfully. Instead, driven by a sense of 'aliveness', destructive affect and associated representations bind together (D) and resist disintegration or splitting. This appears to be Amelia's psychic solution to holding on to her 'dead alive' self. When Amelia would become distressed and start to dissociate she would attack my attempts to understand her. In the example above, the chairs being too close, although impossible to explore, appeared to represent a symbolic equation (Segal, 1978) communicating an anxiety that things were getting terrifyingly intimate for her. We could understand her attack as a straightforward attack on the good object, a lifeless void for her. But based on the preponderance of narrative derivatives that seem to suggest a need to cling, hold on to, her destructive potential, I came to understand her attacks as not only being an attack on my containing function, but also a desperate attempt to 'take back', rescue, a part of herself associated with vitality that she felt I was taking away.

The problem with this solution, however, is that it sets up a parasitic situation and a potential impasse in treatment. Because potentially good understanding objects are felt to deaden the self, their potential to expand the patient's ability to tolerate unbearable states of mind is diminished and experienced by the patient as being more like concrete immutable objects. This sets up a perverse dynamic where an intimate connection with potentially good objects leads to the proliferation of psychic elements that approximate beta-elements which further overwhelm the patient's capacity to think. The organization of this area of mind seems similar to those of destructive aspects of narcissism, or negative narcissism, as described by Rosenfeld (1971) and Meltzer (1968) where psychic states are dominated by the idealization of destructiveness. Here, however, I am emphasizing the link between destructiveness and a sense of 'aliveness'.

The clinical picture is one of increasing levels of dissociation. Given the above situation, the patient's ability to think about, represent, destructive aspects of herself appears more developed than life-giving, nurturing 'good' parts of the self. In Bion's terms, this part of the situation is parasitic because the container–contained interact in a way that produces a third object, dissociative experience (the proliferation of beta-elements), that becomes destructive to both patient and therapist.

We have established that understanding or focusing on destructiveness is problematic. So too is a perceived attempt to help or make the patient feel understood. Is there a way through this conundrum? I am not sure. Sometimes the level of destructiveness is so idealized and intense that it leads to an immediate rupture in the therapeutic relationship without any possibility of falling back on a productive therapeutic working relationship. From my experience, however, it is futile to try and unbundle the link between destructiveness and 'aliveness' through interpreting. Before this becomes possible it is much more about trying to travel alongside the 'dead alive' self, tolerating attacks, thinking about them as attempts to revive the self while attempts are made to build new ways of experiencing. As long as I could respond to Amelia's destructive behaviours without following my impulse to retreat, bouts of anger appeared important to her, important to get through and tolerate as signs of life.

Amelia (revisited)

Amelia continued to struggle to tolerate most things I tried to communicate to her about her difficulties. Often she openly attacked what I was trying to say or appeared not to acknowledge what I had said to try to reach her. This made it very difficult to feel like we could sustain a useful mental connection for any period of time. It felt as though we constantly evaded or 'missed' each other. Trying to think about her actions as a way of attempting to get through to me appeared to help me tolerate some of these attacks. At other times I seemed to lose the will to want to connect with her and felt unmotivated to meet with her. I noticed that at times like this there was a pessimism and barrenness to my thinking. I wondered a little about feeling attacked and therefore making less of myself available to her but there was little curiosity in the process.

Not all sessions were like this, however, and perhaps due to the relative calm in one of our sessions I became more aware of how the emotional tone of our relationship tended to shift throughout the session. More importantly, I began to notice how easily I would unsettle her. Sometimes very slight movements, when I spoke, looked away, gestured, seemed to unsettle her. At times this was very apparent with her becoming agitated. But most of the time it was simply about her seeming to look troubled by my presence and her apparent attention to any slight change in the analytic field, a kind of hypervigilance. I began to think about these points in our interaction as a kind of 'approach–avoidance dynamic'. Some line of communication would be established as if to approach some kind of mental connect, but then something would shift, leading to her breaking off contact and becoming unsettled by me until she or I found another way of engaging.

Knowing that she could not tolerate direct interpretations aimed at understanding this 'approach–avoidance dynamic', I started to make simple comments about how I may be influencing the process. In particular, they were comments about how I thought certain things that I did in the session appeared to affect Amelia, changing the emotional field in some way. These were not direct suggestions about what had changed. I had no clarity on that. They were just markers that 'something' seemed to shift. They were a version of analyst-centred interpretations (Steiner, 1994) and focused mainly on trying to get her to talk about what happened to her when I started to say something to her. At first she resisted this approach, but I persisted, relying on my intuition, and her responses over time appeared to gather more meaning. Over a number of sessions her response to how she felt when I spoke developed as follows: 'distracted', 'there is nothing there', 'you are trying to take something away from me', 'dominating my thoughts', 'an unbearable place', 'I feel dead like you are taking things away', 'if I listen I feel terrified, invisible', 'there is nothing there, I am lost'. At times these thoughts and intuitive inquiries would lead us nowhere. But it did open up a different way of engaging that eventually seemed to expand Amelia's capacity to tolerate a sense of unbearable emptiness that was felt to be at its height when I intervened or conveyed concern. This more collaborative approach to tentatively trying to 'name' what might be occurring, as well as being open to how I may be contributing to 'making' her feel certain things, appeared to put us on a more even footing.

There were times when it took a lot more work to re-establish a mental connection through which unmetabolized experience could start to be thought about. I will recount one such occasion. It occurred when Amelia had forgotten to bring payment for a session and looked very uneasy about this. I found myself trying to ease her discomfort and said, 'It doesn't matter, it's fine to bring the money next time'. Throughout the session, however, Amelia insisted that I was irritated with her and seemed convinced that I was behaving differently towards her. I said that I wasn't aware of feeling irritated and that I would tell her if I was, but this had no effect. Nothing I said seemed to change her view. Her immediate assumption was that I was irritated with her and wanted her to leave treatment. After the session she made several phone calls to my office leaving messages saying she was feeling suicidal. I returned her call to let her know that I had received her message. I reflected to her how difficult it was to tolerate such feelings and reminded her of the crisis plan we had agreed upon earlier, reiterating to her that we could discuss this further in two days' time when we were scheduled to meet. After our conversation Amelia did not arrive for her next session. Instead, she called the psychiatrist who wanted to hospitalize her again. The next session I informed her that the psychiatrist had been in touch with me but did not address the issue of hospitalization directly as I wanted to try and work with the precipitants of her current state.

Amelia arrived for her next session filled with insistence that I thought she was better and wanted her to leave treatment. If I wanted her to stay, she reasoned, I would have hospitalized her. She said she took 'lots of pills' over the weekend and almost died. Things got even more strained when she added that if I really cared I would lower my fees so she could better afford to come. At the time I found myself submerged in her reasoning: Perhaps she was right. Perhaps I should have hospitalized her. I even wondered if it may be pro- ductive to offer her a reduction in fees to minimize further emotional turmoil. I ended up responding without much conviction, but tried to reiterate that we had agreed we would make use of a crisis plan and go through the steps we had put in place, which included using hospitalization as a last option. I was also trying to look for some common ground but this approach felt like a cop- out and a move away from what she was trying to tell me.

Later in the session I was able to say that I thought she felt I wouldn't be there for her at all times and suggested she may have been feeling neglected by what I said. Clearly still angry, she said I had not helped her at all and she was much better off handling things her own way. I asked if we could try and stop for a minute and think about what had happened over the course of the last two sessions, beginning with her forgetting to bring payment. She agreed.

I suggested that it had occurred to me that she had begun to feel very uncomfortable with me from that point and asked her if she could recall what she felt at the time. She said she had realized after the session that she felt terrible about not paying even though she knew I didn't seem bothered. She said it felt like I didn't care if she paid or not and it made her feel alone. I said to her that I was not aware of how this had felt. I said I remembered that she thought I was irritated, but I missed that she felt bad about not paying. I also wondered if I was not able to see the connection between me saying 'it didn't matter' and how it made her feel like she did not matter. Amelia responded by saying she had been having images of walking into my consulting room and throwing things at me so she would feel better and not so invisible. There was no miraculous turning point attached to this exchange, but it seemed to simply re-engage us in the process and address the rupture that had occurred between us.

Discussion: 'creating a contemplative object'

Amelia's engagement with me appears to reflect her ambivalence in engaging with her own terrifying internal barrenness as it is projected into me. On the one hand it is attacked, on the other there is a craving, a need, for the object. People are needed but experienced as empty echoing receptacles, dead spaces, that could not be thought about, only attacked in attempts to revive the self and make things feel real. There is a desperate craving for grounded experience in psychical sensation because thought cannot be trusted or tolerated. In this way 'deadness' is always linked to 'aliveness' in convoluted ways.

These psychic states could be understood as being generated by the psychic processes of splitting and projective identification. In Amelia's case it seemed as though I had become a receptacle for a terrifyingly emptied-out evaded self. My saying something appeared to be the vehicle that signalled to her that I could no longer play this role and she became more aware of her own empty dead self. This also appears to explain why Amelia said once in responding to a forthcoming holiday break, 'If you leave me I feel I lose myself'. Here, containing the projection breaks down threatening greater fragmentation.

I would not discount these as possible explanations of what was going on at the level of unconscious phantasy. But it is the debris of this process that needs engagement in the moment-to-moment exchanges in the clinical encounter. The need to cling on to her hostility (D) and her inability to make use of thinking, understanding, indications of help, make Amelia's experience chaotic and exacerbate the dissociative nature of her experience. In Bion's terms, because she cannot make use of the container function, alpha-elements and beta-elements gather no coherence and meaning and further contribute to overwhelming alpha-function. Due to the level of unmetabolized experience, the clinical picture is chaotic. We often seemed to miss each other in terms of making mental contact and Amelia displayed a hypersensitive responsiveness to my every move although she remained largely unconscious of this. This appears to be similar to what Bion (1967) refers to as a 'thin' transference found to occur with borderline and psychotic patients where they display awareness and sensitivity to the feelings, thoughts, gestures of the analyst, but all are treated equally with little capacity shown to discriminate between more meaningful stimuli that would deepen the transference relationship.

Unmetabolized experience is often described by patients suffering from borderline states to feel like an ever-present build-up or exploding pressure. The patient is only vaguely conscious of such primitive units of experience but they are often associated either with a sense of persecution or depression (Bion, 1967). Although their presence is always felt in this way they cannot be thought about in a productive, cohesive manner. This situation seems to further contribute to Amelia's sense of being 'dead alive': to feel so much but to feel nothing at all. We have already touched on this feature of borderline experience in exploring beta-mentality in violent men.

In Amelia's case, deficiencies in being able to track her own psychic states led to experiences of psychic deadness and emptiness from which she is constantly trying to escape. It should be noted in passing that in patients with less enfeebled capacities to represent their experience one might expect clear phenomenological distinctions between a sense of 'emptiness' and 'deadness', but in Amelia's case finer distinctions such as this could not be easily grasped. The vague but constantly present nature of this experience is aptly captured by Green's (2005b) reference to these states being like 'waking terrors' that borderline patients constantly attempt to avoid and cannot think about.

Without being able to productively use a containing object, borderline patients often display deficits in their ability to generate an ongoing unconscious commentary so necessary for orientating the self in time and space. My attention to moments in our interaction where there was a shift in the emotional field appeared to allow Amelia to slowly begin to track and 'name' experiences in the room and addressed constant lapses in her ability to mentalize, or generate meaningful thought content. In very small ways I believe interventions of this nature helped begin to develop a commentary on her own emotional and mental states. The containing function here is conveyed through drawing the patient's awareness to the therapist's curiosity about slight changes in the emotional field. From a theoretical point of view, when adequate containing is available, it is this unfolding and changing narrative about the self *in interaction* that contributes towards developing a more contemplative stance. Alpha-elements, the basic components of thought, come together to form narratives (D) and then disintegrate (Ps) to form different meanings dependent largely on intuitions about what is on the other's mind and the experience of the particular situation at hand. As mentioned earlier, the fluidity of this process is arrested in Amelia's experience. But I think that the process of questioning affective changes in response to my actions gently helped her to collaboratively think about her 'terrifying invisibleness' and move to other perspectives and possibilities (Ps) that her fixed solution of 'destroying to live' (D) did not allow.

It seems to me that in order to be acutely attuned to borderline experience, it is important to constantly track, the very process of experiencing. This, along with collaborative attempts to 'name' unmetabolized experiences, is more demanding than it may appear. It is often easy to miss the mental exhaustion that comes from constantly tracking the patient's experience, having to make the therapeutic encounter more tolerable through trying to find ways in which the therapist can, in effect, gently remind the patient that he has a mind. This is not unlike the mental exhaustion that comes from trying to track an infant's experience, where parents are constantly required to rely on their own intuitive responses to track the needs, desires and intentions of the infant to confirm that they are indeed thinking and following.

Client-centred and experiential theorists call the 'thinness' of the borderline patient's connection with reality 'fragile process' (Warner, 1991). This understanding seems to aptly capture the real-time experience of borderline functioning where they have great difficulty attending to and staying with their own experience. In this sense, even their own experience, as they are having it, is felt to be abandoning them and they forever feel fragmented and isolated from their own internal world. Due to this, the borderline experience is not one of having emotions; emotions *happen* to them. The 'itness' of Amelia's experience, as expressed in her poem, seems to express how she would move in and out of a depersonalized world. Often borderline patients describe this as an experience of being 'other', a sense that they inhabit an alien body, an alien container.

In my view, helping Amelia 'gather' her experience became a key therapeutic objective in helping her begin to attend to her own experiencing capacity within an optimal affective environment. As Vanaerschot (2004), another experiential-orientated therapist, so eloquently puts it, in such cases we should focus on 'helping the client hold onto experiencing without falling into extreme intensities . . . helping the client to continue the experience long enough to feel the meaning of it and to be able to explicate it in words' (p.115). In my understanding, this process leads to tolerating the emergence of a contemplative object, in whose creation both patient and therapist play their part.

The incident about payment touches on many controversial issues in working with borderline patients. I include it to illustrate Amelia's acute sensitivity to internal and external cues, often leading to a rupture in the therapeutic process. Without being able to attend to their own experience, borderline patients are faced with difficulties in regulating affect. This often leads to hypersensitivity to environmental cues and constant misperception of others' intentions, further contributing to their emotional lability. Due to these characteristic ways of experiencing, borderline patiens often feel invalidated by reactions that do not mirror their mercurial inner world. Such reactions are felt to have a constant impact on the experiencing self and are felt to constitute an attack on their ability to generate their own experience.

My response to Amelia forgetting her money and an inability to contain her terror seemed to have unwittingly invalidated her experience. Even more, from her perspective it seemed to re-enact a personal 'truth': that she is invisible or dead to others, forcing her to mobilize destructive affect in order to hold herself together. From her perspective, something terrifying had gone unnoticed. It seems that the lightness of my comment 'it doesn't matter' had been equated with her feeling that she did not matter. I have tried to illustrate how I attempted to work to re-establish my containing function. First, I actively tried to 'get back behind' the rupture that had occurred and tried to explore what may have happened *from the patient's point of view* by helping her consider what had disrupted her ability to think or contemplate her experience at the time. I think that one can only do this effectively if the therapist is able to genuinely grasp the fragile nature of borderline experience. If he is able to act from this position there should always be a sense that there is 'a grain of truth' to every flare-up and it is not simply about the patient attempting to manipulate the therapist. Ruptures in the treatment process are often indicators of when the containing function breaks down and indicate a place where analyst and patient need to focus their attention. As I hope to have illustrated, attention is focused on experiencing prior to the 'testing' behaviours, not the behaviours themselves.

Amelia (revisited)

Three years into her psychotherapy, Amelia had made some significant progress in being able to better tolerate a crippling sense of emptiness. She was no longer cutting, and although she spoke of 'wiping herself out' regularly, had not acted on this and had begun a relationship. The relationship lasted about six months, at which point Amelia ended it because she disliked the way she had to control her boyfriend's every move and constantly needed reassurance that he loved her. Often this could only be confirmed after copious amounts of sex. 'It made things real', she said, 'even though it seemed to drain the life out of him'.

After the relationship break-up Amelia started to goad me about needing more sessions and wanting to meet for lunch. I responded by saying that I was worried she would see whatever I had to say as a rejection, but reiterated that my responsibility was to help her understand her feelings and her need to meet more often. She fought with me about being insensitive, but surprisingly, after I asked her to try and explore the feeling of wanting more contact with me, she began to reflect and said, 'I need to feel and be touched . . . I'm tired of feeling nothing, just nothingness. I now know that if I push you enough here you react and I don't feel so dead, we can fight, I have a kind of purpose.'

In the following session Amelia returned to a growing awareness of carrying a deadness, an absence, inside her that later she called 'the zombie in me'. She broke down at this point, saying she hated the fact that she had to use people to make her feel alive. 'Why do I have to create such mayhem to feel real, to feel like a person?' she said. I said I was aware of her telling me something different today but I wasn't sure what it was. It was something about a deep sadness when she spoke. We sat in silence for a while and I remembered a few words of a song I had listened to recently: 'when I see you, I see me'. The feelings I had related to these words made me think about the 'intuitive sense' of feeling real, validated, once seen in the eyes of an other. I wondered if I was sensing a deeper connection with Amelia. My dream-thoughts seemed to reflect something about what Amelia desperately craved, but also, at the same time, there appeared to be something catastrophic about sensing real aliveness. I found myself thinking about accounts of how borderline patients detest looking at themselves in a mirror. This seemed to put me more in touch with an ambivalence that I sensed Amelia was experiencing. I said that I wondered if she felt more real in my presence today, but she was also worried about what she might find. 'Well it won't be love', she replied in a moment of humour that made us both laugh.

In the following session she began to speak about how she felt love was always empty, hollow, she could not trust it. Referring to her love for aesthetic objects she said, 'I can love something but not someone, it's a kind of "thing love".' While listening to her, fragments of a poem written by a favourite poet of mine, Stevie Smith, came to mind. After the session I re-read the poem and it seemed to aptly elaborate what Amelia was beginning to describe.

Love Me!

Love me, love me, I cried to the rocks and the trees,
And love me, they cried again, but it was only a tease.
Once I cried love me to the people, but they fled like a dream,

And when I cried love me to a friend, she began to scream.
Oh why do they leave me, the beautiful people, and only the rocks
remain,
To cry love me, as I cry love me, and love me again.

On the rock a baked sea-serpent lies,
And his eyelids close tightly over his violent eyes,
And I fear that his eyes will open and confound me with a
Mirthless word,
That the rocks will harp on forever, and my love me never be
Heard.

(Stevie Smith, in MacGibbon, 1978, p.104)

It seemed uncanny that in the following session Amelia began to describe similar feelings of 'never having love returned'. She described the sense of emptiness that left her with a sense that 'there is something already dying . . . already dead inside'. She said this with great difficulty and found it hard to continue. I was curious about how I was responding to Amelia. I no longer felt I had to make reassuring comments to try and accommodate her distress. There was also an almost inappropriate vitality and excitement to how I felt listening to her. Amelia went on to say that she was going to have to move house in November that year and was worried about being permitted to take her dogs with her to her new residence. She also reported a dream (her first) that disturbed her greatly: *She was kissing a man, it was like she was in some Hollywood romantic movie. She recalls the thought while she was dreaming: 'this was the best kiss'. But when they both turned towards the camera their faces looked ravaged and bloody.* I said the last image in the dream was difficult for me to think about. Amelia agreed. I asked her about the Hollywood romantic aspects of the dream. She said, 'It was me being romantic, but at a distance, in a movie'.

I said I was thinking about the fact that she could at least have the thought of intimacy without running, although she appeared very worried about finding a place for her anger. Amelia agreed and said it always gets in the way. She felt herself withdraw and we seemed to return to a previous point in the therapy where Amelia felt that she disappeared when I spoke. She was aware of this and said she felt terrified but was at least able to feel it.

Discussion: 'moving towards symbolization'

Recently Amelia said to me, 'Do you know I can't see myself, that is frightening, it's like I need my thoughts to hold me together.' This appears to me to be a succinct way of expressing how our identity is (or is not) carried in ourselves, and between ourselves, through time, as a mental projection. This is a core problem for borderline patients due to an enfeebled ability to generate psychic representations. Without this capacity they struggle to process and understand affective experience. The above statement also seems to be an illustration of her being in touch with an emerging vitality and a commentary on a new-found continuity in her experiencing capacity that had felt previously chaotic and constantly interrupted.

The 'bloody kiss' excited and intrigued me in the sense that I felt like a witness to something beautiful unfolding, the birth of her own experiencing, despite the difficulty of the image. It appeared to be her 'dead alive' self in a thinkable form, with all its trauma. In fact it was in the following session that she brought the poem to therapy which appears in the introduction. The 'bloody kiss', among others things, seems to express the emergence of depressive anxieties, worries about damaging her object via the intimate connection of being held in the mind of an other. This appears to have a particular meaning for Amelia given that her destructive affect held so much meaning and vitality. Later we returned to the dream, seeing it as raising an eternal question for her: 'How much can I allow the kiss to be about life?'

Clearly the 'bloody kiss' is a powerful transference reference that seemed to draw upon unconscious confusions between love, sex, support, intimacy, vitality, parasitic destructiveness, and anxiety about what this would do to me. Importantly, I think, I deliberately held off interpreting the transference directly and used it rather as a template to organize my thoughts about her anxiety, helping me better connect with her thinking. My sense is that the dream held within it multiple undeveloped meanings and thoughts. Drawing attention to the transference appeared to detract from what she would, at the time, be able to tolerate regarding how she was experiencing and developing the mental connection between us. In short, it felt as though it would simply precipitate uncontained affect that would rupture or overwhelm the containing and meaning-making process. Earlier, we considered how the therapist's containing function attempts to titrate the relationship between effusive affect and slippages of meaning (symmetry) and limiting its scope (asymmetrical) so as to render the specific experience digestible and meaningful. There is merit here in trying to intuit the level at which the patient can consider affective experience while still being able to think about it. It is a kind of 'witnessing' that is important here and there is no value in drawing attention to every transference move. Eventually, when I felt I could say something that would be tolerated by Amelia, we spoke about it as an intimate connection between us always under threat by her need to take control and 'bloody' it.

More generally, there had been a marked shift in the way Amelia had become able to tolerate my presence. She started to feel held in my mind, thought about in a meaningful way, and could connect with me without much need to fill or disrupt the therapeutic space with her 'lively' destructiveness. As well as starting to think about her emptiness in meaningful ways without projecting it, it was evident that Amelia began to use symbolic thought and reports her first dream. There are also moments of genuine humour. Apart from this perhaps being a sign of 'aliveness' that is not perverted, it is also an indication that she is better able to track the mental states of self and other.

Due to these shifts I am better able to engage with my own private thoughts and musings and consider how they may help me better understand and connect with what is going on in the room. At some points – particularly when I am drawn to reading the Smith poem – it appears uncanny to see that we have similar things on our minds, a sign of two minds connected trying to use each other to process experience. I am not sure of what exactly led to a shift in the 'emotional register' of our relationship from a chaotic attack on the link between us (H) to a more intimate curious connection (K). I think there were a number of things, not all linked to the therapeutic relationship. Amelia's memory of events, however, appeared significant. She said it seemed to hinge on a fond memory of feeling that I could 'see' her sadness but sat in silence and did not try to change it. I think of this as one of those rare moments when Amelia was able to truly feel something different to what her own preconceptions would previously allow. It seemed to lead to a momentary but important mental connection, allowing her to feel profoundly understood while remaining in touch with her own experience.

Concluding comments

The case of Amelia illustrates fertile links between the use of negative affect to generate a sense of self, poor representational capacity, and the phenomenology of a sense of 'deadness' and 'aliveness' in borderline experience. The interminable dilemmas this sets up for the patient and the therapeutic relationship are often chaotic and volatile, making it difficult for the therapist not to be drawn into treating 'acting out' as simply being manipulation. I hope to have shown that our ability to 'go on thinking' about, and attuning to, these dilemmas is the key to addressing difficulties related to making use of a containing object.

A number of treatment implications are suggested by my work with Amelia. It impressed on me how easily 'fragile process', signs of the 'dead alive self', can be missed in the therapeutic process. As a result, it is often assumed that borderline patients have a greater capacity to understand their predicament. But constant ruptures in their experiencing can usually be detected in subtle shifts in attention or in non-verbal occurrences: looking away, changes in one's posture, changes in the tone and cadence of the verbal exchange, and so forth. This occurs especially when there has been some form of perceived invalidation (often unconscious) triggering further fragmentation. We saw this in the case of Amelia when I unknowingly made demands on her about what she had tried to change about her behaviour and when the issue of payment became central to this problem.

Some understanding that the 'dead alive self' is the best way that such patients are able to generate a sense of coherence is important. In the face of a fragile ability to create mental representations this strangely represents some sense of hope. Because borderline patients have been shown to have enfeebled representational capacities, they have great difficulty selectively attending to and metabolizing experience. As a result, they often feel bombarded by primitive affect and unprocessed mentation with little sense of the passing of time. It creates a feeling of being trapped in the present moment. This explains why complex interpretations about understanding defences, Oedipal relations and so forth risk invalidating the patient's experience because they lack the mental capacity to make use of them.

I hope to have demonstrated the importance of working from this starting point with Amelia. Meeting borderline patients in the 'here-and-now' is an attempt to assist them in processing affect and undeveloped thoughts, building representations of experience and thereby extending their ability to attend to their own mental life. Working in the present moment helps the therapist to mobilize current 'trapped' affect while mediating its intensity through enquiring about momentary shifts in the therapeutic relationship.

References

Abraham, K. (1913). A constitutional basis of locomotor activity. In K. Abraham *Selected Papers* (pp.235–243). New York: Basic Books.

Allen, J., Fonagy, P. and Bateman, A.W. (2008). *Mentalizing in Clinical Practice.* Washington, DC: American Psychiatric Publishing, Inc.

American Psychiatric Association (APA, 1994). *Diagnostic and Statistical Manual of Mental Disorders.* Washington, DC: American Psychiatric Association.

Anzieu, D. (1989). *The Skin Ego.* New Haven, CT: Yale University Press.

Anzieu, D. (1993). Autistic phenomena and the skin ego. *Psychoanalytic Inquiry, 13,* 42–48.

Ballenger, J.C. (1997). Discussion and overview: what can we learn if we view panic disorder across the life span and across different presentations and contexts? *Bulletin of the Menninger Clinic, 61,* 95–103.

Baranger, M. (1993). The mind of the analyst: from listening to interpretation. *International Journal of Psychoanalysis, 74*(1), 15–24.

Baranger, B., Baranger, W. and Mom, J. (1983). Process and non-process in analytic work. *International Journal of Psychoanalysis, 64,* 1–15.

Bateman, A.W. and Fonagy, P. (2001). Treatment of borderline personality disorder with psychoanalytically oriented partial hospitalization: an 18-month follow-up. *American Journal of Psychiatry, 158,* 36–42.

Bateman, A.W. and Fonagy, P. (2004). *Psychotherapy with Borderline Personality Disorder: Mentalization Based Treatment.* Oxford: Oxford University Press.

Bateman, A.W. and Fonagy, P. (2006). *Mentalization-Based Treatment For Borderline Personality Disorder.* Oxford: Oxford University Press.

Beebe, B., Alson, D., Jaffe, J., Feldstein, S. and Crown, C. (1988). Vocal congruence in mother–infant play. *Journal of Psycholinguistic Research, 17*(3), 245–259.

Beebe, B., Lachmann, F.M. and Jaffe, J. (1997). Mother–infant interaction structures and presymbolic self- and object representations. *Psychoanalytic Dialogues, 7,* 133–182.

Beebe, B., Knoblauch, S.H., Rusten, J. and Sorter, D. (2005). *Forms of Intersubjectivity in Infant Research and Adult Treatment.* New York: Other Press.

Benjamin, J. (1990). An outline of intersubjectivity: the development of recognition. *Psychoanalytic Psychology, 7,* 33–46.

Benjamin, J. (1998). *Shadow of the Other. Intersubjectivity and Gender in Psychoanalysis.* New York: Routledge.

Benjamin, J. (2005). Creating an intersubjective reality: commentary on paper by Arnold Rothstein. *Psychoanalytic Dialogues*, *15*, 447–457.

Bezoari, M., Ferro, A. and Politi, P. (1994). Listening, interpreting and psychic change in the analytic dialogue. *International Forum of Psychoanalysis*, *3*, 35–41.

Bick, E. (1968). The experience of the skin in early object relations. *International Journal of Psychoanalysis*, *49*, 484–486.

Bick, E. (1986). Further considerations on the function of the skin in early object relations: findings from infant observation integrated into child and adult analysis, *British Journal of Psychotherapy*, *2*(4), 292–299.

Billow, R.M. (2000). Bion's 'passion'; the analyst's pain. *Contemporary Psychoanalysis*, *36*, 411–426.

Billow, R.M. (2003). *Relational Group Psychotherapy: From Basic Assumptions to Passion*. New York: Jessica Kingsley Publishers.

Bion, W.R. (1954). Notes on the theory of schizophrenia. *International Journal of Psychoanalysis*, *35*, 113–118.

Bion, W.R. (1956). Development of schizophrenic thought. *International Journal of Psychoanalysis*, *37*, 344–346.

Bion, W.R. (1957). Differentiation of the psychotic and the non-psychotic personalities. *International Journal of Psychoanalysis*, *38*, 266–275.

Bion, W.R. (1958). On arrogance. *International Journal of Psychoanalysis*, *39*, 144–146.

Bion, W.R. (1959). Attacks on linking. *International Journal of Psychoanalysis*, *40*, 308–315.

Bion, W.R. (1961). *Experiences in Groups*. London: Tavistock Publications.

Bion, W.R. (1962a). A theory of thinking. *International Journal of Psychoanalysis*, *43*, 306–310.

Bion, W.R. (1962b). *Learning From Experience*. London: Heinemann.

Bion, W.R. (1963). *Elements of Psychoanalysis*. London: Heinemann.

Bion, W.R. (1965). *Transformations*. London: Heinemann.

Bion, W.R. (1967). *Second Thoughts*. London: Heinemann.

Bion, W.R. (1970). *Attention and Interpretation*. London: Tavistock Publications.

Bion, W.R. (1976). Evidence. *Bulletin British Psycho-Analytical Society No. 8, 1976*. Reprinted in *Clinical Seminars and Four Papers* (1987).

Bion, W.R. (1987). Making the best of a bad job. In F. Bion (ed.) *Clinical Seminars and Four Papers* (pp.247–257). London: Karnac.

Bion, W.R. (1989). *Two Papers: The Grid and Caesura*. London: Karnac. First published 1977. Rio de Janeiro: Imago Editora.

Bion, W.R. (1992). *Cogitations*. London: Karnac.

Bion, W.R. (2005a). *The Italian Seminars*. London: Karnac.

Bion, W.R. (2005b). *The Tavistock Seminars*. London: Karnac.

Blacking, J. (1976). *How Musical is Man?* London: Faber and Faber.

Blanchot, M. (1969). *The Infinite Conversation*. Minneapolis: University of Minnesota Press.

Bollas, C. (1983). Expressive uses of the countertransference – notes to the patient from oneself. *Contemporary Psychoanalysis*, *19*, 1–33.

Bott Spillius, E. (ed.) (1988). *Melanie Klein Today*. London: Routledge.

Bourdieu, P. (1997). *The Logic of Practice*. Cambridge: Polity Press.

Bowlby, J. (1985). The role of childhood experience in cognitive disturbance. In

M.J. Mahoney and A. Freeman (eds) *Cognition and Psychotherapy*. New York: Plenum.

Bråten, S. (2003). Participant perception of others' acts. Virtual otherness in infants and adults. *Culture and Psychology*, 9(3), 261–276.

Brenman, E. (1985). Hysteria. *International Journal of Psychoanalysis*, 66, 423–432.

Brenman Pick, I. (1992). The emergence of early object relations in the psychoanalytic setting. In R. Anderson (ed.) *Clinical Lectures on Klein and Bion* (pp.24–33). London: Routledge.

Brenman Pick, I. (1995). Concern: spurious or real. *International Journal of Psychoanalysis*, 76, 257–270.

Britton, R. (1989). The missing link: parental sexuality in the Oedipus complex. In R. Britton, M. Feldman and E. O'Shaughnessy (eds) *The Oedipus Complex*. London: Karnac.

Britton, R. (1992a). Keeping things in mind. In R. Anderson (ed.) *Clinical Lectures on Klein and Bion* (pp.102–113). London: Routledge.

Britton, R. (1992b). The Oedipus situation and the depressive position. In R. Anderson (ed.) *Clinical Lectures on Klein and Bion*. London: Routledge.

Britton, R. and Steiner, J. (1994). Interpretation: selected fact or overvalued idea? *International Journal of Psychoanalysis*, 75, 1069–1078.

Bucci, W. (1985). Dual coding: a cognitive model for psychoanalytic research. *Journal of the American Psychoanalytic Association*, 33, 571–608.

Bucci, W. (1997a). Pattern of discourse in 'good' and troubled hours: a multiple code interpretation. *Journal of the American Psychoanalytic Association, 45*, 155–187.

Bucci, W. (1997b). *Psychoanalysis and Cognitive Science: A Multiple Code Theory*. New York: Guilford Press.

Busch, F.N. (1995). Agoraphobia and panic states. *Journal of the American Psychoanalytic Association*, 43(1), 207–222.

Busch, F.N., Milrod, B., Rudden, M., Shapiro, T., Singer, M., Aronson, A., *et al.* (1999). Oedipal dynamics in panic disorder. *Journal of the American Psychoanalytic Association*, 47, 773–790.

Caper, R. (1999). *A Mind of One's Own: A Kleinian View of Self and Object*. London: Routledge.

Carnochan, P.G.M. (2006). Containers without lids. *Psychoanalytic Dialogues*, 16(3), 341–362.

Carpy, D.V. (1989). Tolerating the countertransference: a mutative process. *International Journal of Psychoanalysis*, 70, 287–294.

Carr, I. (1991). *Keith Jarrett: The Man and the Music*. London: Da Capo Press.

Cartwright, D. (1997). Some aspects of countertransference disclosure. *Psychoanalytic Psychotherapy in South Africa*, 5, 2–23.

Cartwright, D. (1998). Patient receptivity and projective identification. *British Journal of Psychotherapy*, 15(1), 3–18.

Cartwright, D. (2002). *Psychoanalysis, Violence and Rage-Type Murder: Murdering Minds*. London: Brunner-Routledge.

Cartwright, D. (2004a). Anticipatory interpretations: addressing 'cautionary tales' and problem of premature termination. *Bulletin of The Menninger Clinic*, 68(2), 95–114.

Cartwright, D. (2004b). The psychoanalytic research interview: preliminary suggestions. *Journal of the American Psychoanalytic Association, 52,* 1–30.

Cartwright, D. (2006). Autistic defenses in agoraphobic syndrome: 'flat' objects and the retardation of projective identification. *Journal of the American Psychoanalytic Association, 54*(1), 109–135.

Charles, M. (1999). Patterns: unconscious shapings of the self and experience. *Journal of Melanie Klein and Object Relations, 17*(2), 367–388.

Charles, M. (2004). *Learning From Experience.* London: Analytic Press.

Clarkin, J.F. and Levy, K.N. (2006). Psychotherapy for patients with borderline personality disorder: focusing on the mechanisms of change. *Journal of Clinical Psychology, 62*(4), 405–410.

Clarkin, J.F., Foelsch, P.A., Levy, K.N., Hull, J.W., Delaney, J.C. and Kernberg, O.F. (2001). The development of a psychodynamic treatment for patients with borderline personality disorder: a preliminary study of behavioral change. *Journal of Personality Disorder, 15*(6), 487–495.

Cleary, M., Siegfried, N. and Walter, G. (2002). Experience, knowledge and attitudes of mental health staff regarding clients with a borderline personality disorder. *International Journal of Mental Health Nursing, 11*(3), 186–191.

Clyman, R.B. (1991). The procedural organization of emotions: a contribution from cognitive science to the psychoanalytic theory of therapeutic action. *Journal of the American Psychoanalytic Association, 39,* 349–382.

Cohen, D. and Jay, S.M. (1996). Autistic barriers in the psychoanalysis of borderline adults. *International Journal of Psychoanalysis, 77,* 913–933.

Cohen, P., Crawford, T.N., Johnson, J.G. and Kasen, S. (2005). The Children in the Community Study of developmental course of personality disorder. *Journal of Personality Disorder, 19*(5), 466–486.

Coltart, N. (1992). *Slouching Towards Bethlehem.* New York: Guilford Press.

Compton, A. (1992). Agoraphobia and other phobias of adults. *Psychoanalytic Quarterly, 61,* 400–425.

Compton, A. (1998). An investigation of anxious thought in patients with DSM-IV agoraphobia/panic disorder: rationale and design. *Journal of the American Psychoanalytic Association, 46*(3), 691–721.

Davison, S. (2002). Bion's perspectives on psychoanalytic method. *International Journal of Psychoanalysis, 83,* 913–917.

Deleuze, G. (1968/1994). *Difference and Repetition* (P. Patton, Trans.). London: Athlone Press.

Deutsch, H. (1929). The genesis of agoraphobia. *International Journal of Psychoanalysis, 10,* 51–69.

Ehrenberg, D.B. (1995). Self-disclosure: therapeutic tool or indulgence? – countertransference disclosure. *Contemporary Psychoanalysis, 31,* 213.

Eliot, T.S. (1963). *T.S. Eliot: Collected Poems 1902–1962.* New York: Harcourt Brace.

Emde, R.N. (1993). Epilogue: a beginning-research approaches and expanding horizons for psychoanalysis. *Journal of the American Psychoanalytic Association, 41,* 411–424.

Fairbairn, W.D. (1952). *Psychoanalytic Studies of the Personality.* London: Tavistock Publications.

Feldman, M. (1992). Splitting and projective identification. In R. Anderson (ed.) *Clinical Lectures on Klein and Bion* (pp.74–88). London: Routledge.

Ferenczi, S. (1988). *The Clinical Diary of Sándor Ferenczi.* Cambridge, MA: Harvard University Press.

Ferro, A. (2002). Narrative derivatives of alpha elements: clinical implications. *International Forum of Psychoanalysis, 11,* 184–187.

Ferro, A. (2004). Interpretation: signals from the analytic field and emotional transformations. *International Forum of Psychoanalysis, 13,* 31–38.

Ferro, A. (2005a). *Seeds Of Illness, Seeds Of Recovery.* London: Brunner-Routledge.

Ferro, A. (2005b). Bion: theoretical and clinical observations. *International Journal of Psychoanalysis, 86,* 1535–1542.

Ferro, A. (2005c). Which reality in the psychoanalytic session. *Psychoanalytic Quarterly, 74,* 421–442.

Ferro, A. (2006). Clinical implications of Bion's thought. *International Journal of Psychoanalysis, 87,* 989–1003.

Fonagy, P. (2004). *Affect Regulation, Mentalization and the Development of the Self.* London: Karnac.

Fonagy, P. and Target, M. (1996). Understanding the violent patient: the use of the body and the role of the father. *International Journal of Psychoanalysis, 76,* 487–501.

Fonagy, P., Gergely, G., Jurist, E.L. and Target, M. (2004). *Affect Regulation, Mentalization, and the Development of the Self.* New York: Karnac.

Fonagy, P., Moran, G. and Target, M. (1993). Aggression and the psychological self. *International Journal of Psychoanalysis, 74,* 471–486.

Freud, S. (1895). On the grounds for detaching a particular syndrome from neurasthenia under the description 'anxiety neurosis'. *Standard Edition, 3,* 114.

Freud, S. (1900). The interpretation of dreams. *Standard Edition, 4,* 1–338.

Freud, S. (1910). The future prospects of psycho-analytic therapy. *Standard Edition, 11,* 139–152.

Freud, S. (1911). Formulations on the two principles of mental functioning. *Standard Edition, 12,* 213–226.

Freud, S. (1914). From the history of an infantile neurosis. *Standard Edition, 17,* 7–123.

Freud, S. (1923). The ego and the id. *Standard Edition, 19,* 1–66.

Gabbard, G.O. (1992). Psychodynamics of panic disorder and social phobia. *Bulletin of the Menninger Clinic, 56,* 3–13.

Gabbard, G.O. (1998). Treatment-resistant borderline personality disorder. *Psychiatric Annals, 28,* 6651–6656.

Gaddini, E. (1992). *A Psychoanalytic Theory of Infantile Experience.* London: Routledge.

Gallese, V. (2003). The roots of empathy: the shared manifold hypothesis and the neural basis of intersubjectivity. *Psychopathology, 36,* 171–180.

Gentile, J. (2007). Wrestling with matter: origins of intersubjectivity. *Psychoanalytic Quarterly, 76,* 547–587.

Gilligan, J. (1997). *Violence: Reflections on a National Epidemic.* New York: Vintage.

Ginot, E. (2007). Intersubjectivity and neuroscience: understanding enactments and their therapeutic significance within emerging paradigms. *Psychoanalytic Psychology*, *24*, 317–332.

Gleick, J. (1987). *Chaos: Making a New Science*. New York: Penguin.

Godbout, C. (2004). Reflections on Bion's 'elements of psychoanalysis': experience, thought and growth. *International Journal of Psychoanalysis*, *85*, 1123–1136.

Goldstein, A.J. and Chambless, D.L. (eds) (1982). *Agoraphobia: Multiple Perspectives on Theory and Treatment*. New York: Wiley.

Gooch, J. (2001). Bion's perspectives on psychoanalytic technique. Paper presented at the 42nd Congress of the International Psychoanalytical Association, Nice.

Green, A. (1999). *The Work of the Negative* (A. Weller, Trans.). London: Free Association Books.

Green, A. (2000). The intrapsychic and intersubjective in psychoanalysis. *Psychoanalytic Quarterly*, *69*, 1–39.

Green, A. (2005a). *Key Ideas for a Contemporary Psychoanalysis*. London: Routledge.

Green, A. (2005b). *Psychoanalysis: A Paradigm for Clinical Thinking*. London: Free Association Books.

Grinberg, L., Sor, D. and Tabek de Bianchedi, E. (1993). *New Introduction to the Work of Bion*. New York: Jason Aronson.

Grotstein, J.S. (1979). Who is the dreamer who dreams the dream and who is the dreamer who understands it – a psychoanalytic inquiry into the ultimate nature of being. *Contemporary Psychoanalysis*, *15*, 110–169.

Grotstein, J.S. (1983a). *Do I Dare Disturb the Universe: A Memorial to W.R. Bion*. London: Karnac.

Grotstein, J.S. (1983b). A proposed revision of the psychoanalytic concept of primitive mental states: Part II. The borderline syndrome. Section 1: The disorders of autistic safety and symbiotic relatedness. *Contemporary Psychoanalysis*, *19*, 571–609.

Grotstein, J.S. (1990). The 'black hole' as the basic psychotic experience: some newer psychoanalytic and neuroscience perspectives on psychosis. *Journal of the American Psychoanalytic Association*, *18*, 29–46.

Grotstein, J.S. (1991). Nothingness, meaninglessness, chaos, and the 'black hole' III – self- and interactional regulation and the background presence of primary identification. *Contemporary Psychoanalysis*, *27*, 1–33.

Grotstein, J.S. (2000). *Who is the Dreamer Who Dreams the Dream?* London: Analytic Press.

Grotstein, J.S. (2004). The seventh servant: the implications of a truth drive in Bion's theory of 'O'. *International Journal of Psychoanalysis*, *85*, 1081–1101.

Grotstein, J.S. (2005). 'Projective transidentification': an extension of the concept of projective identification. *International Journal of Psychoanalysis*, *86*, 1051–1069.

Gunderson, J.G. and Ridolfi, M.E. (2001). Borderline personality disorder. Suicidality and self-mutilation. *Annals of the New York Academy of Sciences*, *932*, 61–73.

Gunderson, J.G., Daversa, M.T., Grilo, C.M., McGlashan, T.H., Zanarini, M.C., Shea, M.T., *et al.* (2006). Predictors of two-year outcome for patients with borderline personality disorder. *American Journal of Psychiatry*, *163*(5), 822–826.

Hamilton, N.G. (1990). The containing function and the analyst's projective identification. *International Journal of Psychoanalysis*, *71*, 445–453.

Heimann, P. (1950). On counter-transference. *International Journal of Psychoanalysis*, *31*, 81–84.

Heimann, P. (1956). Dynamics of transference interpretations. *International Journal of Psychoanalysis*, *37*, 303–310.

Horowitz, M.J., Fridhandler, B. and Stinson, C. (1990). Person schemas and emotion. *Journal of the American Psychoanalytic Association*, *39*, 173–208.

Hyatt-Williams, A. (1998). *Cruelty, Violence and Murder: Understanding the Criminal Mind*. New York: Jason Aronson.

Jaffe, J., Beebe, B., Feldstein, S., Crown, C.L. and Jasnow, M.D. (2001). Rhythms of dialogue in infancy: coordinated timing in development. *Monographs of the Society for Research in Child Development*, *66*(2), 1–132.

Jaques, E. (1953). On the dynamics of social structure. *Human Relations*, *6*, 3–23.

Kernberg, O.F. (2003). The management of affect storms in the psychoanalytic psychotherapy of borderline patients. *Journal of the American Psychoanalytic Association*, *51*(2), 517–545.

Klein, M. (1932). *The Psycho-Analysis of Children*. London: Hogarth Press.

Klein, M. (1935). A contribution to the psychogenesis of manic-depressive states. *International Journal of Psychoanalysis*, *15*, 145–174.

Klein, M. (1940). Mourning and its relation to manic-depressive states. In *The Writings of Melanie Klein* (Vol. 1, pp.34–69). London: Hogarth Press.

Klein, M. (1946). Notes on some schizoid mechanisms. *International Journal of Psychoanalysis*, *27*, 99–110.

Klein, M. (1955). On identification. In *The Writings of Melanie Klein* (Vol. 3, pp.141–175). London: Hogarth Press.

Klein, M. (1957). *Envy and Gratitude*. London: Tavistock.

Klein, S. (1980). Autistic phenomena in neurotic patients. *International Journal of Psychoanalysis*, *61*, 395–402.

Knoblauch, S.H. (2000). *The Musical Edge of Therapeutic Dialogue*. New York: Analytic Press.

Kohut, H. (1950). On the enjoyment of listening to music. *Psychoanalytic Quarterly*, *19*, 64–87.

Kohut, H. (1972). Thoughts on narcissism and narcissistic rage. In P. Ornstein (ed.) *The Search for the Self: Selected writings of Heinz Konut, 1950–1978* (vol. 1, pp. 205–232). New York: International Universities Press.

Lacan, J. (1977). *Ecrits: A Selection*. London: Routledge.

Lacan, J. (2004). *Le séminaire, Livre X: L'angoisse [The Seminar, Book 10: Anxiety]*. Paris: Seuil.

Lafarge, L. (2000). Interpretation and containment. *International Journal of Psychoanalysis*, *81*(1), 67–84.

Lamanno-Adamo, V.L. (2006). Aspects of a compliant container: considering narcissistic personality configurations. *International Journal of Psychoanalysis*, *87*, 369–382.

Langer, S.K. (1951). *Philosophy in a New Key*. New York: New American Library.

Langs, R. (1982). *Psychotherapy: A Basic Text*. New York: Jason Aronson.

Lansky, M.R. (2005a). The impossibility of forgiveness: shame fantasies as instigators of vengefulness in Euripides' Medea. *Journal of the American Psychoanalytic Association*, *53*(2), 437–464.

Lansky, M.R. (2005b). Hidden shame. *Journal of the American Psychoanalytic Association*, *53*(3), 865–890.

Lansky, M.R. (2007). Unbearable shame, splitting, and forgiveness in the resolution of vengefulness. *Journal of the American Psychoanalytic Association*, *55*(2), 571–593.

LeFevre, J.A., Smith-Chant, B.L., Fast, L., Skwarchuk, S.L., Sargla, E., Arnup, J.S., *et al.* (2006). What counts as knowing? The development of conceptual and procedural knowledge of counting from kindergarten through Grade 2. *Journal of Experimental Child Psychology*, *93*(4), 285–303.

Lewin, B.D. (1935). Claustrophobia. *Psychoanalytic Quarterly 2*, 227–233.

Lewin, B.D. (1952). Phobic symptoms and dream interpretation. *Psychoanalytic Quarterly*, *21*, 295–322.

Lewis, M. (2008). *Shame: The Exposed Self*. New York: Free Press.

Linehan, M. (1993). *Cognitive-Behavioral Treatment of Borderline Personality Disorder*. New York: Guilford Press.

Linehan, M.M., Comtois, K.A., Murray, A.M., Brown, M.Z., Gallop, R.J., Heard, H.L., *et al.* (2006). Two-year randomized controlled trial and follow-up of dialectical behavior therapy vs therapy by experts for suicidal behaviors and borderline personality disorder. *Archives of General Psychiatry*, *63*(7), 757–766.

Luzuriaga, I. (2000). Thinking aloud about technique. In P. Bion Talamo, F. Borgogno and S.A. Merciai (eds) *W.R. Bion: Between Past and Future* (pp.145–163). London: Karnac.

MacGibbon, J. (ed.) (1978). *Stevie Smith: Selected Poems*. London: Penguin.

Malloch, S. (1999). Mother and infants and communicative musicality. Unpublished manuscript.

Mancia, M. (2003). Dream actors in the theatre of memory: their role in the psychoanalytic process. *International Journal of Psychoanalysis*, *84*, 945–952.

Mancia, M. (2006). Implicit memory and early unrepressed unconscious. *International Journal of Psychoanalysis*, *87*, 83–103.

Marks-Tarlow, T. (1999). The self as a dynamical system. *Nonlinear Dynamics, Psychology, and Life Sciences*, *3*(4), 311–345.

Matte-Blanco, I. (1975). *The Unconscious as Infinite Sets: An Essay in Bi-Logic*. London: Duckworth.

Matte-Blanco, I. (1983). Reflecting with Bion. In J.S. Grotstein (ed.) *Do I Dare Disturb the Universe?* Beverly Hills: Caesura Press.

Matte-Blanco, I. (1988). *Thinking, Feeling and Being*. London: Routledge.

Meloy, J.R. (1992). *Violent Attachments*. New York: Jason Aronson.

Meltzer, D. (1968). Terror, persecution, dread – a dissection of paranoid anxieties. *International Journal of Psychoanalysis*, *49*, 396–400.

Meltzer, D. (1974). Mutism in infantile autism, schizophrenia and manic-depressive states: the correlation of clinical psychopathology and linguistics. *International Journal of Psychoanalysis*, *55*, 397–404.

Meltzer, D. (1975a). 'Adhesive identification'. *Contemporary Psycho-Analysis*, *11*, 289–310.

Meltzer, D. (1975b). *The Kleinian Development*. Strath Tay: Clunie Press.

Meltzer, D. (1986). *Studies in Extended Metapsychology: Clinical Applications of Bion's Ideas*. Strath Tay: Clunie Press.

Meltzer, D. (1992). *The Claustrum: An Investigation of Claustrophobic Phenomena.* Strath Tay: Clunie Press.

Meltzer, D. and Bick, E. (1960). Lectures and seminars in Kleinian child psychiatry. In D. Meltzer (ed.) *Sincerity and Other Works* (pp.35–89). London: Karnac.

Meltzoff, A.N. and Decety, J. (2003). What imitation tells us about social cognition: a rapprochement between developmental psychology and cognitive neuroscience. *Philosophical Transactions of the Royal Society B: Biological Sciences, 358*(1431), 491–500.

Meltzoff, A.N. and Moore, M.K. (1977). Imitation of facial and manual gestures by human neonates. *Science, 198*(4312), 74–78.

Milrod, B. (1995). The continued usefulness of psychoanalysis in the treatment armamentarium for panic disorder. *Journal of the American Psychoanalytic Association, 43,* 151–162.

Mitchell, S.A. (2000). *Relationality: From Attachment to Intersubjectivity.* London: Analytic Press.

Mithen, S. (2005). *The Singing Neanderthals.* London: Weidenfeld & Nicolson.

Mitrani, J.L. (1992). On the survival function of autistic manoeuvres in adult patients. *International Journal of Psychoanalysis, 73,* 549–559.

Mitrani, J.L. (1998). Unbearable ecstasy, reverence and awe, and the perpetuation of an 'aesthetic conflict'. *Psychoanalytic Quarterly, 67,* 102–127.

Mitrani, J.L. (2001). 'Taking the transference': some technical implications in three papers by Bion. *International Journal of Psychoanalysis, 82,* 1085–1104.

Modell, A.H. (1980). Affects and their non-communication. *International Journal of Psychoanalysis, 61,* 259–267.

Money-Kyrle, R.E. (1956). Normal counter-transference and some of its deviations. *International Journal of Psychoanalysis, 37,* 360–366.

Money-Kyrle, R.E. (1971). The aim of psychoanalysis. *International Journal of Psychoanalysis, 52,* 103–106.

Newirth, J. (2003). *Between Emotion and Cognition: The Generative Unconscious.* New York: Other Press.

Nozick, R. (1971). *Anarchy, State, and Utopia.* London: Basic Books.

Nozick, R. (2001). *Invariances: The Structure of the Objective World.* London: Harvard University Press.

Ogden, T.H. (1986). *The Matrix of the Mind: Object Relations and the Psychoanalytic Dialogue.* Northwale, NJ: Jason Aronson.

Ogden, T.H. (1992). *The Primitive Edge of Experience.* London: Karnac.

Ogden, T.H. (1997). *Reverie and Interpretation.* New York: Jason Aronson.

Ogden, T.H. (2004a). The analytic third: implications for psychoanalytic theory and technique. *Psychoanalytic Quarterly, 73,* 167–195.

Ogden, T.H. (2004b). On holding and containing, being and dreaming. *International Journal of Psychoanalysis, 86,* 1349–1364.

Pam, A., Inghilterra, K. and Munson, C. (1994). Agoraphobia: the interface between anxiety and personality disorder. *Bulletin of the Menninger Clinic, 58*(2), 242–261.

Quinodoz, J.-M. (1997). Transitions in psychic structures in the light of deterministic chaos theory. *International Journal of Psychoanalysis, 78,* 699–718.

Racker, H. (1957). The meanings and uses of countertransference. *Psychoanalytic Quarterly, 26*(3), 303–357.

Rey, J.H. (1979). Schizoid phenomena in the borderline. In E. Bott Spillius (ed.) *Melanie Klein Today: Volume 1, Mainly Theory*. London: Routledge.

Rocha Barros, E. (2000). Affect and pictographic image: the constitution of meaning in mental life. *International Journal of Psychoanalysis, 81*, 1087–1099.

Rose, G.J. (2004). *Between Couch and Piano*. New York: Brunner-Routledge.

Rosenblatt, A. (2004). Insight, working through, and practice: the role of procedural knowledge. *Journal of the American Psychoanalytic Association, 52*(1), 189–207.

Rosenfeld, H. (1952). Notes of the analysis of the superego conflict in an acute catatonic schizophrenic. *International Journal of Psychoanalysis, 33*, 111–131.

Rosenfeld, H. (1964). On the psychopathology of narcissism: a clinical approach. *International Journal of Psychoanalysis, 45*, 332–337.

Rosenfeld, H. (1971). A clinical approach to the psychoanalytic theory of the life and death instincts: an investigation into the aggressive aspects of narcissism. *International Journal of Psychoanalysis, 52*(2), 169–178.

Rosenfeld, H. (1987). *Impasse and Interpretation: Therapeutic and Anti-therapeutic Factors in the Psychoanalytic Treatment of Psychotic, Borderline, and Neurotic Patients*. London: Tavistock Publications.

Roth, M. (1996). The panic-agoraphobic syndrome: a paradigm of the anxiety group of disorders and its implications for psychiatric practice and theory. *American Journal of Psychiatry, 152*(7), 111–124.

Ruddick, B. (1961). Agoraphobia. *International Journal of Psychoanalysis, 42*, 537–543.

Schafer, R. (2000). Reflections on 'thinking in the presence of the other'. *International Journal of Psychoanalysis, 81*(1), 85–96.

Schroeder, M. (1991). *Fractals, Chaos, Power Laws*. New York: Freeman.

Searles, H.F. (1979). *Countertransference and Related Subjects: Selected Papers*. New York: International Universities Press.

Segal, H. (1978). On symbolism. *International Journal of Psychoanalysis, 59*, 315–319.

Segal, H. (1981). *The Work of Hanna Segal: A Kleinian Approach to Clinical Practice*. New York: Jason Aronson.

Segal, H. (1991). *Dream, Phantasy and Art*. London: Routledge.

Shear, M.K. (1996). Factors in the etiology and pathogenesis of panic disorder: revisiting the attachment–separation paradigm. *American Journal of Psychiatry, 153*(7), 125–136.

Shengold, L. (1989). *Soul Murder: The Effects of Child Abuse and Deprivations*. New Haven, CT: Yale University Press.

Shengold, L. (1991). *"Father, don't you see I'm burning?"*. New Haven, CT: Yale University Press.

Silver, D. (1985). Psychodynamics and psychotherapeutic management of the self-destructive character-disordered patient. *Psychiatric Clinics of North America, 8*(2), 357–375.

Skodol, A.E., Gunderson, J.G., Shea, T.M., McGlashan, T., Morey, L.C., Sanislow, C.A., *et al.* (2005). The collaborative longitudinal personality disorders study (CLPS): overview and implications. *Journal of Personality Disorders, 19*(5), 487–504.

Sloboda, J.A. (1985). *The Musical Mind: The Cognitive Psychology of Music*. Oxford: Clarendon Press.

Sorensen, P.B. (1995). Thoughts on the containing process from the perspective of infant/mother relations. *Melanie Klein and Object Relations*, *13*(2), 1–16.

Stadler, M.A. (1989). On learning complex procedural knowledge. *Journal of Experimental Psychology: Learning, Memory and Cognition*, *15*(6), 1061–1069.

Steiner, J. (1993). *Psychic Retreats: Pathological Organizations in Psychotic, Neurotic and Borderline Patients*. London: Routledge.

Steiner, J. (1994). Patient-centred and analyst-centred interpretations: some implications of containment and countertransference. *Psychoanalytic Inquiry*, *14*, 406–422.

Steiner, J. (2000). Containment, enactment and communication. *International Journal of Psychoanalysis*, *81*, 245–255.

Stensson, J. (2006). Aniara, mimicry and aspect-seeing. *International Forum of Psychoanalysis*, *15*, 157–161.

Stern, D.N. (2000). *The Interpersonal World of the Infant*, 2nd edn. London: Basic Books.

Stern, D.N. (2004). *The Present Moment in Psychotherapy and Everyday Life*. New York: Norton.

Stolorow, R., Atwood, G. and Orange, D. (2002). *Worlds of Experience: Interweaving Philosophical and Clinical Dimensions in Psychoanalysis*. New York: Basic Books.

Symington, J. and Symington, N. (1986). *The Clinical Thinking of Wilfred Bion*. London: Routledge.

Symington, N. (1983). The analyst's act of freedom as agent of therapeutic change. *International Review of Psychoanalysis*, *10*, 283–291.

Trevarthen, C. (1993). The self born in intersubjectivity: the psychology of an infant communicating. In U. Neisser (ed.) *The Perceived Self: Ecological and Interpersonal Sources of Self Knowledge* (pp.121–173). Cambridge: Cambridge University Press.

Trevarthen, C. (1999). Musicality and the intrinsic motive pulse: evidence from human psychobiology and infant communication. Unpublished manuscript.

Tustin, F. (1972). *Autism and Childhood Psychosis*. London: Hogarth Press.

Tustin, F. (1986). *Autistic Barriers in Neurotic Patients*. New Haven, CT: Yale University Press.

Tustin, F. (1990). *The Protective Shell in Children and Adults*. London: Karnac.

Vanaerschot, G. (2004). It takes two to tango. On empathy with fragile processes. *Psychotherapy: Theory, Research, Practice, Training*, *41*(2), 112–124.

Warner, M.S. (1991). Fragile process. In L. Fusek (ed.) *New Direction in Client-Centerd Therapy: Practice with Difficult Client Populations*. Chicago: Chicago Counseling and Psychotherapy Center.

Weiss, E. (1935). Agoraphobia and its relation to hysterical attacks and to traumas. *International Journal of Psychoanalysis*, *16*, 59–83.

Weiss, E. (1964). *Agoraphobia in the Light of Ego Psychology*. New York: Grune & Stratton.

Willingham, D.B., Nissen, M.J. and Bullemer, P. (1989). On the development of procedural knowledge. *Journal of Experimental Psychology: Learning, Memory and Cognition*, *15*(6), 1047–1060.

Willoughby, R. (2001). 'The dungeon of thyself': the claustrum as pathological container. *International Journal of Psychoanalysis*, *82*, 917–932.

Winnicott, D.W. (1949). Hate in the counter-transference. *International Journal of Psychoanalysis*, *30*, 69–74.

Winnicott, D.W. (1958). The capacity to be alone. *International Journal of Psychoanalysis*, *39*, 416–420.

Winnicott, D.W. (1965). *The Maturational Processes and the Facilitating Environment*. London: Hogarth Press.

Winnicott, D.W. (1971). *Playing and Reality*. London: Tavistock Publications.

Winnicott, D.W. (1975). *Through Paediatrics to Psycho-Analysis*. London: Hogarth Press.

Winnicott, D.W. (1988). *Babies and their Mothers*. London: Free Association Books.

Wisdom, J.O. (1983). Metapsychology after forty years. In J.S. Grostein (ed.) *Do I Dare Disturb the Universe: A Memorial to W.R. Bion* (pp.601–624). London: Karnac.

Young, R.M. (1994). *Mental Space*. London: Process Press.

Zanarini, M.C., Frankenburg, F.R., Hennen, J., Reich, D.B. and Silk, K.R. (2005). The McLean Study of Adult Development (MSAD): overview and implications of the first six years of prospective follow-up. *Journal of Personality Disorder*, *19*(5), 505–523.

Zanocco, G., De Marchi, A. and Pozzi, F. (2006). Sensory empathy and enactment. *International Journal of Psychoanalysis*, *87*, 145–158.

Zizek, S. (2003). Fantasy reloaded. On 'The Matrix' movies. *Journal of European Psychoanalysis*, *16*. Retrieved July, 2004 from www.psychomedia.it/jep/pages/number16.htm.

Index

Page numbers in *italic* indicate figures.